MARIO PUZO

An American Writer's Quest

M. J. Moore

 Heliotrope Books

New York

ISBN 978-1-942762-63-8

Cover Design by M. J. Moore and Naomi Rosenblatt
Typeset by Naomi Rosenblatt

MARIO PUZO

An American Writer's Quest

For Daniel

Table of Contents

Author's Note 9

PRELUDE 11

INTRODUCTION 17

CHAPTER 1 . . . . 25 ~ Forward Motion

CHAPTER 2 . . . . 53 ~ Active Player

CHAPTER 3 . . . . 72 ~ Short Stack

CHAPTER 4 . . . . 87 ~ Up the Ante

CHAPTER 5 . . . . 107 ~ Side Game

CHAPTER 6 . . . . 132 ~ All In

CHAPTER 7 . . . . 163 ~ Jackpot

CHAPTER 8 . . . . 181 ~ Coming Over the Top

CHAPTER 9 . . . . 211 ~ Wrap

EPILOGUE 243

BIBLIOGRAPHY . . . 245

Author's Note

No university or college archive of Puzo materials was available for research, comparative analysis or other interpretive purposes during the time I wrote this book. Future biographers, however, will surely benefit greatly from a collection of Mario Puzo's papers acquired by Dartmouth College in 2018. As for this book, it is neither an academic study nor a complete biography. I prefer to think of it as a portrait—in words.

When writing, I had one captivating polestar which I strove to follow. Carl Van Doren's *Swift* (first published in 1930) shows that even in the absence of archival resources commonly considered essential, one can still evoke and explicate a writer's life—as long as there's a judicious deployment of the subject's verified words; and provided that a thoroughgoing familiarity with the subject's oeuvre is demonstrated.

In two out-of-print nonfiction books, Puzo left behind abundant autobiographical passages, personal essays, mid-life reflections, and ruminations. Thus, in addition to his newspaper and magazine interviews, as well as credible anecdotes in memoirs by Peter Bart, Carol Gino, Bruce Jay Friedman, Erica Heller, and Joseph Heller, most of the quotations attributed to Mario Puzo in this book are gleaned from pieces he selected for *The Godfather Papers and Other Confessions* (a 1972 collection) or from *Inside Las Vegas* (Puzo's text complemented that illustrated chronicle).

For an encyclopedic array of reasons, the works and days of Mario Puzo have affected me deeply—much as Carl Van Doren was affected by Jonathan Swift. "A biographer looks in his heart as a poet does. Now Swift rose in my imagination, substantial and alive, and compelled me," Carl Van Doren recalled in his personal essay "Private Depression."

My hope is that the writer's quest of Mario Puzo is illuminated here. If it's not, then the fault is mine.

MJM
January 1, 2019

Prelude

"If only I could write as poorly as *he* does," Norman Mailer once groused, while sipping drinks with author Bruce Jay Friedman at a party. The "he" at issue was Mario Puzo, who in that season had another best-selling novel on his hands. It was a remark typical of Mailer, whose competitive zeal turned to fury when others went ahead and actually did what he always promised, but rarely delivered. Mario Puzo was not the only fellow writer that ol' stormin' Norman had trashed. More than once, in gleefully spiteful ad hominem attacks presented as literary criticism, Mailer had tweaked, insulted, challenged, derided, and dumped on his peers.

If ever he heard about such a snarky remark—"If only I could write as poorly"—Mario Puzo would not have winced. Nor cared very much. Puzo had long since given up any dream of being welcomed or esteemed by the sparkling literati. And yet, when Gay Talese reviewed Mario's new novel in 1984, singing the praises of Puzo and *The Sicilian*, he made it clear to readers that his admiration abounded.

But it wasn't just Gay Talese who broke ranks and took Puzo seriously, in contrast to the highbrows who swatted him with pejorative summations and dismissive cant in the wake of his record-breaking commercial success with *The Godfather*. There were others who went against the grain. Camille Paglia asserted in her 1997 *New York Times* profile of Mario that . . . well, let her words be reprinted here: "As an Italian-American writer who reveres Mr. Puzo, I feel like a fortunate pilgrim myself in being invited," she wrote, upon visiting his home for one of his rare interviews.

It's no accident that Paglia echoed *The Fortunate Pilgrim*, which was the second of Puzo's early literary novels. First published in 1965, its fate was then as doomed as 1955's *The Dark Arena*, Puzo's debut novel. Both books earned royal critical praise from important literary critics, failed to sell, and barely earned Puzo seven thousand dollars. The rest was history.

With his 50th birthday looming (and debts in the many tens of thousands burdening him), the next novel Mario wrote was *The Godfather*, which from the get-go (and for three years prior to the premiere of the first of the films induced by that work) not only sold millions of copies worldwide, but also (for reasons still debated) evolved into an entrenched cultural touchstone—our primary American myth.

In short, Camille Paglia's adroit reference to *The Fortunate Pilgrim* was a deft reminder that Mario Puzo had once been a meticulous literary sculptor, poor and bloodied (but unbowed). And then, as editor and publisher Jonathan Karp once explained: "He changed his approach and focused more on his skills as a storyteller."

In that way, author Puzo broke records, more than once, for the prices paid to issue his books as paperbacks; and his most celebrated novel yielded two Oscar-winning Best Pictures that he co-wrote the scripts for (thus earning himself two Academy Awards as a screenwriter).

Yet for decades, ever since the first two *Godfather* films were released to record-setting box-office success and rhapsodies of critical acclaim, a perennial cliché has been that director Francis Ford Coppola deserves the lion's share of the credit, and that Puzo's novel as source material was, at best, a piece of mediocre commercial schlock. No matter how vehemently Coppola disavowes that notion, the cliché persists.

To understand the degree to which the work of Coppola and his filmmaking colleagues was entirely interdependent with Mario's writing, one need only look closely at a single page of the massive "prompt book" assembled and annotated by Francis himself. As a former Hofstra University theater major (it was there that Coppola's whirlwind energy and take-charge personality first manifested), the use of a "prompt book" had been learned sedulously. What Coppola did for the making of *The Godfather* was to tear out each page of Puzo's text from a hard-cover copy of the novel; then he pasted each page onto a blank scrapbook page that was large enough to accommodate notes, cues, reminders, and ideas in regard to the details in Mario's prose that needed to be replicated on the screen. The result is startling to observe: We learn quickly that Puzo's text informs almost every frame of the film.

Let's cite one vivid, infamous example: The pivotal scene where Michael Corleone (a.k.a. the Al Pacino character) shoots the crooked cop, McCluskey, as well as the drug-trafficking Virgil Sollozzo whose henchmen twice tried to kill Michael's father, Don Vito) unfolds on page 152 of Puzo's novel. Coppola's annotations include . . .

"Important: The audience knows he is not following Clemenza's instructions," Francis wrote in the top margin, right above the line where Puzo had reminded the readers that Clemenza had instructed Michael "to come out of the toilet and blaze away. But either out of some warning instinct or sheer funk he had not done so. He felt that if he had made one swift move he would have been cut down. Now he felt safe and he must have been scared because he was glad he was no longer standing on his legs. They had gone weak with trembling." One word of advice to himself was penned by Coppola next to that passage, and his one-word cue was meant to indicate a plethora of elements regarding tone and mood. The one word was: *"Hitchcock."*

Again and again, deploying the word *"Detail!"* (often with multiple exclamation marks), Coppola took note of Mario's precise observations. Next to the line reading "Underneath the table his right hand moved to the gun tucked into his waistband," Francis cued himself to *"get this detail for the audience!"* And adjacent to the words "shoved the gun almost against Sollozzo's head," Coppola instructed: *"Really close."*

Similarly, wherein Puzo wrote that the "bullet caught Sollozzo squarely between his eye and his ear and when it exited on the other side blasted a huge gout of blood and skull fragments onto the petrified waiter's jacket," Coppola reminded himself at the bottom of the novel's page to *"Design!!!"* and to be sure to catch something key: *"Image: Blood all over the waiter's white jacket."*

Critical moments in the film that last merely seconds are made to feel eternal due to the ways in which Coppola and his cohort zeroed in on the specifics Mario had written in his novel, especially the details that allowed Puzo to show off the best of his action-oriented magazine writing. For example, Mario had written this: "Only one second had gone by as Michael pivoted to being the gun to bear on McCluskey." And Coppola cued himself about that line: *"Extend time."*

With laser-like focus on one single paragraph in Puzo's book, a menu of telling details was annotated by Coppola.

Mario wrote: "His veal-covered fork was suspended in his hand," and Coppola noted: "[McCluskey's] *fork frozen in mid-air"* along with *"Frozen time."* And because the first shot to hit Captain McCluskey "was bad, not mortal" according to Puzo's prose, "Michael fired the next shot through the top of his white-haired skull." About which Coppola made these notes next to the paragraph: **"Hit hard and bloody!!"** and **"He chokes."**

Finally, where Mario had spelled out that "the air seemed to fill with a fine mist of sprayed blood," Coppola followed by writing in the margin: **"Image: Mist of Blood."**

These "prompt book" illuminations were not limited to certain scenes. Coppola did this with every film-related page of the novel. His "prompt book" is as fat as an old-time Sears catalog. And in latter-day documentaries about the making of *The Godfather* (the first of the three movies derived from Mario's book), Francis freely admits that it was not the screenplay typed up in a traditional manner that he depended on. Instead, what he did was to make the film with Puzo's novel's pages staring up at him, because his "prompt book" was always within reach, serving as a blueprint. According to Coppola, he co-wrote "the script from this notebook . . . I could have made the movie just from this notebook."

The scope of Puzo's achievement (and the ramifications of what his third novel spawned) is best summed up in *The Godfather Effect: Changing Hollywood, America, and Me*, a remarkable work of social history, personal memoir, and Hollywood lore published in 2012 by Tom Santopietro. His conclusions are precise and stirring:

> The lasting effect of The Godfather *ran even deeper, however, because in detailing the saga of the Corleones, author and screenwriter Puzo was examining nothing less than the state of America. His vision filled with an understanding of the fundamental contradictions inherent in all human beings, Puzo's singular achievement lay in his ability to celebrate the virtues of the Italian family while never losing sight of the tragedy at the heart of* The Godfather *and America alike. What Puzo and screenwriter/director Coppola delivered—brilliantly—was nothing less than a disquisition on the madness, glory, and failure of the American dream.*

> Upon publication, the impact of The Godfather *proved to be so powerful that it changed not only how real-life mobsters interacted with one another but also the very vocabulary with which both law enforcement agencies and the general public discussed organized crime. For the purposes of his novel, Puzo actually invented the term "godfather" as an expression of mobster respect . . . even the FBI now uses the term to describe the heads of the crime families,*

an appropriation of his fictional term that proved to be a source of much amusement to Puzo during his lifetime.

Puzo's post-*Godfather* novels—published at wide intervals—usually made it to the #1 spot on the best-sellers list (sometimes for weeks; often they sat among the top ten or twenty best sellers for months). Such success had nothing to do with celebrity or notoriety. Mario Puzo shunned most publicity and avoided scandals of any kind. He never made a public spectacle of his ego or his distress.

No wonder Norman Mailer lambasted him. Puzo had conquered the culture.

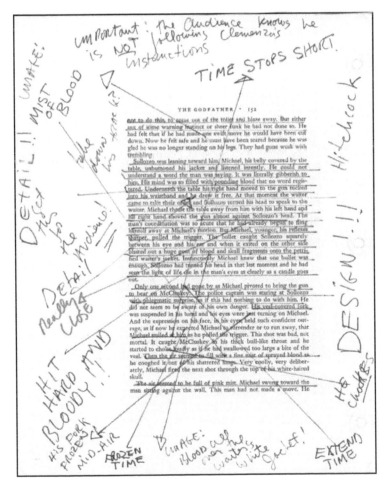

Annotations of Puzo's novel by filmmaker Francis Ford Coppola

Introduction

Toward the end of summer in 1996, a discernible lack of excitement and a dull sense of predictability slowly blanketed the presidential campaigns then underway.

Few were the politicos (and fewer still the pundits) who thought that Republican challenger Sen. Robert Dole (a stalwart Kansas conservative who was old enough to have been wounded in Italy in World War Two, which had ended more than 50 years earlier) stood any chance of unseating Democratic incumbent President Bill Clinton (America's first Baby Boomer president and a charter member of a demographic that had once fancied itself Woodstock Nation, so to speak).

The chronological and cultural divide between the two candidates represented by default the chasms separating a great many Americans: Class of '45 vs. Class of '70.

For Generation Dole, the soundtrack of youth was summed up by names like Glenn Miller, Tommy and Jimmy Dorsey, and Sinatra when he was called "Frankie." For Generation Clinton, music began with Elvis and led straight to the Beatles, Bob Dylan, and Fleetwood Mac.

Not only was Sen. Dole a wounded veteran of the Second World War, he was also, once upon a time, a hawk on Vietnam—whereas sitting President Bill Clinton had publicly protested America's war in Vietnam when he was a Rhodes Scholar at Oxford back in 1969.

Indeed, the two men dominating the news that summer of 1996 were formed by backgrounds and iconic national images as wildly disparate as any could be. What could be stranger than a presidential race between two American males whose profiles of manhood were as dissimilar as the ones beheld by Clinton and Dole? After all, for Generation Dole, manhood and its protocols had been personified by Humphrey Bogart: From speech patterns to hat choices, Bogie had shown the way.

In the realm of Generation Clinton, manhood was anything but a still-life photo in glorious black and white. It was more like a longhair "on the cover of the *Rolling Stone*," where Clinton had been featured, in fact, as the political rock star he was.

The two candidates seem to reflect (and to speak for) voters on different planets.

However, in the late summer of 1996, as the Clinton-Dole contest was played out 24/7 on CNN, with the national conventions that did their level best to amp up the electorate for the campaigning scheduled to erupt right after Labor Day, and not to cease until the first week in November, another man was thriving in the media.

Novelist Mario Puzo, at the age of 75, had gone and done it again. Written a blockbuster, that is. And to have done so in his mid–70s was quite extraordinary.

Almost six years had passed since the publication of his last novel, and all of a sudden in July and August of 1996 the author often referred to as "the father of *The Godfather*" was appearing on the celebrated talk shows hosted by Charlie Rose and Larry King. And then National Public Radio broadcast a lengthy interview with Puzo. One by one, a number of magazines unfolded in their illustrated pages an array of photo-essays highlighting "the return of Mario Puzo," whose new novel—*The Last Don*—was set for a gargantuan debut in September.

Random House planned a first printing in excess of 200,000 copies, and already the Book-of-the-Month Club was touting it as a Main Selection. Meanwhile, a bidding war for the film rights was won as CBS Television paid a whopping $2.1 million dollars for the chance to transform *The Last Don* into a mini-series. All the big impressive numbers aside, though, what made Puzo's renaissance unique was that Mario was out there talking, helping to sell the book through interviews and personal appearances—all for the first time.

In prior decades, Puzo (both shy and modest) declined publicity efforts.

Putting on no airs whatsoever, speaking slowly and often with self-deprecating wit, and exuding nothing like the arrogance, the egomania, the competitive fury or the sheer bloviating upchuck of other authors who grandstanded on TV or on radio, the long-awaited televised conversations between Puzo and the likes of Larry King and Charlie Rose met with tremendous audience appreciation. Mario answered endless questions not just about his new so-called "Mafia novel," but he also addressed the usual medley of inquiries about

Don Vito Corleone and his sons: Santino ("Sonny"), Michael, and Fredo; along with *consigliere* Tom Hagen, plus Tessio and Clemenza, all their great one-liners—and the horse's head, too.

In short, more than a quarter century after his novel *The Godfather* had exploded in America's consciousness when published in March 1969, the American masses were still joyfully and loyally attached, on a first-name basis, to the members of the Corleone Family and their allies, enemies, aides and adversaries. And now, with an ambitious new novel featuring a different Mob-connected family, Mario was back.

Puzo's comeback was an authentic American phenom. And equally authentic was the trans-generational admiration and love that greeted Mario Puzo as *The Last Don* quickly rose to the top of all the best-sellers lists, where it stayed in the #1 spot (or in its vicinity) well into 1997, when the CBS mini-series topped all network ratings.

If there was one thing—and only one thing—that might be agreed upon between Generation Dole and Generation Clinton, it was that the narrative powers and the storytelling gifts of Mario Puzo were superb, unforgettable, and timeless.

Regardless of age or any other demographic issues, *The Godfather* prevails as a beloved cultural treasure all over the world and it was Academy Award-winning director Francis Ford Coppola who ultimately insisted that Paramount Pictures redesign the credits to read "Mario Puzo's *The Godfather.*" The ultimate tribute.

And it couldn't have happened to a nicer guy.

The Yiddish word *mensch* derives from the German word *mensch,* and by definition is "a person of integrity and honor." That's what Mario Puzo was: a *mensch.*

"He was the kindest, sweetest man," recalls Jonathan Karp, who was merely at the beginning of his career as a New York editor and publisher when he first had the chance to meet Mario Puzo. It was startling to Karp that an author so celebrated for novels with explicit violence happened to be the ultimate gentleman. "It was always so striking to me how gentle he was," Karp once said, "because he would write these scenes full of revenge and bitter irony. But in person he was one of the nicest people I've ever met."

By the time *The Last Don* was published in 1996, Puzo and Jon Karp had a full-fledged author-editor relationship. But how they met and the way in which their rapport was cultivated is telling. It all harked back to early 1990, when Karp was closing in on his thirtieth birthday and had abandoned a fledging journalism career.

Having left newspaper writing behind, Jonathan Karp's career trajectory led to being an assistant to a number of Random House's top-tier editors. One day, as Karp tells the story, he was "answering the phones, filling in for the receptionist at lunch," and he happened to "be the first person seen by publisher Joni Evans when she exited the elevator as she returned from lunch." At that serendipitous moment, Karp recalls, "[Joni] saw me standing right in front of her, and said, 'I need a guy to read this novel I'm working on.' And I was the guy."

Indeed, he was. Jonathan Karp was then handed a printout of *The Fourth K*, which was Mario Puzo's sixth novel (and scheduled for publication in the winter of 1991). He spent a weekend giving the novel a close reading and he wrote a ten-page report for his superiors: "what was good about it, what I thought needed to be improved," and so forth. "Joni showed it to Puzo," as Karp remembers, "and we all agreed that the manuscript still needed work."

The Fourth K was in certain ways a new kind of novel for Mario Puzo, who had become so exclusively identified with *The Godfather* that "gangster tales" or "Mafia stories" were seemingly all that readers really wanted from him. When Mario had published *Fools Die*, a massively entertaining, digressive, nonlinear, picaresque, autobiographical novel back in 1978, the reaction of many readers expecting some kind of *Godfather* reprise was one of disappointment (or confusion). Everything that makes picaresque novels what they are (sprawling, plotless, and largely driven by the unreliable, lower-class narrator's force of personality) failed to hook a great many readers who yearned for a tightly-knit narrative, which is the form that Puzo returned to with *The Sicilian* in 1984. Accordingly, *The Sicilian* was not just a best seller but commanded the #1 spot on the most prestigious best-sellers lists.

However, as Jonathan Karp read *The Fourth K*, he realized that Mario was in new territory. And, this time, his richly imagined fiction dovetailed with the Kennedys.

When summing up what *The Fourth K* was all about, Karp said: "It was a thriller set in Washington [D.C.]—Puzo's only Washington novel. It was about a [nephew] in a great political family [i.e., the

Kennedy clan] who is a very unpopular president. He's the second president in his family and, to strengthen his popularity, he allows an act of terrorism to occur in the United States, thereby seizing dictatorial power. This was in 1990."

More than a decade later, in the aftermath of the 9/11 catastrophes, it appeared that Puzo had shown a touch of the clairvoyant, as *The Fourth K* featured terrorist debacles and the machinations of power as practiced by a president whose dynastic family pedigree is both a blessing and a curse. Ironically, however, at the time it first appeared in 1991, while *The Fourth K* did well enough (thanks to Puzo's name, brief best-seller status was assured), it never caught on in a great big way. Its convoluted plot seemed—again, at that time—decidedly surreal. And though the legacies of John and Robert Kennedy are alluded to several times over, Mario's decision not to veer too closely to the works and days of JFK or RFK prevented the novel from trending in sync with the Kennedy revival that was galvanized by the relentless arguments induced later in 1991, due to Oliver Stone's conspiracy film *JFK*.

Nonetheless, it was a pivotal work in more ways than one for Puzo and for Karp.

"I loved *The Fourth K*," a glowing Jon Karp later recounted: "This was during a time when publishers sometimes traveled to be with their authors." As Karp explains:

> I still can't get over this, but Joni [Evans], Julie Grau, and I flew to Las Vegas, where we edited Mario Puzo in person because Mario felt that he did his best work in Vegas. He liked to gamble. So Mario's walking around Vegas in his sweatpants. During the day we worked around the table and edited, and then at night he took us gambling. I had never gambled in my life, and he decided that he wanted to introduce me to the game of baccarat. He gave me a hundred dollars and said, 'Have some fun.' I proceeded to lose the hundred dollars. I felt horrible about this . . . But he gave me another hundred dollars and something remarkable happened: I began to win. I think I won about five hands in a row. I paid back the two hundred dollars, which was good, but what was really good was that Mario had been gambling along with me while I won my five hands, and he'd made about seven thousand dollars on it. So he felt very good about it.

Long story short: Not long after those halcyon days, both Joni Evans and Julie Grau left Random House. Puzo knew no other mavens there, but a team of senior editors certainly wanted to be in league with him. Mario, though, was calling the shots. He told the CEO at Random House that he preferred to work with Jon Karp, not just due to his editorial savvy but also because Karp represented luck.

"And that is how I became Mario Puzo's editor," a laughing, delighted Karp said.

Unsurprisingly, then, it was Jonathan Karp who went on the record with *Publishers Weekly* in the summer of 1996, touting *The Last Don* with unconditional brio: "It works on an almost mythic level," he explained, adding that "savage wit and subtle moral irony" were combined as "Mario contrasts the morality of the modern American mob family and the Hollywood establishment. It's a combination of mob family values and a fierce, funny, wickedly honest look inside Hollywood."

Three years later, when Puzo's death in July 1999 yielded innumerable obituaries all over the world, the bulk of all such notices consisted of *Godfather*-related lore. But a myriad of references also were made to the ways in which *The Last Don* had been welcomed by the public at large as a "comeback" for Puzo, who wrote that novel in the years following a massive coronary topped by quadruple-bypass surgery in the early 1990s. "He definitely [viewed *The Last Don*] as a comeback with a vengeance," Jonathan Karp averred.

And yet, in none of those many obituaries did readers ever get a real sense of the long and winding road that Puzo traveled in order to achieve *The Godfather* and its life-transforming success. It still seems to many readers that prior to *The Godfather*, the career of Mario Puzo, and his life, as well, were (and are) a blur. Even a mystery.

The Los Angeles Times said it best: "Puzo [was] a man who . . . remained in the shadows throughout his long career as a novelist and screenwriter, only rarely speaking to the press." That may not seem like such an oddity until one is reminded that during the mid-1970s *The Godfather* sold more copies per year than any other book except the Bible. Somehow, though, Puzo stayed under the radar, save for the occasional photo-essay in a national magazine: *LIFE* in 1970, *New York Magazine* in 1972, and a *TIME* cover story in 1978. He was a modest man with a great talent

He was also a writer who struggled for decades before any success occurred; and only after age 50 was he an author whose success was so prodigious that it affected, tainted, defined, and pigeonholed the artist who, out of economic desperation and romantic imagination (plus will power and the ability to follow through), created the single most recognizable of American protagonists.

In the life of Puzo, all roads led to *The Godfather*. No other writer of his generation created such an internationally embraced, mythic, beloved tale. As a writer born in 1920, Puzo was chronologically in the cadre that included Norman Mailer, James Jones, William Styron, and James Baldwin (all of whom were born between 1921 and 1925). We can add Gore Vidal, Truman Capote, and Richard Yates to the list.

And yet, while their writers' careers ascended as they segued from their mid–20s to age 40, Puzo's quest to be a successful author was akin to the Myth of Sisyphus. Although Mario Puzo received major critical praise for his first two novels (1955's *The Dark Arena* and 1965's *The Fortunate Pilgrim*), sales were all but flat. Then: Badly indebted, with five children, pushing 50 and plagued by stress, he vowed to write a best-seller. His third novel was *The Godfather*.

Boom! Long before the first film premiered in 1972, Puzo's *Godfather* sold millions of copies. Subsequently, his co-screenwriting gigs with Francis Ford Coppola on the three *Godfather* movies ensured that Mario Puzo was central to what's now considered America's ultimate mythology. In fine: *The Godfather* has superseded Colonial narratives, Westerns, and the Civil War as a blueprint for understanding America's dreams, disasters, and ethos.

Yet, Puzo has never been given the credit he deserves vis-à-vis his generation's World War Two-era novels. *The Dark Arena* is no less important than Mailer's *The Naked and the Dead* or James Jones's *The Thin Red Line*. Indeed, like Mailer and Jones (and sixteen million other Americans between 1940 and 1945), there were significant years of Puzo's young adult life spent in uniform. And from the woman he married to the narrative he structured for his debut novel, the epoch of the Second World War was transformative for him.

Similarly, *The Fortunate Pilgrim* has yet to receive the critical and commercial success it deserves. Although dubbed "a small classic" by an astute *New York Times* critic when first published in 1965, *The Fortunate Pilgrim* ought to be firmly placed on the same shelf as Henry Roth's *Call It Sleep*, James T. Farrell's *Studs Lonigan* trilogy, Toni Morrison's *Song of Solomon*, and other major novels encapsulating ethnic Americana.

Besides living one of the America's most vivid examples of a rags-to-riches success story, there is this: Mario Puzo's life story is a heroic tale. Against all odds, the quiet, self-effacing, socially awkward son of poor, illiterate, Southern Italian immigrants made himself into an author whose collected works fill a whole shelf . . . and a writer whose most famous novel—*The Godfather*—has seeped into America's psyche and soul to a degree that is unique.

And yet, there has never been a biography of Mario Puzo. This portrait, I hope, will lead the way.

Hell's Kitchen in the 1930s. Puzo was born and raised in this New York City neighborhood; photographer unknown

1

Forward Motion

Mario talks about "having a thousand years of illiterate Neapolitan peasants" behind him. He craved his life as if it were a fantastic meal, even when it hurt the heart out of him.

~~~ Seymour Krim

I fell to my knees in the dark street. The pain radiated all over my back. I flattened out onto the ice-cold pavement. There wasn't a soul around, so no one could help me. The entrance to the hospital was a hundred feet away ... And now I could see the Christmas lights decorating a nearby store. The pain receded a little. I lay there thinking I was a fucking animal. Here I was an artist, a book published ... and I was dying like a dog in the gutter.

~~~ Mario Puzo, *Fools Die*

When he got out of the taxi, he collapsed curbside. It was Christmas Eve, 1955.

By now the cold air was frigid enough to sting his face whenever the wind blew. And New York City, of course, with its routine hurly-burly drastically diminished by the grand pause that only certain major holidays can induce, had that unmistakable overlay of forlorn Yuletide stillness. December 24th was hardly the ideal night for a major gall-bladder crisis.

Somehow, though, it was an apt night for the kind of private, thoughtful mental reckoning that a bout of illness often produces. The man who fell by the curb that night was neither old nor feeble. He had no chronic medical problems. In general, like most other men of his generation, this 35-year-old man (who crumbled as soon as he hauled himself out of the taxi) was assumed to be in the prime of his life.

In the magazine-saturated and advertising-centric TV culture of 1955, it was the men of this demographic—the guys of the G.I. Bill generation, supposedly rising in the world ten years after the war ended; the ex-soldiers and former sailors, airmen, and Marines—who, ostensibly, had the world by the tail. They were newly-minted executives, in many cases. Or ambitious attorneys. Untold numbers were striving salesmen. Some were future judges. Freshly appointed assistant professors were in their ranks; and in all other jobs and career fields (from factory work to scientific research) the thirty-something demographic represented the largest aggregate of the postwar generation of male Americans, many millions of them, who served in the military during the Second World War.

Now, on Christmas Eve in 1955, this 35-year-old ex-G.I. (who'd spent several years in uniform during World War Two, sometimes attached to the Fourth U.S. Armored Division in Europe, and who was now married with four children) looked skyward from the curb out in front of the VA hospital at which he'd arrived alone. For him, 1955 was definitely ending with symbolic distress.

Earlier that year—back in February of '55—Random House published this man's first novel. A more powerful publisher didn't exist. And the novel, over which he labored for several years, had been reviewed in high-profile venues.

Positive critics hailed the new author, comparing his debut work to the first novels of Norman Mailer (*The Naked and the Dead* was his 1948 best seller) and James Jones (his *From Here to*

Eternity remained a perennial best seller after its blockbuster 1951 publication). Negative critics had argued that the new writer was even "dirtier" than either Mailer or Jones, both of whom received much criticism for the profanity-laced chapters that formed their respective novels. Nonetheless, both Mailer and Jones (though critics were divided on their merits) enjoyed hefty sales.

The vagaries of the book business being what they were, no such luck shone upon the man who could now scarcely rise from the ground. In his case, despite several glowing reviews and a big push from the Random House publicity machine, the sales for his novel, *The Dark Arena*, were not just slight. They were meager. In addition to his book sales being minimal, Hollywood had shown no interest in buying the film rights to *The Dark Arena*, a somber novel about moral ambiguities in the postwar U.S. Army ranks of occupied Germany.

Well, so much for any hope of quitting his civil-service administrative job. TIME

More than twenty years later, the man who fell out of the cab that night would recall that it was then—*just then*—that he had an epiphany: "It was Christmas Eve and I had a severe gall-bladder attack. I had to take a cab to the Veterans Administration Hospital on 23rd Street, got out and fell into the gutter. There I was lying there thinking, here I am, a published writer, and I am dying like a dog. That's when I decided I would be rich and famous."

By the time novelist Mario Puzo offered that anecdote to *TIME* magazine for its 1978 cover story entitled "Paperback Godfather," things had changed. But not overnight. Not quickly. After 1955, it took another decade and a half of struggle, persistence, solitary writing, and visionary intuition . . . and when *The Godfather* (Puzo's third novel) was published in March 1969, a phenomenon emerged.

It was such a phenomenon that when Mario Puzo reflected in 1978 on what it was like to find himself "dying like a dog" at 23rd Street on Christmas Eve back in 1955, he did so knowing that there were more copies in print of *The Godfather* than any other book on the planet, except the Bible. He did so knowing that because of his third novel's international success, and with two extraordinary films forever reinforcing interest in the book, there were now trust funds for all of his children. Perhaps most poignant of all was that Puzo ruminated on Christmas Eve '55—surely one of the low points in his twenty-year struggle to achieve success as a writer—while knowing full well that his wife, Erika, was dying of breast cancer.

Only three months after the August '78 *TIME* Magazine cover story appeared, Erika Puzo died. It was a morose Thanksgiving. They had been married more than 30 years. They raised five children. They met under unusual circumstances at the end of World War Two (Erika was a German citizen; Puzo was the G.I. she fell in love with) as the U.S. Army shifted its focus from combat to occupation. If anyone had hinted to the uniformed Puzo and his war bride that they and their children would one day appear in a *LIFE* Magazine photo-essay, rich guffaws would have erupted.

Laughter was in short supply throughout the early years of Mario Gianluigi Puzo.

He was born on October 15, 1920. And contrary to the vaudeville stereotype of singing, excitable Italians that was perennially in vogue on the stage (and would later prevail on popular radio shows like "Life with Luigi" in the 1930s and 1940s, as well as in the films of that era and the TV shows of the future), there was not just a lack of laughter in Puzo's milieu, but also a lack of tuneful gaiety. About that happy "Que Sera Sera" lightheartedness for which the stereotyped Italians were known? Forget it. What Mario Puzo and his family knew was poverty. And grim work.

Hell's Kitchen is the name of the area where Puzo was born. The name itself still conveys a mythic intensity. There was a murky, complicated socio-economic history to Hell's Kitchen—which in the 1920s was still a gritty neighborhood from West 29th Street to West 55th Street, between Eighth Avenue and the Hudson River.

Throughout the 1800s, that particular pocket of New York was infamous for its ethnic gang wars, with the hordes of Famine-fleeing immigrant Irish pitted against every other incoming immigrant group: Italians, Poles, Germans, and whoever else took an interest in issues of turf, local politics, and power and control in the urban maze of 19th-century New York. Prostitution, gambling, drunken excess, vice of all sorts, and, perhaps most of all, the perpetual corruption of seemingly upright men were Hell's Kitchen's claims to fame.

Impoverished living conditions were the norm. Filth was everywhere. Neither the police nor the local clergy were immune from the contamination of the area, simply because the admixture of alcohol and wanton women and the chronic availability of self-destructive indulgences made Hell's Kitchen a swamp, sucking in everyone.

It was a locale upon which social reformers often focused. When Mario Puzo was a boy there in the 1920s, the realm in which he lived was quite an improvement over the squalor of the 1800s. Nonetheless, it was still a rough, intimidating, dangerous place to be. It was still, in effect, a world within a world. It was also where the vast majority of immigrants from Southern Italy settled, struggled, and made their lives.

Thus from his earliest days onward, Puzo observed the tensions induced by class distinctions and economic inequalities between the Southern Italians and the immigrants who hailed from Northern Italy (and everywhere else). All over Hell's Kitchen in the 1920s and the 1930s, the lines were drawn clearly. Toward the end of his life, Mario Puzo remarked that the varied neighborhoods within Hell's Kitchen at large were akin to "contained medieval cities."

He elaborated on this when admitting that his youth had nothing to do with what most Americans assumed about Italians by looking at popular movies or magazines:

"As a child and in my adolescence, Puzo once explained, living in the heart of New York's Neapolitan ghetto, I never heard an Italian singing. None of the grown-ups I knew were charming or loving or understanding. Rather they seemed coarse, vulgar, and insulting. And so later in my life when I was exposed to all the clichés of lovable Italians, happy-go-lucky Italians, I wondered where the hell the moviemakers and storywriters got all their ideas from." They certainly never obtained any ideas from Avellino, Italy. Located twenty-six miles from Naples, in one of the southernmost provinces of Italy, it was from the hardscrabble, dry plains of agrarian Avellino that both of Mario Puzo's parents emigrated.

"Italy," Puzo sardonically explained later in his life, "the golden land, so loving to vacationing Englishmen . . . has never cared for its poor people. My father and mother were both illiterates. Both grew up on rocky, hilly farms in the countryside adjoining Naples." All of her life, Puzo's mother would bitterly remember that in her youth neither she nor her family could ever "taste the ham from the pig they slaughtered every year." And why not? Economics. "It brought too high a price in the marketplace," Mario later explained: "cash was needed."

Puzo was raised as one of seven children who were born to Maria Le Conti Puzo. "My family and I grew up together on Tenth Avenue," he noted precisely, "between Thirtieth and Thirty-first streets, part of the area called Hell's Kitchen."

What made their family unique in comparison to other clans in their realm was that Maria had had four children with a first husband who died young due to an accident at work. Like many male Italian immigrants of that era, Maria's first husband had been a day laborer who earned little and risked life and limb working on the docks. Dangerous conditions were the norm, along with long hours, very low wages, no benefits, and the inevitable exhaustion resulting from perennial hard physical work; compounded by the fatigue brought on by trying to raise children in a realm where amenities were minimal. Hot water? Air-conditioning? Dishwashers? They were dreams. Beyond dreams. They were Sci-Fi fantasies.

Later, after Maria took Antonio Puzo as her second husband, she gave birth to another three children within the next decade. A hint of the charisma, strength, intelligence, and beauty of Maria Le Conti Puzo can be ascertained by the fact that she succeeded at finding a second husband, when four young children, already wholly dependent on her, came along with any marriage to Maria herself.

Antonio Puzo worked for the New York Central Railroad, which employed a great many of the uneducated, low-skilled workingmen of Hell's Kitchen. As a railway trackman, the work Antonio was required to do for the railroad always involved brute physical exertion, dust and dirt enough to last a lifetime, and perhaps most of all a mentally draining way of passing 12-hour shifts. Sometimes much longer.

For laborers, the eight-hour workday was not commonplace. No one had any rights to sick days, personal days, or vacation time. The very idea of daily work being in any way commensurate with happiness, pleasure, or at the very least contentment would have sounded alien. In Hell's Kitchen in the 1920s, when Mario Puzo's first memories were formed, it was considered a monumental step up just to have a steady job and a legitimate income.

Of course a legitimate income for the menial wages paid to unskilled laborers was rarely enough to make ends meet. Corners were cut. Accommodations were made. And as a child, young Puzo had his eyes wide open. "The older boys," he recalled, "the ones just approaching voting age, made their easy money by hijacking silk trucks that loaded up at the garment factory on Thirty-first Street. They would then sell the expensive dresses door to door, at bargain prices no discount house could match. From this some graduated into organized crime, whose talent scouts alertly tapped young boys versed in strong arm. Yet despite all this, most of the kids grew up honest, content with fifty bucks a week as truck drivers, deliverymen, and white-collar clerks in the Civil Service."

It was considered a sacred obligation to work hard so that one's children might receive an education, which surely promised better lives in their American futures.

Maria Le Conti and Antonio Puzo were illiterate Southern Italian immigrants, but all of their seven children were raised to attend school and learn at least the basic skills of reading, writing, and arithmetic. Such basic skills represented significant progress toward the ultimate goal of full American assimilation.

That was the ticket: Assimilation. As for "the American dream" or any fanciful projections about career possibilities, well, dreams were not just impractical, they were unaffordable. Nonetheless, Mario Puzo was always a born dreamer.

"As a child," Puzo recalled later in his life, "I had the usual dreams. I wanted to be handsome, specifically as cowboy stars in movies were handsome. I wanted to be a killer hero in a worldwide war. Or if no wars came along (our teachers told us another was impossible), I wanted at the very least to be a footloose adventurer."

Such dreams may have been normal childhood reveries, but such spontaneous mental meandering did not thrive easily in the tense milieu of Puzo's youth. On any given day, when Puzo was young, the atmosphere was dominated by harried, unhappy, stressfully temperamental adults, because "all the fathers and mothers that I knew," Puzo recounted, "were a grim lot; always shouting, always angry, quicker to quarrel than embrace." And it wasn't just parents who were livid. "My oldest sister was just as unhappy," Puzo remembered. She was "a dressmaker in the garment industry," he recalled, but "she wanted to be a schoolteacher."

As a small child in the heavily populated Neapolitan neighborhood that was sandwiched between 30th and 31st Streets on Tenth Avenue in Hell's Kitchen, the free-floating imagination of young Puzo was forever being jolted out of his boyhood daydreams. The crowded tenements had a clamorous soundtrack all their own. And the bellowing of distressed adults was often the primary sound. All of their discontents bewildered Puzo, who hadn't yet gone to work in any fashion. He later surmised: "I did not understand that their lives were a long labor to earn their daily bread and that physical fatigue does not sweeten human natures."

Long before he reached his teen years, Puzo formed some very definite ideas about how his life would be lived in contrast to the clashing, acrimonious lives around him. Above all else, he was in possession of one ironclad conviction: "I dreaded growing up to be like the adults around me." He had his reasons. Most of all, however, he had no life experiences yet that would temper his judgments about his elders.

As a child who still was allowed (chores at home and school notwithstanding) a basic freedom to roam, to play, and to live primarily in his imagination, he was able to enjoy the temporary luxury of believing in his heart that his life would be different.

What's most telling is that these youthful convictions—which Puzo recalled taking hold in his mind "even as a very small child"— partly resulted from his innate gifts not only as a born dreamer, but as a born writer. Already, "the child [was] the father of the man," as poet William Wordsworth put it.

Puzo's gift for careful listening was evident in his childhood, and he eavesdropped successfully enough on the adults around him to conclude that he "heard them saying too many cruel things about their dearest friends."

In addition to cultivating his natural gift for listening, he also observed with great intensity, and thus "saw too many of their false embraces with those they had just maligned." Inevitably he also "observed with horror their paranoiac anger at some small slight or a fancied injury to their pride. They were, always, too unforgiving. In short, they did not have the careless magnanimity of children."

It is some kind of tribute to the gods of innocence that Puzo could define the first decade of his life as a time when children (in his memory) were able to enjoy such "careless magnanimity." Consider briefly the world Puzo had been born into and some of what was in the air as 1920 segued to 1930.

First and foremost, by 1920, the millions of veterans of the First World War were no longer "Over There" and the short-lived glories of newsreels showing faraway battles and big parades had faded fast. Throughout the 1920s, many of the four million former Doughboys whose lives had been upended by conscription (or enlistment) and perhaps traumatized by the final year of war on the Western Front (in 1918) struggled with employment searches, housing issues, aborted academic programs, and truncated careers.

Like all veterans of each war, the Doughboys who'd gallantly marched off to "Make the World Safe for Democracy!" in 1917-1918 returned to a nation full of states, cities, towns, and rural hamlets that had managed to thrive without them.

Jobs that were supposedly "to be held" for many veterans were now jobs that had been permanently inherited by their juniors. On top of everything else making life after World War One anything but a "return to normalcy" (avidly promised in 1920 campaign speeches by President Harding), there was not just the war's lingering tension and evidence in the shell-shocked faces and the grievously injured bodies of hundreds of thousands of wartime casualties (missing limbs, disfigured faces, and thousand-yard stares isolated a great many ex-soldiers).

There was also the dread that lingered on in the aftermath of the worldwide influenza epidemic of 1918-1919, a pandemic in two awful waves that caused 50 to100 million deaths around the world. In America, 28% of the population was affected and well over 500,000 citizens died. In the America of Puzo's infancy, the recent influenza pandemic had taken more lives than battles on the Western Front had. And in addition to the dread fear and panic induced by the influenza outbreak, other crises abounded.

A rash of severe race riots erupted in America throughout 1919-1922, not just in Chicago (where urban violence was the worst) but in many other rural and metropolitan areas. Vast numbers of African-Americans who had migrated from the South to the North to work in the wartime factories and industrial centers weren't planning on any return to the South. Hence competition for jobs, housing, and all other aspects of urban life was exacerbated by the intensities of racial hatred.

All of which was compounded by the emergence throughout the so-called Roaring Twenties of an authentic new phenomenon in America. It would soon be dubbed "organized crime." And the reason it naturally arose in the Twenties can be summed up by this word:

Alcohol. Or, to put it more precisely: Prohibition.

Once the Volstead Act of 1919 became the law of the land and was implemented to enforce the Eighteenth Amendment as of January 1920, the doomed effort to make the manufacture, sale, or transport of alcohol as taboo as prostitution led to the immediate rise of urban gangs and notorious gang leaders whose fortunes rose with each succeeding year. America's craving for booze was simply unquenchable.

An entire culture of illegal "bootleg" liquor and its relentless swilling ensured the violent evolution of city-based hierarchical criminal networks that guaranteed the production, the distribution, and the sale of alcohol—from the very finest imports to the worst kind of homemade "rotgut." One way or another, Americans from Boston to Boise, Idaho, wanted their whiskey, gin, and Scotch. And they got it, despite the manifest efforts of all authorities (including J. Edgar Hoover and his newly reorganized FBI, which J. Edgar began looming over in 1924).

Controversial new music was also in the air, and "jazz" (which used to be a "Negro" euphemism for sex, as in "to jazz someone") became the term to describe the blues-based big-city music causing youth to invent a wildly popular new dance: "The Charleston" scandalized America's elders due to the erotic physicality required to swing one's arms, move two legs, and flap about energetically. It was hot.

Women dancing "The Charleston" were a sight to behold. Their breasts not only jiggled, they bounced. And the same with their ample derrieres. It was considered outrageous, immoral, and worse than "unladylike." Such dancing represented a breakthrough (or a breakdown, depending on perspective) in the 1920s that was comparable to the outrage and chagrin caused by "The Twist" forty years later.

Meantime, silent films were more and more popular, with the movies of Charlie Chaplin, Buster Keaton, Harry Langdon, Harold Lloyd, and Roscoe "Fatty" Arbuckle creating a Golden Age of Comedy (although Arbuckle's career was eclipsed by scandal, due to dubious sex-abuse charges that erased him from the nation's screens by the mid–1920s). Considered a novelty only one decade earlier, motion pictures were now one of America's paramount new cultural forces, and stars like Mary Pickford, Douglas Fairbanks, Rudolph Valentino, John Gilbert, Clara Bow (*The "It" Girl*) and, by decade's end, Greta Garbo, enthralled the public with their romantic dramas and adventures.

And though films remained silent until later in the Twenties, the newfound technological miracle of radio brought a whole new soundtrack of worldwide news, modern music, comedy and drama programs, advertisements, sports coverage, and political opinion into America's burgeoning households. "My older brothers listened to a crystal radio on homemade headsets," Puzo recalled decades later.

By the end of the 1920s, any American home with both a radio and a telephone was as cutting-edge and "connected" as one could possibly be. Young people, of course, considered such amenities essential. Many elders were annoyed and befuddled.

In no way was the so-called Generation Gap of the 1960s a new phenomenon. Back in the 1920s and 1930s, young Puzo ascertained such a vast chasm between all the immigrant parents and grandparents populating his neighborhood, and the brash, judgmental, sometimes harsh assessments of his fellow first-generation American kids. The elders were often perceived in a less than charitable manner: "They wore lumpy work clothes and handlebar mustaches," Mario remembered, "they blew their noses on their fingers, and they were so short that their high school children towered over them. They spoke a laughable broken English and the furthest limit of their horizon was their daily bread. Bent on survival, they narrowed their minds to the thinnest line of existence."

On the other hand, with the passage of time and after enduring his own perennial struggles as a husband and father in later decades, Puzo came to the conclusion that the elders in his neighborhood were nothing short of heroic; and the older he got, the more he marveled: "How did they ever have the balls to get married, have kids, go out and earn a living in a strange land, with no skills, not even knowing the language?" He asked such questions in retrospect, and then added with vehemence: "They made it without tranquilizers, without sleeping pills, without psychiatrists, without even a dream. Heroes. Heroes all around me. [But] I never saw them."

As always, however, money determined everything. And, while America in the 1920s roared on with its stock market rising and its new radios blaring and all those telephones literally ringing in a new epoch, the lack of money in the family of Mario Puzo had much to do with how and why his life became that of a witness to chronic frustration. As a careful listener and intent observer, what Puzo mostly did in his pre-teen years was alternate between the "careless magnanimity" that he shared with other children on the streets of New York (within the strict confines of their neighborhood's specified turf) and the witnessing of his mother's angry discontent.

"It was inevitable that my mother and I became enemies," Puzo said later in his life. "With my father gone, my mother the family chief, I, like all the children in all the ghettos of America, became locked in a bitter struggle with the adults responsible for me."

When he was twelve years old, Mario Puzo's father vanished from the family home. His behavior had been increasingly erratic. On some nights, after work hours, he would wander the local neighborhood streets, lost in his own world of silent and mysterious distress.

Puzo's father was a trackman laborer for the locally predominant New York Central Railroad, a vast complex that served as that neighborhood's primary employer for males: "Nearly all the Italian men living on Tenth Avenue supported their large families by working on the railroad," Puzo recalled. "Their children also earned pocket money by stealing ice from the refrigerator cars in summer and coal from the open stoking cars in winter." One day he was told by his foreman to go fetch enough water to slake the thirst of a crew on duty. Antonio Puzo wandered away in search of buckets of water, and he kept wandering. He did not look back. And he did not return to work. "He was a mystery," Puzo later concluded: "a Southern Italian with blue eyes, who departed from the family scene . . . when I was twelve."

By the time Mario was thirteen, his father was institutionalized as a schizophrenic and the family was forced to go on Home Relief to make ends meet. The confusing, frightening, disorienting aspects of such a major shake-up in a large, poor, immigrant family were offset by the grit, the mental toughness, and the sheer force of personality exuded by Maria Le Conti Puzo.

She not only stepped up to the many challenges now facing her family and herself, she evolved into a maternal sergeant. And while Puzo's wildfire imagination was sustained by his frequent trips to the nearest public library, as well as the cozy library housed within the Hudson Guild Settlement House (whose social benefits swiftly became stabilizing and beneficent forces throughout Puzo's early teen years), each day at home was a reality check.

"I never came home to an empty house," Puzo reflected when he was fifty years old. Not only was there "always the smell of supper cooking." Something equally vivid and compelling set the agenda. Puzo's mother's stern presence was almost always ruling the roost. "My mother was always there to greet me, sometimes with a policeman's club in her hand (nobody ever knew how she acquired it). But she was always there, or her authorized deputy, my older sister, who preferred throwing empty milk bottles at the heads of her little brothers when they got bad marks on their report cards."

Throughout his boyhood in the Depression-plagued 1930s, Puzo never experienced a lack of food or lousy food. No matter what, his mother figured out how to manage otherwise. Maria Le Conti Puzo "would never dream of using anything but the finest imported olive oil, the best Italian cheeses." It certainly helped that all of her sons at varied times were employed by the New York Central Railroad, which was a short walking distance from Tenth Avenue. Puzo's oldest brother was a brakeman for the railroad; and another of his brothers worked as a clerk. Before he was sent away, the job that Puzo's father had held gave him "access to the fruits coming off ships, the produce from railroad cars, all before it went through the stale process of middlemen." Surely such "access" was enjoyed by the sons Antonio left behind.

After all, as Puzo confirmed with a shrug and fundamental sense of honesty when looking back on his childhood, "teen-agers were expert hijackers back then." And Maria Le Conti Puzo did not hesitate to step forward as "their best customer." In 1931, when Mario was eleven, one incident literally brought the issue home. A local youth had been pursued by the police, who chased the chicken-snatching petty thief up six flights of stairs and right into the Puzo's apartment. They began to beat the boy. And the temper of Puzo's mother exploded. She screamed at the police. She intervened and prevented the boy's arrest. "She believed he was entitled to steal the chickens," Puzo explained, "and she was entitled to buy them." The boy was let go.

Such a basic philosophy proved to be a great asset to Puzo's mother, whom he once described as "like most Italian women . . . a fine cook in the peasant style."

The pleasures of food were not just known to young Mario Puzo within the confines of his mother's kitchen. For six summers in a row, between 1929 and 1935, as Puzo later reflected, the Hudson Guild "was also responsible for absolutely the happiest times of my childhood . . . they sent me away as a Fresh Air Fund kid." He qualified to participate in the Fresh Air Fund's program for poor urban children. "This was a program where slum children were boarded [with] private families in places like New Hampshire for two weeks." And for those summer weeks, Puzo spent blissful days and nights in a bucolic setting with a childless couple in New Hampshire. There he marveled at the vegetables grown in their own backyard garden, while also enjoying the splendors of relaxed, royal picnic lunches.

The Fresh Air Fund was a privately funded opportunity that was made available under the auspices of the Hudson Guild Settlement Project. Much like the Catholic Youth Organization (the CYO) in Chicago and elsewhere, the Hudson Guild served a variety of needs for the poorer families in the milieu of Puzo's youth. Athletic teams were organized and educational programs were offered. A band program and a theater group were sponsored by the Hudson Guild. But the Fresh Air Fund exceeded the possibilities that those daily in-house programs made available.

Puzo was extricated from his stone laden and increasingly hot, humid Tenth Avenue neighborhood. Suddenly removed from the crowded family home and the stressful pressures of life on the streets of New York, those six boyhood summers provided Mario with trips to a safe, clean, utterly wholesome wonderland. The program never failed to live up to its promising name.

The clean air struck young Puzo—who was used to the grimy odors, the sooty filth, and the oily stenches emanating from the New York Central Railroad, which was located adjacent to his apartment building—as nothing less than miraculous. And just as miraculous were the endless fields of green. Fresh apples and oranges fell from their trees. There were clean, often empty country roads. Cows roamed here and there. And most of all there was quiet. The home of the older Baptist couple who hosted Puzo offered him a serene, orderly, polite, soft-spoken, conflict-free environment. Nobody shouted at each other. No fights broke out (within the home or outside of it). All urban tensions dissolved. Mario considered it a haven.

"When I got to New Hampshire," he recalled, "when I smelled grass and flowers and trees, when I ran barefoot along the dirt country roads, when I drove the cows home from pasture, when I darted through fields of corn and waded through clean brooks, when I gathered warm brown-speckled eggs in the henhouse, when I drove a hay wagon drawn by two great horses—when I did all of these things—I nearly went crazy with the joy of it. It was quite simply a fairy tale come true."

Puzo had no formal (or even informal) religious training as a child, and yet his fortnights in the countryside caused him often to define events with religious language: "A cucumber or a strawberry in the earth was a miracle," he averred.

During the summers when the Fresh Air Fund sent him to New Hampshire, his host couple held to their strictly scheduled Baptist protocols. And that involved much more than their Thursday night prayer meetings. To honor their religious tenets, the host couple refused to see movies. In fact, as Mario once clarified, they "had never seen a movie. They disapproved of dancing, they were no doubt political reactionaries; they were everything that I came later to fight against. And yet they gave me those magical times children never forget."

There was a three-hour church service on Sunday mornings, followed by a Bible study class. And rather than resist or rebel, Puzo enjoyed those, too. Why not? He knew his host couple would soon indulge his passion for extended picnic outings. All that was required was a bit of rhetorical revision, none of which was lost on the wide-open ears of young Puzo: "When they saw how much I loved picnics, the sizzling frankfurters on a stick over the wood fire, the yellow roasted corn, they drove me out on Sunday afternoons to a lovely green grass mountainside. Only on Sundays it was never called a picnic; it was called 'taking our lunch outside.'" Such a euphemism was needed in a realm where enjoying picnics on Sunday was sinful.

For the bookish young man who was dreading the fact that by age 16 he'd have to join his brothers at the New York Central Railroad and begin what looked to be a life of menial toil and low-income drudgery, the Baptist services on Sunday (there was a second church gathering after the long midday meal) struck Puzo as further examples of safely calibrated and ultra-civilized patterns.

He marveled at the generosity and thoughtfulness that his hosts exuded. They bought him his first pair of brand-new pajamas. They bought him new clothes each year. Throughout the school year, when Puzo was ensconced in the concrete jungle of Hell's Kitchen and steeped in the noisy, hectic, noxious environment that he had no choice but to accommodate each day, reminders of his summertime privilege would arrive in the mail. His host family sent him birthday presents in October and Christmas gifts in December. Mario Puzo remembered their kindness all of his life.

The man hosting young Puzo had a complete inventory of tools and he knew how to use them. As those six summers unfolded, he gradually built for Puzo a playground of special amenities. Before the end of this phase of their lives, a seesaw and some swings and sliding ponds had all been constructed. "I believed then, as a child," Puzo later confirmed, "that the state of New Hampshire had some sort of gates at which all thieves and bad guys were screened out. I believed this . . . because [their] house was left unlocked when we went to church on Sundays and Thursday nights. I believed it because I never heard anyone curse or quarrel with raised voices. I believed it because it was beautiful to believe."

Opting again to make use of religious terminology, Puzo once summed up: "From this Paradise I was flung into Hell. That is, I had to help support my family by working on the railroad."

Before entering the world of work, however, Puzo's early life offered unto him one other major element that for years provided a buffer between tensions at home and the frightening insecurities of the world at large. That element was the Hudson Guild Settlement House. It was far more than an agency that helped facilitate the all-important two-week summertime trips to New Hampshire in league with the Fresh Air Fund. Much closer to home, on a daily basis, the Hudson Guild served as a place to go to. A retreat. And the benefits to Puzo were all about body, mind, and soul.

"As rich men escape their wives by going to their club, I finally escaped my mother by going to the Hudson Guild Settlement House," Mario recalled.

The Hudson Guild was a five-story edifice that combined almost all the aspects of a social club with a social-service mission. On one floor were large rooms with pool tables, ping-pong tables, and other recreational games. Elsewhere there was a shop where youngsters could relax and learn the craft of making lamps. A theater was thriving on another floor, and plays were always in the process of being either rehearsed or studied, and occasionally performed. And the gym, of course, was a beloved resource for physical exercise.

Athletics came naturally to Puzo in his teens. He vigorously played on teams that the Hudson Guild sponsored. Baseball. Basketball. Football. He played fast and he played hard. The weight problems that would plague him later in life were not an issue in his teen years. He was, like a great many of the Italian-American urban male youth of his generation, a muscular, sculpted, dark-haired, dark-eyed young man.

And his participation in the varied sports programs that the Hudson Guild offered induced in young Puzo a period of leadership efforts. Just playing was not enough. He captained more than one team. He forced himself to try as hard as possible to be not just an excellent player—whatever the sport—but also a dynamic leader.

"At the age of eleven," he once explained, "I became captain of my club football team for seven years and president of the Star Club, an office I held for five. I enjoyed that success more than any other in my life. And learned a great deal from it. At the age of fifteen I was as thoroughly corrupted by power as any other dictator until I was overthrown by a coalition of votes; my best friends joining my enemies to depose me. It was a rare lesson to learn at fifteen."

Other lessons were being learned, too. A certain holiday tradition harking back to earlier years had incrementally shaped an entirely non-academic side of Puzo's learning curve. "In my childhood," he once reported, "Christmas Eve was a time for all the family and relatives to play cards, it was one of the holiday treats." And for Mario, it wasn't a treat limited to Christmastime.

He discovered a definite knack for the tempo and strategies required for playing cards. It's not for everyone. Sitting impassively and not letting all sorts of physical tics, twitches, and other signals give away one's hand by way of "tells" demands focus and real attention.

Remembering others' "tells" (and not indicating with chuckles, sudden smirks, or any other sign of competitive energy that one has noted the tics and twitches of other players) is essential. It is crucial is to tamp down one's emotions and wildfire thoughts of easy winnings, thus never allowing an adrenaline rush to dictate one's choices.

"In my childhood I squeezed in a lot of card playing while becoming a sports hero on Tenth Avenue and reading Dostoyevsky," said Puzo. It's fascinating to think that he may have read and reread the brooding Russian's novella *The Gambler*. No less fascinating is the image of young Mario Puzo—barely in his teens—and already quite at home not just with a deck of cards, but with the protocols and the basic flow of older men whose lives revolved around sitting at card tables (indoors or out). "I was playing poker with very tough workingmen beneath lampposts in the streets of New York or in the backs of local candy stores," he later recounted.

As for the Star Club: In its informal way, they were something of a gang that in Puzo's estimation "had been pacified by the Hudson Guild Settlement House." They had their own football, basketball, and baseball teams. And best of all, they enjoyed a special room at the Hudson Guild where they could meet, make plans, schedule games, and be safe. It was the ultimate urban tree house.

The Hudson Guild also provided a volunteer guidance counselor, usually a young man attending college. One of them was Ray Dooley— "whom I remember with affection to this day," Puzo wrote decades later. Ray Dooley had a car and during wintertime he'd take Mario and his Star Club pals on weekend outings to the Hudson Guild Farm in nearby New Jersey, "where we hitched our sleds to his car, towed at thirty miles an hour."

The four seasons had much to do with whatever Puzo's priorities were. "In the summertime I was one of the great Tenth Avenue athletes, but in the wintertime I became a sissy," Mario sardonically explained: "I read books. At a very early age I discovered libraries." The Eleventh Avenue public library was but a few steps away.

At the Hudson Guild, where a small library was highlighted by comfortable reading chairs in which he could spend as much time as he pleased (or as much time as was possible), no stigma was attached to reading. "I loved reading in the Hudson Guild, where the librarian became a friend," he fondly noted.

And through voracious reading, the imagination of Mario Puzo was born and fully sustained, not just in his youth, but also for the rest of his life. At first the works of adventure writer Rafael Sabatini (*Captain Blood*, *The Sea Hawk*) enthralled him. "Part of my character to this day is Scaramouche, I like to think," he said at age 50.

Popular well-known "boys' books" hit the spot, with Jack London and Robert Louis Stevenson transporting Puzo to other times, exotic places, and royal epochs by way of their words. But it was Dostoyevsky's dark novels that touched Mario's soul.

Puzo had a truly impassioned reaction in his mid–teens when reading the works of Dostoyevsky, a reaction that he would reflect upon with special emphasis until the end of his life: "I wept for Price Myshkin in *The Idiot*, I was as guilty as Raskolnikov [in *Crime*

and Punishment]. And when I finished *The Brothers Karamazov* I understood for the first time what was really happening to me and the people around me. I had always hated religion even as a child, but now I became a true believer. I believed in art. A belief that has helped me as well as any other."

Meantime, there was the glare of Maria Le Conti Puzo, whom Mario remembered as looking "on all this reading with a fishy Latin eye. She saw no profit in it." And yet the compassionate streak that Dostoyevsky was helping to draw forth from young Puzo also compelled him to realize that "there may have been some envy. If she had been able to, she would have been the greatest reader of us all."

Mario's own passion for reading doubtless provided him with many a window onto the world he was reluctantly moving toward as his teenage years segued to young adulthood. When not immersed in chapters of Dostoyevsky or when he wasn't rereading (as he would throughout his life) the tales of King Arthur that had entranced him since boyhood, he had more than ten daily newspapers all around him on the streets of New York in the 1930s. On any given day, whether by glancing at headlines or actually reading the stories (maybe just by scanning the lead paragraphs), Puzo's voracious reading habits paid off by allowing him quickly to apprehend the extraordinary variety of information in the daily newspapers.

When set against the historical backdrop of the 1930s, it becomes obvious that Mario Puzo's coming-of-age years were anything but a time of innocence.

Puzo's 13th birthday occurred in October 1933, when Franklin D. Roosevelt's legendary First 100 Days were already half a year gone by. And before the end of the year, major stories like the repeal of Prohibition and the violent attacks by U.S. Army troops on the World War One veterans (known as the Bonus Marchers) who had made their way to Washington, D.C. to petition for the token fiscal bonus that they'd been promised when their war ended, were already fast receding.

Now the embryonic New Deal programs were the talk of the nation, but it would take months and even years before programs translated into progress for most individual citizens. FDR's fireside chats provided hope to the country's radio listeners, but from the get-go President Roosevelt also had plenty of enemies. While perceived as a unifying force by his admirers, FDR was also a highly divisive figure. So divisive, in fact, that when he ran for re-election in 1936 he cheerily said of those who despised him: "I welcome their hatred!"

In between those milestone years—that is, in between 1933 and 1936—as Puzo made his way through Commerce High School at 60th Street, gradually chalking up his fourteenth, fifteenth, and sixteenth birthdays, the individual markers in his life were matched by cultural signposts in the life of the country. When he turned 14 in 1934, he was one of those young American boys—many millions of whom went to the movies each week, where a ticket cost a nickel or a dime, depending on whether or not there was also a "Live!" stage show of one kind or another—who enjoyed the rise of Clark Gable as America's new male icon. That was the year when the newly crowned King of Hollywood caused the sale of men's undershirts to nosedive in the marketplace, because women and girls collectively swooned over Gable's Academy Award-winning performance in Frank Capra's *It Happened One Night*, and a crucial scene found him bare-chested after he removed his button-down dress shirt.

By the time of Mario's fifteenth birthday in 1935, the radio airwaves were filled with the exciting new swing music being played by Benny Goodman. After many years of struggle, the clarinet-playing Goodman now helmed a highly charged new band modeled on the instrumental protocols perfected years earlier by Duke Ellington and others. Swing music was buoyant. It sizzled. It was thrilling to dance to, but for many equally satisfying to listen to. And if one didn't have the cash to buy any of the new records coming out, there was always the radio.

Benny Goodman's weekly "Camel Caravan" radio shows would soon be complemented by similar half-hour broadcasts starring other great new bands led by Tommy Dorsey, Glen Gray, Artie Shaw, Jimmy Dorsey, and by decade's end, Glenn Miller and a host of others. America's leading cigarette companies sponsored such programs with vigorous advertising (Old Gold and Artie Shaw or Glenn Miller and Chesterfield were spoken of over the radio as if the brand and the bandleader's name were one word), and before he finished high school Puzo had become a smoker. Hollywood glamorized cigarette smoking and there were no stigmas about pipes or cigars, either.

One English teacher, Mrs. Tyler, told Mario, with no qualms whatsoever, that his essays indicated a talent for writing. His compositions, she insisted, were "good enough to be published." And for such words to be offered to him at the same time that classic novels were informing his mind, uplifting his heart and filling his soul—well, the timing was exquisite.

Other English teachers at Commerce High School galvanized

Puzo's imagination just as much as Dostoyevsky or anyone else. They instilled in him a sense of *possibility*. And, perhaps most important of all, they planted in him the seed of an idea that he was nurturing and nourishing long before graduation day: *He* would be a writer.

No matter what. Someday. Although he was surrounded in his neighborhood (and inside his home) with a legion of others who were sure to find the notion absurd, his conviction was visceral. Some way, somehow, no matter what it took, Mario Puzo vowed that his life would be different. He was meant for something else. He was neither destined nor doomed to a life of toil on the New York Central Railroad. If Jane Austen (a writer he adored) could create books, so would he.

It was in the season of his sixteenth birthday, in the early autumn of 1936, that this blazing personal ambition was at last admitted to his mother and the world at large. He did not receive a round of applause. Instead, "when I let everybody know that I was going to be a great writer, my friends and family took the news quite calmly, my mother included," Puzo later remembered. "She did not become angry. She quite simply assumed that I had gone off my nut. She was illiterate, and her peasant life in Italy made her believe that only a son of the nobility could possibly be a writer." Meantime, the novels of Edith Wharton elucidated America's socio-economic class schisms, which intensified Puzo's observations about class.

Author Tom Santopietro reminds us that Puzo's mother was representative:

Early in the twentieth century, immigrant Italian women stayed at home, perhaps working as seamstresses while mixing almost exclusively with fellow immigrants. Forced to observe and listen, information became their currency. Seldom venturing beyond the confines of their immediate neighborhood, these women were much more likely than male immigrants to lack any true fluency in the speaking, let alone reading or writing, of English. When these women did in fact travel out of the Italian ghetto, they were faced with constant reminders, both verbal and visual, that their social values, clothes, and gregarious manner of speech were considered inferior to those of the refined ruling class descended from English stock. Outsider status proved the order of the day for the women, just as surely as it did the men.

Meantime, work. That's what mattered the most. For Maria Le Conti Puzo, the ideal situation for Mario—now that he was sixteen—was for him to apprentice to be a railroad clerk. "And that was her *highest* ambition," Puzo later observed; "she would have settled for less." The world was pressing in around him. Economically and geographically. After all, it's not as if his first job involved bold new journeys. Quite the other way. "Beneath our windows," he later mused, "were the black iron gardens of the New York Central Railroad, absolutely blooming with stinking boxcars freshly unloaded of cattle and pigs for the city slaughterhouse." It was all nearby. It had been for as long as he could remember. Now he had to go to work.

So, throughout the remainder of his junior and senior years at Commerce High School, each day when classes ended at three o'clock in the afternoon, Mario "went to work in the freight office as a messenger. I also worked Saturdays and Sundays when there was work available. I hated it."

As always, reading was the ultimate succor. Fortunately, in addition to the libraries he had access to on Eleventh Avenue, at school, and at the Hudson Guild, there was also at Puzo's disposal the plethora of newspapers and magazines that were available everywhere.

And by way of new issues of *LIFE* magazine, the most amazingly vivid and current photos of what was happening in the world—from the Spanish Civil War to Jesse Owens's triumphant running in Berlin at the 1936 Olympics; and from the bouts of Joe Louis to the ominous overseas images of Nazi Germany and Imperial Japan, already on the march in stricken parts of the world, ensuring that another international war was imminent—were complemented by often lengthy articles.

Back then, any young American with a hunger to write could not help but be aware that in the mid–to–late 1930s, in the major magazines as well as on the New Books shelves in the public libraries, there were newly published groundbreaking works by authors who at the time were controversial, often critiqued harshly, and in many ways just hitting their stride. Long before they were canonized by academe, they were "new writers."

Between the time Puzo turned sixteen in 1936 and his twentieth birthday in October of 1940, American letters were galvanized, scandalized, and to some extent rebooted by a stunning array of innovative works. John Steinbeck was making his mark, and shorter books like *Of Mice and Men* paved the way for *The Grapes of Wrath*, which in 1939 made his name a household word.

In that same four-year period between 1936 and 1940, after a career lull earlier in the 1930s, Ernest Hemingway roared back to life by publishing *To Have and Have Not* in 1937, quickly followed by his omnibus of collected short stories in 1938, all of which was topped off by *For Whom the Bell Tolls* in 1940. In those years, Papa was king of the hill (though he was scarcely 40 years old).

Similarly, there were inspiring, important new works from Richard Wright, whose *Native Son* in 1940 truly put him on the map. And it seemed as if John Dos Passos could not help but publish one chronicle after another.

The late Thomas Wolfe (who had died in 1938) was more popular than ever, thanks to *The Web and the Rock* and *You Can't Go Home Again*, the two massive posthumous novels that appeared in his name in 1939 and 1940. And so many other literary voices were in the air: James T. Farrell and William Faulkner; Clifford Odets and young Irwin Shaw; and during the same years the preponderance of captivating writers was matched by the surplus of phenomenal Swing bandleaders and their legions of virtuoso sidemen (when Benny Goodman's band performed the first-ever Jazz Concert at Carnegie Hall on January 16, 1938, the ensemble helmed by Goodman featured drummer Gene Krupa, piano man Teddy Wilson, trumpet-legends Harry James and Ziggy Elman, vibraphonist Lionel Hampton and other top-tier players, and they were all within the band itself or highlighted in Benny's smaller combos . . . but all part of one aggregation).

In short, there were cultural peaks being scaled. Yet in young Mario Puzo's realm—regardless of what he daydreamed about and irrespective of his wishes or how much he knew about the percolating arts scene that in many ways was New York's status quo—something more mundane formed his daily agenda.

School followed by work.

Nonetheless, his pronouncements about being a writer someday were not followed by ennui or procrastination. In between his school hours and his shifts at work, he started writing short stories. "One of my first short stories was about how I hated that job," he later noted. "But of course what I really hated was entering the adult world. To me the adult world was a dark enchantment, unnatural. As unnatural to the human dream as death. And as inevitable."

In the privacy of his mind, young Puzo harbored understandable fears about his future. "I really thought that I would spend the rest of my life as a railroad clerk," he once said. "That I would be married and have children and go to christenings and funerals and visit my mother on a Sunday afternoon. That I would never own an automobile or a house. That I would never see Europe, the Paris and Rome and Greece that I was reading about in books from the public library. That I was hopelessly trapped by my family, by society, by my lack of skills and education."

In his second novel, 1965's *The Fortunate Pilgrim* (which Puzo considered his best work, certainly his own favorite), the character of younger brother Gino gets a glimpse of the freight office where his older brother Vinnie works at a desk. The scene makes clear that so-called white-collar work was no panacea either:

> *It was like a nightmare in which a man sees a prison that he knows he will someday come to live in. There were long rows of desks with billing machine typewriters spewing forth rolls of multiple lading accounts. The men who operated these machines were all in vests and white shirts and loose, dangling ties. They were older than Vinnie, and they were very quick. The machines clattered blindly. Each desk had its own yellow lamp . . . There was no sound of voices. There was no hint of daylight outside. It was as if these people were all entombed above the rumbling of the coupling freight trains that moved below in the pit of the building. Gino looked, and at last he spotted Vinnie.*

> *Vinnie was the only man without a vest, and he wore a colored shirt so he could use it two or three days without changing.*

Despite being young, healthy, employed, and surrounded by family and friends, not to mention a bona-fide high school graduate—which was then a major milestone for Americans, many of whom never earned a diploma—Mario Puzo was miserable between ages eighteen and twenty-one. "I hated my life," he simply stated.

From any angle whatsoever, that is truly one hell of a thing for a person to say about his or her emergence into adulthood. Nonetheless, Puzo was adamant: "I hated my life." Between 1938 and 1941, those four words (even after the passage of a great deal of time) summed up his post-high school period, which for many others is a time of excitement, perhaps adventure (going off to college, joining the military, traveling somehow—if one can afford to) or at least a sense of hope and growth.

There was, however, one notable exception in this period of discontent. In 1939, the year he turned nineteen, with high school behind him and nothing but "a drudge job" on the railroad on his agenda, Puzo was accepted into the Civilian Conservation Corps (CCC). This New Deal program afforded him a glorious opportunity to do what has long been considered essential for a young American man. To go West. And he did. Out in Lovelock, Nevada, young Puzo's sense of self was considerably enhanced when he discovered that he felt right at home in the world of casinos.

At that time, it was Reno (most famous for its quickie divorces) that allowed for the bulk of legal gambling in the state of Nevada. Only after World War Two would Las Vegas emerge in all of its neon, gaming glory. "But Lovelock was only a couple of hours from Reno," as Puzo recounted, "which was then *the* gambling city."

When the young men in the CCC were not preoccupied with their tree planting, bridge building, and other restorative projects, the environs of Lovelock, Nevada, offered certain opportunities.

Two whorehouses were located just outside of town: One was named "My Place" and the other was called "Jo Ann's." Puzo would laugh with everyone else when attending one of the local movie theaters, because it seemed inevitable that at one point a character would say: "Let's go over to my place." At which point the audience would erupt in cheers and whistles.

Once again Mario discovered how centered and how utterly *right* he felt in the milieu of cards, dice, and other compelling distractions. One night, as he "sat in a casino in Reno decorated like Hell, rock-red walls, hostesses wearing devils' tails, mascaraed eyes under devil-horned caps," on the cusp of his 19th birthday, Mario was so smitten with a "pretty hostess" that he spent his last three dollars buying "sucker drinks" and remained blithely unaware that for a mere two dollars extra, she would have taken him to bed.

"She was so beautiful that it never occurred to me that she was a hooker," Puzo later revealed. He then added: "But now I realize I was never a degenerate gambler. A degenerate gambler would never spend his last three dollars buying drinks . . . He would have tried to get lucky at craps."

Mario did get lucky that night, nonetheless. After briefly crashing and dozing fitfully for hours in a back-room furnished with wooden tables for broke customers to sleep on, Puzo made his way to the local train station. There his background with railroad work held him in good stead. He befriended some decent men, and they set him up for a free ride on a locomotive headed back to Lovelock. To ensure his safety, they made sure that Mario met the train's engineer. He granted Puzo a stirring early-morning episode resembling a page out of the novels of Jack London.

"I rode beside the engineer and will never forget that ride through the desert with dawn breaking," Mario gratefully recounted. "A teenaged, busted-out gambler coming home just in time for camp breakfast. No money in my pockets, no worries in my head. Enjoying the stunning morning air and light. Two years later my CCC camp would be an Army camp and we'd be at war. A lot more important things would happen to me, but I never forgot that night ride through the desert."

However, in Puzo's case, there was no moving away from home in order to lead his own life. Not only would that have been too costly but it would have burdened his mother with increased fiscal stress due to his breakaway.

Unlike many young men and women who light out on their own—one way or another—in the years after completing high school, Mario did not exit the family home. Which was, of course, the tenement apartment that he'd called home for the longest time.

"Not even my gift for retrospective falsification can make my eighteenth to twenty-first years seem like a happy time," he later remarked. And it was no random quirk or fabricated funk that caused him to define three entire years as a loss. There were specific and all-encompassing personal reasons why young Puzo felt that his life was shrinking, not developing. Contracting, instead of expanding. Drying up. And making him depressed.

"I was being dragged into the trap I feared and had foreseen even as a child," he said.

And it's important to highlight that when Puzo as a child looked all around him and noted the bad tempers, the fatigue, and the despondency of the exhausted relatives, neighbors or others in his midst, he had a child's freedom to go and play; or to let his imagination carry him away for extended periods of unencumbered time.

Now, each day's schedule was determined by work. And that also applied to the weekends. In addition to which his presence was expected for traditional family meals (especially on Sunday).

Incrementally his life's course was being set by the calcified routines and ossified patterns around him.

"It was all there, the steady job, the nice girl who would eventually get knocked up, and then [there would be] the marriage and fighting over counting pennies to make ends meet," he later recalled with a sense of having barely escaped. Puzo also said: "I noticed myself acting more unheroic all the time. I had to tell lies in pure self-defense, I did not forgive so easily." In short, his life did not match his vision.

It is during such transitions from one life phase to another (whether it's after high school and into the world of work or after one marries and then "settles down" or following a military hitch and then the return to civilian life) that one is likely to hear the clarion call of all those voices that say, more or less: "Time to grow up!"

And usually such mandates are followed by the Give Up Your Dreams lecture. It is at such times that one unexpected pregnancy or one arrest or a single turning point of one sort or another can vehemently jolt a young person's life. Fortunately, in Puzo's case, there was never a pregnancy caused by any recklessness or an arrest on his record. Even though he was in the prime of youth, he already believed in caution.

Meantime, his imagination was the weapon with which he fought to be himself. It was at this crucial time that Puzo discovered a personal knack for what he later dubbed "retrospective falsification." He used it as a tool for self-preservation.

"At the age of eighteen," he explained later in life, "I started dreaming about the happiness of my childhood. As later at the age of thirty I would dream about the joys of my adolescence . . . I had the most valuable of human gifts, that of retrospective falsification: remembering the good and not the bad."

And one other dream-based gift kept Puzo from succumbing to anything resembling despair: His writing. About which he continued to make personal vows. "I still dreamed of future glory," he admitted. "I still *knew* I would be a great writer, but I was beginning to realize that accidents could happen and my second choice, that of being a great criminal, was coming up fast."

He also realized that his lack of panache with romance ensured that his sex life would remain thwarted. Even as a young man, Puzo was a great listener (a trait that in his later years would be his hallmark). "I listened to female conversations that made my head ache," he once reflected, "[and] I fell in love with women who tenderly told me that I was their best friend and so, therefore, they could never be my bedmate. These same women [went] to the ends of the earth to sleep with guys I could beat in handball, chess and IQ tests . . . I bought young girls countless theater dinners, rode the subway with them to the farthest outposts of the Bronx . . . and received in return never more than a friendly kiss on the cheek."

Mario Puzo in the mid-1940s; photographer unknown.

2
Active Player

She went on. "My son sleeps in the house of his mother, his brothers, his sisters. Until he has a wife. That, or he goes off to reform school to enjoy his pleasure. At eighteen let him leave and I will not be his mother. But until he is of age I have no choice. None of my children will be pimps or jailbirds or murderers."
~~~ Mario Puzo, *The Fortunate Pilgrim*

"I evacuated French civilians under shellfire."
~~~ Mario Puzo, *Fools Die*

It stands as a tribute to Puzo's common-sense reticence and also to his mother's overbearing presence that while he entertained fantasies of "being a great criminal," he never came close (at that time) to trouble with the law. In his milieu, it would not have been difficult to find his way into illegal activities. To use the jargon perfected by Hollywood gangster films that dominated American movie screens throughout Puzo's youth (from *The Public Enemy* with James Cagney in 1931 to *High Sierra* with Humphrey Bogart in 1941, plus dozens of other gangster movies starring Bogart or Cagney—sometimes together—or Edward G. Robinson or Paul Muni or George Raft) a "life in the rackets" was always an option. After all, as Mario once remarked about his environment: "[My] particular neighborhood could have been a movie set for one of the Dead End Kid flicks or for the social drama of the East Side in which John Garfield played the hero. Our tenements were the western wall of the city."

Besides, in many of those neighborhood poker games of his youth, it wasn't just the older workingmen sitting opposite Puzo. Also welcomed to some of those games were "local strong-arm punks and nickel-and-dime stickup artists." Without at all missing the ironic undertone of his reflections on this phase of his youth, Mario flat-out insisted (from the vantage point of his mid–fifties) that he believed gambling was one of the forces that kept him "out of jail." Puzo elaborated: "I grew up in a tough neighborhood with a lot of opportunities to get into serious trouble. While some of my buddies were out late burglarizing and strong-arming, I was trying to break the candy store owner in [games of] casino."

Were those late-night excursions sanctioned by Puzo's mother? No. She was unaware of his precise activities, and assumed that more biological urges were at play. After staying out until all hours in his later teens, Maria Le Conti Puzo ranted at Mario. "My mother screamed that I would be forced to marry the girl, that I would get her into trouble. I only wished she was right. I was too shy with girls to have any luck or any dates. I was out until 4 A.M. still trying to make my fortune in poker."

If Puzo's life had gone in another direction and if he had apprenticed as a numbers runner or the ally of a small-time crook instead of as a railroad clerk, a sequence of courtrooms and judges could have found him on a dubious path. Instead, limiting his local gambling forays to games risking no more than "nickels, dimes, and quarters," it later occurred to Puzo that not only did his passion for cards keep him "out of jail"; such immersions also provided mental respite from the stress of his young male adulthood. "It made me forget for a few moments that my sex life was incomplete," he said. "Sometimes at the enamel-topped card table at the back of a candy store I would think of the stories I would write that would make me a rich and famous author," he mused when he was much older. "I never misled myself for a moment, even then, that I could make my fortune gambling."

Thus he stayed the course with the job he hated, buoyed by his imagination. He continued to write short stories. True, he was frustrated and unhappy and fearful about living his life that way forever. "But for the young everything goes so slowly," he realized. "I could wait it out. The world would wait for me. I could still spin out my life with dreams."

Until December 7, 1941. That's when the dreaming stopped for Puzo's generation. Once FDR declared war on Japan in the immediate aftermath of the attack on Pearl Harbor, reality set in with a vengeance. And yet, for Puzo (and for untold numbers of other frustrated, thwarted young men), this was also a time of new beginnings.

"I was delighted . . . terrible as it may sound," Puzo confessed. "My country called. I was delivered from my mother, my family, the girl I was loving passionately but did not love. And delivered WITHOUT GUILT. Heroically. My country . . . ordered me to defend it. I must have been one of millions—sons, husbands, fathers, lovers—making their innocent getaway from baffled loved ones."

Similarly, along with millions of others—eventually there would be fifteen million American men in uniform when the war hit its peak in 1945—there was for Puzo the jolting transition out of civilian life and into his new life in the U.S. Army. At age 21, now standing five feet and six inches tall, Puzo was transformed into a soldier.

Contrary to the tons-of-fun comedy films of the era (Abbott and Costello's wildly popular *Buck Privates* made induction and basic training seem like a vaudeville show), the life-transforming process later anatomized by author James Jones as "The Evolution of a Soldier" (which serves as the leitmotif of his nonfiction chronicle

WW II: A Chronicle of Soldiering, published in 1975) most definitely applied to Mario and his new cohort.

Jones later reflected on the speed with which innumerable lives were upended:

> *These were the young men who hastened joyously to enlist in the early days after Pearl Harbor, and for some months after. There is always that exciting feeling about the beginning of a war, or even of a campaign. I guess the closest way to depict the feeling is to liken it to a school holiday. All restraints are off, everyday life and its dull routines, its responsibilities are scratched and a new set of rules takes over. True, some people are going to die, but probably it will not be oneself. And for a while, at least, adventure will reign.*

> *In any case, the new enlistees, and new draftees . . . got a pretty rude awakening. With the induction ceremony the honeymoon got over pretty quickly. Men who had been raised to believe, however erroneously, in a certain modicum of free thinking were being taught by loud, fat, devoted sergeants to live as numbers, by the numbers.*

One thing's for sure. Mario doubtless missed the first-rate cooking and the nutritious meals always provided by Maria Le Conti Puzo. There would be no use of "the best olive oils" in the military. Nor would there be endless quantities of fresh bread, delectable pastas, protein-laden meatballs, and exquisite sauces. In general, the shift from his civilian eating patterns to the army's exceedingly basic culinary menu had to be a bit shocking to Puzo. Future fellow author James Jones summed it up well when he wrote to his brother about the army's breakfast offering on Thanksgiving Day back in 1939, when Jones was a newly enlisted inductee.

On that day, Jones's breakfast consisted of one tiny box (a manufacturer's sample) of cereal, plus a mere half-pint of milk, along with a butter pat (limited to one per man). The main dish was a piece of toast that was slathered in leftovers from the prior night's dinner. Between the toast (which Jones remembered as "rubbery") and the slop ladled upon it, he noted that "the stomach-churning dish [is] rather aptly described by the soldier's word for it: shit on a shingle."

And in every other way—from its all-male environs to its clockwork precision with schedules and all agendas—the Army was a parallel universe wherein most of the daily amenities that even a working stiff could take for granted did not prevail. Any sense of personal freedom regarding the ability to come and go was taboo. Like it or not, one's personal rhythms were of no interest to the barking sergeants.

Unlike some of his fellow draftees, however, Puzo had plenty of experience with demanding, tough, tiresome physical work. He may have once apprenticed as a messenger boy for the New York Central Railroad, but inevitably he had done other kinds of work involving brute strength and long hours. That was a huge advantage.

Contrarily, there were other future writers in the ranks (or there would be as the draft calls increased exponentially as the war reached its apex in 1944 and 1945), and for some of those writers— who had enjoyed years of comparative pampering on college campuses prior to induction—the military transition was shocking. After his four years at Harvard, for example, young Norman Mailer (a Brooklyn mama's boy if ever one existed) felt pummeled by the physical demands of basic training.

In the case of Mario Puzo, the years he had spent as a railroad employee helped him considerably. He was not allergic to dirt, dust, grime, or sweat.

But he surely did not care for it. Furthermore, he quickly ascertained that the fundamental and chronic physical courage required to be gung-ho as a soldier was not his forte.

Like many city kids who assumed that their street smarts and their "turf wars" back at home were enough to have made them rugged, Mario found out quickly that such was not always the case.

There were times when the corn-fed rural farm boys had the edge. More than a half-century after the war's end, when interviewed for the *New York Times* by cultural critic Camille Paglia, this transition period was noted: "In the Army during World War II, Mr. Puzo had what he calls a 'rude awakening.' As a veteran of street fist fights, he thought he was a 'tough guy' until he was tossed head over heels by strapping farm kids in the hand-to-hand combat of basic training."

It certainly helped that the country boys hadn't begun smoking as teens.

Like many of his urban-bred peers, Puzo had been puffing away for years. And thanks to the ubiquitous availability of cigarettes in the service (when not given away for free they could be bought for a nickel a pack in any PX), a generation of heavy smokers was now evolving. By the time he was thirty, Puzo would switch effortlessly between cigarettes and cigars. But he respected certain boundaries.

Shortly before he was "about to go into the Army," Puzo paid a final visit to the home of the New Hampshire couple whose environs had been his haven in earlier summers. Now twenty-one, Mario was—as always—acutely aware of life's dichotomies: "The young were excessively grateful then," he noted, "so I did not smoke in their house nor did I follow up on a local maid who seemed promising."

Equally promising in Puzo's case was the possibility of surviving the war, even though he eventually served with the 4th Armored Division of the U.S. Army at the peak of the Second World War in Europe. A number of factors (both geographical and chronological) allowed Puzo to be up close and yet skin-of-his-teeth removed from several violently active, dangerous, hectic combat zones throughout the latter half of 1944 and the first half of 1945. He was, simply put, one lucky soldier.

For starters, Mario had poor eyesight. His marksmanship was worse than mediocre. And it wasn't for lack of trying. Like any young man with sensitivity to how he's perceived by others, Puzo would have been mortified if considered a coward or a malingerer. He was neither. He was, indeed, terribly far-sighted and thus a lousy risk in a rifle company. Toward the end of his life, Mario joked: "As a soldier, I was so inept, that it's a good thing I never had to handle a rifle!" So, being assigned to the 4th Armored Division was his first stroke of luck. Of course, plenty of danger and violence attended all those who served in armored units, but another bit of luck came Puzo's way due to his typing abilities. His skills as a clerk emerged.

One of the primary issues often ignored in PBS specials or high school textbooks in regard to the American Army in World War Two is the plain fact that the vast majority of GIs who were in the service were never "up front," let alone on the ever-hazardous front lines. Actually, even for the American soldiers who were on the ground in the European Theater of Operations, in particular, the majority served in a wide array of support services and other capacities. Fewer than twenty percent of the American men in uniform routinely fired weapons or fought in the infantry. In no way is this observation meant to slight anyone. Quite the other way.

It's important to understand that the almighty juggernaut of the combined Allied armies in the war against Hitler depended entirely on a 20-to-1 ratio of support troops to combatants. In short, for every G.I. Joe fighting up front, there were 20 other soldiers supporting him: Quartermaster Corps and their crucial Gas & Supply Companies; untold thousands of combat engineers; a seemingly infinite number of truck drivers ferrying supplies and materiel of all sorts (food, clothing, weapons, spare parts, ammunition, medical inventories), and so forth. Within each combat infantry or armored division, a similar separation of duties abounded.

In his classic study, *Wartime: Understanding and Behavior in the Second World War*, author Paul Fussell (a critic, historian, and combat memoirist) cites the year 1943 as representative of this issue: "In 1943 the Army of the United States grew by two million men, but only about 365,000 of those went to combat units, and an even smaller number ended in the rifle companies." Fussell explains more about this allocation of duties when highlighting that "by [1944] there were 11 million men in the American army, [but] only 2 million were in the 90 combat divisions, and of those, fewer than 700,000 were in the infantry." Fussell then sums up concisely:

> *If most civilians didn't know about these things, most soldiers didn't either, since only a relatively small number did any fighting which brought them into mortal contact with the enemy. For the rest, engaged in supply, transportation and administrative functions, the war constituted a period of undesired and uncomfortable foreign travel under unaccustomed physical and social conditions, like enforced obedience, bad food, and absence of baths. Thus, as William Manchester has said, "All who wore uniforms are called veterans, but more than 90 percent of them [were] as uninformed about the killing zones as those on the home front."*

Where Puzo's luck really held was in the geographical areas and the chronological timetable that delineated the orders of the 4th Armored Division, which trained in America for two solid years between 1942 and 1944. That stateside training was followed by the division's move to England, where intensive maneuvers took place between January and July of 1944. All along, the men knew that their division would soon play its part in the big push across Northwestern Europe that everyone assumed would be the war's decisive phase.

One of the principal clichés about military service is that it makes everyone a cog in the machinery of a vast, impersonal enterprise. An oft-recycled notion suggests that, invariably, the brutal necessities of any large-scale military campaign will transform all the individual human participants into desensitized human tools of destruction. In spite of whatever truth there may be within that colossal set of assumptions, there is an equally compelling flipside of issues to consider. Another way of seeing the big picture, so to speak. Given his lifelong and highly developed gift for observation, it stands to reason that Puzo took note of the phenomenon within which he served.

Contrary to the idea that all men in uniform are ciphers in the service of a faceless marauding juggernaut, the fact is that in certain phases of World War Two many of the GIs realized that their division, with its brigades and regiments, its battalions, companies, platoons, and squads, were nothing less than family-like units.

This is one of the aspects of wartime service that veterans frequently talk about, agreeing that there is simply no way to explain to civilians how unconditionally close and how eternally bonded the soldiers (or sailors or airmen or Marines) feel about each other. It's not a hackneyed "brothers" notion. And it's infinitely more complex than anything most films can suggest, because it's an internalized and ineffable sense of union and mutual devotion.

Of course, it's also chock-full of knotty contradictions.

For example, no American author to emerge out of the Second World War was a more powerful critic of the army's dehumanizing tendencies than novelist James Jones, who anatomized the crucible of his generation with meticulous narratives (*From Here to Eternity*, *The Pistol*, *The Thin Red Line*, and *Whistle*) that were saturated with details and universal in scope. Yet, in his fiction as well as his nonfiction writing about the war (especially in *WW II: A Chronicle of Soldiering*), Jones also heavily emphasized his own individual sense of pride and gratitude for having been able to serve as part of the 25th "Tropic Lightning" Infantry Division. Contradictions abound, as always. Jones detested the army's bureaucratized and technocratic ways of asphyxiating individual self-expression. But, at the same time, he admitted to a tremendous sense of personal exhilaration (at times) when his division, his regiment, his company, or his platoon or squad gelled as a unit.

In Puzo's case, much like Jones's (despite the fact that Jones served in the Pacific and Mario was in the European Theater of Operations), it's important to stress that being part of a highly-trained, aggressively successful division made a big difference. There's simply no comparison (save for national identity and the color of uniforms) between the training regimens, the caliber, or the experiences of the 4th Armored Division and the poorly trained, hurriedly deployed, and disastrously fated 106th Infantry Division, for example, wherein fellow author Kurt Vonnegut served (and within which Vonnegut witnessed blunders, inadequacies, and every type of fuck-up to be found in a massive organization, not to mention becoming a prisoner of war).

Although Mario Puzo's role in his division—that is, his Military Occupational Specialty (or MOS)—involved duties of comparative safety as opposed to the chronic dangers that the infantrymen and tankers or artillerymen and others were exposed to up front—it's equally true that Puzo's duties were crucial in the aggregate. It helps to understand the structure of the 4th Armored Division.

By definition, a battalion is "a large, organized group of people pursuing a common aim or sharing a major undertaking." In military parlance, the definition becomes "a large body of troops ready for battle, esp. an infantry unit forming part of a brigade typically commanded by a lieutenant colonel." Put numerically, a battalion is a military unit that consists of 300 to 1,200 soldiers (or Marines) spread out within two to seven companies.

Well, in Puzo's singular division, there were three separate Tank Battalions, three different Armored Infantry Battalions, and three specific Armored Field Artillery Battalions, plus an Armored Engineer Battalion and the 25th Cavalry Reconnaissance Squadron (Mechanized). Then: All of those elements were supported by the 126th Armored Ordnance Maintenance Battalion, plus the 46th Armored Medical Battalion. In addition to which, Puzo's division was fleshed out by the Headquarters and Headquarters Battery, the Division Artillery, and the Reserve Command.

Where Mario Puzo individually found himself was inside (or often in between) the Division Headquarters Company and the 144th Armored Signal Company, both of which dovetailed with the Forward Echelon, 4th Armored Division Headquarters and the Rear Echelon, 4th Armored Division Headquarters.

As the 4th AD made its way from Utah Beach across Normandy and Brittany and northern France, then to Belgium, Luxembourg, and across the Siegfried Line into Germany (concluding its campaign at war's end in Prague), it furnished Puzo with an extraordinary opportunity to witness the best and the worst of human behavior.

As fate would have it, the 4th Armored Division did not land at Utah Beach until more than one month after the D-Day landings at Normandy on June 6, 1944. But less than a week after landing at Utah Beach on July 11th (staggering logistical difficulties had to be overcome to put an armored division—numbering nearly 10,000 men, hundreds of tanks, and myriad other challenges—on the ground), the 4th AD had its baptism of fire on July 17th. Roped in as part of Operation Cobra, it fell to Puzo's division to secure the area all around Coutances in Northern France, which they did by July 28th.

By August 12th, after pivoting south to capture Nantes, the division succeeded at encircling and in effect cutting off the Brittany Peninsula. Things happened fast.

What made Puzo's situation unique, however, is that his duties kept him at a fairly safe remove from the war's greatest dangers while at the same time he served with an armored division that soon played a pugnaciously active, constantly combative role in the final ten months of the war in Europe. The 4th Armored Division may not have landed at Utah Beach until one month after the pivotal D-Day landings of June 6, 1944, but in short order the 4th AD also plunged headlong into the war's furies. "I evacuated French civilians under shellfire," says Puzo's doppelganger in his novel *Fools Die*, "I don't think I ever killed a German."

Once operations were underway, the division's commander (Lt. General John S. Wood) adamantly refused to approve for the 4th AD any particular nickname. That was unusual. Divisions took great pride in their media-celebrated nicknames: the 45th Infantry Division basked in their aura as "Thunderbirds," and the 42nd Infantry Division's appellation as "the Rainbow Division" harked back to World War One. In the case of the 4th AD, though, the word was put out. When asked by a war reporter how the division ought to be nicknamed, Wood's reply was blunt: "Name enough!" In other words, their formal identity was sufficient because their deeds told the tale.

Ironically, their deeds ended up inspiring (or inducing) at least three different nicknames. Because at specific times—especially when they pulled off a logistical miracle, rerouting and traveling (within one week) nearly 150 miles in horrid winter weather to relieve the beleaguered troops at Bastogne in Belgium at the height of the Battle of the Bulge during Christmas week in 1944—they performed an extraordinary array of duties with phenomenal competence. Regardless of Wood's injunction against nicknames, the 4th Armored Division became known in the press as "Patton's Vanguard," once they were attached to General George S. Patton's Third Army group, which succeeded at varied times with lightning force and progress at the task of knocking the German armies clear across Northern France. So many critical engagements with the enemy found the 4th AD emerging triumphant, with the Nazi forces reeling in defeat after defeat, that the Army press in *Stars & Stripes* called the 4th AD the "Breakthrough" division. And they most certainly were. Even the most cursory glance at their wartime agenda highlights one breakthrough after another.

After liberating their first French town at Coutances and then taking the city of Avranches (a key objective for the Allies), there was brutal fighting at Rennes, followed by rapid advances leading to the capture of Troyes and a breakthrough capped off by creating a bridgehead across the Seine on August 25, 1944 (when the weeklong Liberation of Paris was unfolding in all of its dizzying, ecstatic spectacle).

Again and again in September 1944, the 4th Armored Division led the way and crossed the Meuse and then the Moselle. Those milestones were soon followed by the savage fighting at the Battle of Singling, which climaxed in early December with the triumphant linking up of Patton's Third Army group and the Seventh U.S. Army. It was then that Hitler's last gamble furiously exploded in what's now known as the Battle of the Bulge. Every effort was made to attack the Americans at the weakest links in their chain of armies between Belgium up north and the Vosges Mountains to the south, and the shock and force of Hitler's mid–December counterattacks had extreme short-term success. Just as extreme, though, were the mind-boggling grit and mythic temerity of the American forces that managed, in the end, to defeat Hitler's last great offensive. And it fell to Mario Puzo's division to play a critical part in that crusade. Between December 20 and December 26 in 1944, the 4th AD played a pivotal role in speedily making tracks for Bastogne in Belgium, in effect rescuing the badly outnumbered, undersupplied men of the 101st Airborne Division, who had miraculously held on against all odds throughout ten days of ferocious fighting.

Two months later, the 4th AD smashed through the West Wall of Germany and one month after that crossed the Rhine. For a division that had no officially sanctioned nickname, they were destined to be a decisive force at so many critical junctures that even the Germans singled them out.

The "Breakthrough" division celebrated in *Stars & Stripes* (a.k.a. "Patton's Vanguard" as stateside American papers preferred to call them) was defined differently by the German soldiers. They routinely referred to the 4th Armored Division as "Roosevelt's butchers." They meant that as a compliment. Sort of.

And as rapid progress was made, it was the role of Puzo and his cohort to set up, facilitate, and sustain the temporary military headquarters that each liberated town or city required. Far more than bureaucratic drudgery was involved. Those military headquarters served briefly as the infrastructure and authority of newly liberated domains that had everything from food shortages to Nazi collaborators. Winning battles and chasing the Germans out of France was step one. The next step was to try to establish something resembling social order in the chaos left behind.

As a clerk typist, a reliable driver, and most of all as a soldier who instinctively knew how to exercise caution, Puzo was tailor-made for the type of "occupation" duties that followed the combat episodes necessary to push the Germans out.

By mid–September, having now swung eastward, the 4th Armored Division had quickly made tracks north of the Loire Valley, finally rumbling and crashing across the Moselle River between September 11th and 13th, after which the division flanked the city of Nancy and then captured the town of Luneville.

Continually, as the weeks and months unfolded, Puzo performed his duties with varied operations that always followed the battles. This pattern allowed Mario to be in the wake of the war, but not in its worst aspects. Although he was awarded five battlefield stars for serving in sectors that came under fire, he was spared the terrors of being an infantryman or a tanker.

To the end of his life, Puzo acknowledged his good fortune: "I drove a jeep, [and] toured Europe," he once reflected, "had love affairs, found a wife, and lived the material for my first novel." The paradox was never lost on him.

Europe was a graveyard when the war ended in May 1945. The combat casualties were a fraction in comparison to the civilian deaths, which numbered in the tens of millions.

There were shattered economies, a devastated landscape, stunning numbers of displaced and orphaned and lost individuals, not to mention the revelations of the Holocaust that arose as the Allied armies entered the parallel universe of the concentration camps. Food was scarce, starvation threatened many and diseases metastasized. It would take years for true recovery to commence. "Just after the [German] surrender," wrote historian Paul Fussell, "some 50,000 orphans could be found living in holes like animals." Puzo now witnessed plenty of such catastrophic postwar conditions.

Mario Puzo's twenty-fifth birthday occurred in October of 1945, two months after the grotesquely nicknamed atomic bombs, dubbed "Fat Man" and "Little Boy," put a final end to the Second World War. By the time that Puzo celebrated the birthday that signified his own personal quarter-century mark, the war in Europe had been over for nearly half a year. And unlike the vast majority of his fellow civilian-soldiers, Mario was not tallying up his service points and angling for the earliest possible discharge. Instead, he took stock of his life—past and present.

Doubtless he concluded that his options were few.

One option was to return to America and line himself up bureaucratically for a discharge as soon as possible. By the fall of 1945, the demobilization process was causing heads to spin in Washington, D.C. Now that the war had been won both in Europe and in the Pacific, the pressure put upon members of Congress to speed up the return home of approximately fifteen million soldiers, sailors, airmen, and Marines (the vast majority of whom were post-Pearl Harbor inductees with no interest in staying in the service) was intensifying. General George C. Marshall, the army's Chief of Staff who had been FDR's treasured advisor and would soon devise the Marshall Plan that partly saved postwar Western Europe, was utterly appalled by the numbers. Scant months after the war's end in the summer of 1945, there were 750,000 military discharges *per month* underway in the autumn of 1945.

On the record, Gen. Marshall said: "It wasn't a demobilization. It was a rout."

But the option of a swift discharge (for which Puzo did have the requisite points) didn't appeal to Mario. Now twenty-five years old and having proved himself to be competent at serving in certain capacities within the military, the prospect of being back at work for the New York Central Railroad was hardly a glimmering vision.

Another option was to think about a quick discharge as the necessary step toward using the newfangled GI Bill to acquire a college education. In Puzo's family, a high school diploma was considered a superlative achievement. To secure a college degree would be an extraordinary step up. And Mario was not unique in this regard. At war's end, when a monumental survey was conducted to file as much data as possible on the massive numbers of men and women who were soon to shed their uniforms, it was ascertained that only 25% of those in the military in 1945 were in possession of high school diplomas. The vast majority of individuals who created the armed aggregation that defeated Hitler and Tojo had left high school incomplete.

Now, however, chronology became irksome. Puzo was already twenty-five. And as an avid card player who by his own estimate "dealt a million hands of poker" while in the service for well over three years, he naturally evaluated any and all situations by their percentages. He weighed options. Considered this and that. Pondered the plusses and minuses. Looked for what would give him the edge. And knowing that a college career that commenced in 1946 could very well keep him in classrooms until he was nearly thirty years old . . . well, that held little appeal. First and foremost, he was already a voracious reader and a self-reliant autodidact. Besides, knowing that his ultimate dream was to write and to be published as a professional writer, he also knew that real writers stood to gain minimal benefits from classroom immersions.

The creative-writing cottage industry had scarcely begun, but Puzo had to know (as a New Yorker) that there were course offerings in fiction writing. Young writers were then widely aware of a handful of high-profile university-based instructors a' la Whit Burnett, whose early mentoring of Norman Mailer and J. D. Salinger helped both aspiring authors to get some of their nascent works into *Story Magazine*, which was often a stepping-stone to book publication. There was nothing like the glut of MFA programs in creative writing that would later mushroom throughout academe.

Did Mario see himself as a writer who could do well as a journalist? Absolutely not. He knew in his bones that he was a storyteller. Through and through. The nuts-and-bolts details of newspaper writing weren't for him. How about being an English teacher? Would it make sense to attend college on the GI Bill and earn a degree or two in English and then make a career as a teacher? For others, yes. But not for Puzo. He wisely sidestepped the indignity of lecturing to half-asleep minions.

What then? In a flash of insight that would lead to a slew of benefits both as a man and as a writer, Puzo opted to leave the Army but not entirely disengage from the military. He figured out how to be free of the oppressive challenges inherent to service as part of the Occupation Army, yet still manage to remain in Europe and to do so in a way that induced opportunities for gaining wider experience.

Before the end of 1945, Puzo chose to sign a clerk's civilian-contract with the U. S. Government, at the precise time when the War Department was being rebranded as the Department of Defense. And as a civilian employee of the Defense Department, he was assigned to duties in occupied Germany; duties that made full use of his skills as an administrative clerk with a large understanding of organizational needs and priorities. It may sound dull and by-the-numbers boring to think of clerking as a gateway to anything other than ennui, but postwar Europe was rife with intrigue, dangerous in ways that an ambitious writer would appreciate for sheer narrative intensity, and most of all in postwar Germany the occupying American forces and their civilian cohort were placed on the razor's edge of the new Cold War.

Insecurely, 1946 was unfolding.

And for individuals who looked at the latest news stories for a sense of how things were going in the world, the grim speech made on March 5, 1946, by former British Prime Minister Winston Churchill at a college in Fulton, Missouri, spoke volumes. In his speech, Churchill proclaimed that "from Stettin in the Baltic to Trieste in the Adriatic," there was now a new reality: "An iron curtain has descended across the Continent." In short, the geo-political rivalry between the USA and the USSR was escalating. Lines were being drawn as the map of the world was reconfigured after the war. The eyes of the world were on Eastern Europe most of all, as the Soviet Union consolidated its postwar power with authoritarian policies and geographical incursions that swiftly ended the wartime alliance between Moscow and America.

In Washington, D.C., every new week brought fresh worries about where, how, and when the Soviets might make the slightest move to expand control in what was commonly called their "sphere of influence." Similarly, in Western Europe and elsewhere in the world, the United States took the lead in exerting its power and establishing whatever controlling power it could (by way of installing puppet governments if necessary, but opting at other times to deploy massive quantities of aid and assistance to win over and secure allegiances in the postwar world).

To use the most simpleminded of analogies, the world in 1946 was (for its two mightiest postwar powers: the USA and the USSR) an international chess game, not the idyllic, peaceful, harmonious global family that was dreamed of when the war was being fought. And postwar Germany was a major pawn in the game being played between the White House and the Kremlin. It would be for decades.

There was a toxic atmosphere of intrigue, suspicion, and mutual fears. The Soviets dreaded the fact that America was then alone in its possession of atomic weapons, which were used twice over with devastating consequences in August 1945. On the other hand, America feared the overwhelming numbers present in the Red Army, which had not demobilized after the war and which was poised to attack in Europe at will, save for the restraints imposed by fear of America's atomic arsenal. None of this was lost on Mario Puzo.

He was, after all, a smart young who brought to all of life's situations the mentality of a seasoned poker player. And if the intelligence, skill, strategic wisdom, and tactical maneuvers required to be a good chess player have kin anywhere, it's in the realm of card players who never, ever confuse poker with gambling. It's not. Much like chess players, serious poker players apprehend the world at large through a savvy combination of skills that weigh multiple options, always taking the measure of the opponents with whom one is entangled. And most of all, whether it's a future president like Richard Nixon (whose poker-playing skills in the Navy in the South Pacific were prodigious) or a future novelist like Puzo, the ways of thinking in general by expert card players are often incisive and surprising.

In the case of Mario Puzo, a basic philosophy of life came into focus. The primary idea that took hold in Puzo's mind was that all human behaviors were ultimately negotiations of power. On every level. Public and private. It was as simple as that. In the new Atomic Age, at the highest level, the fate of the world would now hang in the balance as the presidents, prime ministers, generals, and others negotiated power plays and traded this for that (land, oil, steel, gas, or any other commodity). Negotiations of power, in private lives, defined everything as well. Husbands and wives? Parents and children? Siblings? In-laws? Power plays were always afoot.

At the lowest level, all around him in the bombed-out, half-starved, postwar ruins of what was then called West Germany (with East Germany under the USSR's lock and key), Puzo was a daily witness to the same impulse to survive and perhaps to get an edge. Only the stakes appeared to be different. But for the defeated Germans with whom Puzo now interacted on a regular basis, negotiations of power that involved issues of bread, meat, cigarettes, booze, cash dollars or military scrip, bars of soap or bouts of sex, all of it was fundamentally as driven by survival needs and self-interest as the geo-political strategic moves made by the world's leaders.

Puzo's personal vision of how the world worked—this entrenched idea that all human experience, at bottom, was a quest to improve one's position and to secure more power (or presumed power) for oneself with each little victory in whatever negotiation was underway, whether it was bidding war over black market food or a showdown at the poker table—would furnish a blueprint of ideas that in the future informed his novels their unique narrative leitmotifs.

Tellingly, this idiosyncratic vision of how the world really functioned harked back to Mario's years of studying facial twitches, impulsive gestures, personal tics, and all the varied "tells" that he ascertained while sitting at card tables in the back of the candy stores in Hell's Kitchen, and also while playing cards constantly in the army.

"Ask any soldier, sailor, or Marine how he spent most of his time during World War II," Puzo once asked rhetorically. Then he provided details: "Five days on a [troop] train from New York to Oklahoma I was resisting the temptation to deal the Ace of Spades from the bottom of the deck. Three weeks on a troop ship going to Europe I was honest but very lucky."

Mario recalled one negotiation of power that was dramatically vivid: "A not-so-lucky paratrooper put a pistol to my head," Puzo recalled, "which taught me another valuable lesson. You have to be more careful when you are innocent than when you are guilty."

Lesson learned.

As Puzo settled into his new life as a civilian administrator employed by the U.S. Department of War (with free housing, PX privileges, vehicles at his disposal, and other perks enjoyed by the victors), the murky desperations of the populace surrounding him in postwar West Germany presented a template of human behaviors that his card-player's mind was able to understand, without the harsh judgments of a moralist or the gleeful nastiness of a xenophobe. After all, as Mario once noted: "I spent nearly four years in the wartime Army and never fired a shot in anger. But I dealt a million hands of cards." Thus he saw the shattered world around him as a microcosm of life's choices.

While discharging his duties as a War Department civilian clerk amid the wasteland of postwar Germany's stricken population and desiccated landscape, Mario Puzo made choices that further transformed his life. A single black-and-white photograph snapped in the summer of 1948 illustrates this. In the photo, a smiling Puzo (who is now a bit husky) basks in the glow of new love: He had met and married Erika Lina Broske in Germany during 1946, and as the old photograph with its glaring sunlight and simple tones makes plain, they plunged into parenthood swiftly. A little boy sturdily appears in the photograph, and looks happy to be discovering the ability to stand and soon to walk freely. For the time being, though, the toddler is still protected fully by the presence of both parents and most tellingly by the affectionate, effusive, paternal embrace of his father.

Born on June 10, 1947 in West Germany (as it was then known), Anthony Puzo is the center of this vintage picture that shows us plenty about the priorities of Mario Puzo as a married man about to turn 28, who took to fatherhood with commitment and joy. You can see it in the picture. Mario's arm encircles Tony (as he was almost always called), and there is gentleness, pride, affirmation, protection, and unconditional love pouring forth. Similarly, wife Erika smiles with gratitude, hopefulness, and contentment. It's a picnic photograph; you can see an Army-issue blanket spread out beneath the new little family. Telltale stripes on the blanket make it clear that it's Government Issue. But Puzo, of course, is in civilian clothes: a short-sleeved white shirt and lightweight trousers. Erika appears lovely and shimmering—with her swept-up hairstyle and radiant smile she looks as if she could audition for a production of Irwin Shaw's "The Girls in Their Summer Dresses"—and Tony, the little boy on the cusp of toddlerhood, completes the circle.

By 1949, they had left Germany and Puzo moved his trio to New York, where he struggled to balance a slew of writing and literature classes at the New School for Social Research and Columbia University with his need to work full-time to support his growing family. At the New School, Mario was befriended by a novelist named George Mandel. One day in a class taught by the esteemed Brom Weber, they were eyewitnesses to an explosive dispute between Professor Weber and a student named Jack Kerouac. The dispute was ignited by Allen Ginsberg, a young poet visiting the seminar as Kerouac's guest that day. In his usual audacious manner, Ginsberg openly confronted Brom Weber, insisting that he ought to conduct classes in the loving spirit evoked by Columbia University's Mark Van Doren, the Pulitzer Prize-winning poet, essayist, and biographer. Eventually, the disagreement was amplified by Kerouac when he flat-out insisted that literary criticism was all for naught anyway, because any worthwhile writing was "a prayer to God."

Before he left classrooms behind for good, Mario enrolled (between 1949 and 1954) in eight literature courses at the New School taught by Elbert Lenrow, whose impact on Puzo's mind was made evident in 1955 when Mario inscribed a copy of his first novel with these words of appreciation: "For Elbert Lenrow . . . Who influenced this book when he introduced a barbarian to the Greeks. Hope you will like some of the things in it." But all that was years in the future.

Meantime, in August 1950, the birth of a new daughter—Dorothy Antoinette Puzo—made Erika and Mario's family a quartet. Puzo's thirtieth birthday loomed.

Biographer, memoirist, and erstwhile actress Patricia Bosworth (who worked alongside Puzo for a magazine publisher in the 1960s) commented once about this ironclad element in Mario's life. Despite the frustrations of his writer's quest, which was always compounded by his impecunious status as a low-level office employee, when Bosworth was asked if Puzo behaved like a gentleman, she replied: "Was Mario a gentleman? Absolutely. Old-fashioned, a good husband. Mario loved his wife; he loved his kids."

3

Short Stack

The first thing I did after the war was to enroll in writing courses at the New School for Social Research. Everybody then wanted to be a writer, as twenty years later everyone hoped to be a filmmaker . . . I discovered that I read more than anyone else, even the guys going for PhDs in English . . . I wrote some short stories and started a novel about the war.
~~~ Mario Puzo, *Fools Die*

Mario and Erika Puzo circa 1948, with Anthony—the first of their five children

Unlike many of his peers, who had published their first stories or even their breakthrough novels while still in their mid-to-late twenties (Salinger's early stories were in a number of major magazines throughout the 1940s and Norman Mailer's debut novel, *The Naked and the Dead*, appeared in 1948 when Mailer was 25), it was not until 1950, when Puzo was crossing the threshold of his 30th birthday, that his first serious fiction appeared in print. Titled "The Last Christmas" and published in *American Vanguard*, one of the new periodicals devoted to the writing of emerging postwar authors (many of them veterans of World War Two who were now using the G.I. Bill to attend college). Puzo's debut fiction remains a startling, evocative piece of work. It's a bold story very much in the tradition later mastered by John Cheever and John Updike, with its middle-aged male protagonist agonizing over his personal distress, in spite of the ambience of the holiday season and the seemingly successful façade of his life as a husband and father. "The Last Christmas" was one part of what Mario Puzo originally planned as a series of interlinked short stories. (As an admirer of Katherine Anne Porter's masterly short fiction, he later lamented: "I know I'll never write a great short story.")

Puzo's plan was alluded to in a thumbnail sketch of his background, which appeared in 1953 with biographical notes about the other writers whose stories, poems, or essays appeared in a handsome pocket paperback titled *New Voices: American Writing Today*. It was "A Perma Special" paperback (Perma Books was then a division of Doubleday & Company), and the collection was edited by Don M. Wolfe, a professional New York editor and publisher who enjoyed prodigious access to the portfolios then circulating in the creative writing courses at the New School, Columbia University, and also the City Colleges of New York. What's printed on the back of this representative collection of new postwar writing (a collection that includes pieces by William Styron and George Mandel, who had already managed to complete and publish their highly regarded first novels) tells us plenty about the assumptions then that young authors were considered America's spokespersons, its cultural barometers and sharpest social observers:

"Here are the young writers of today . . . poignant and powerful, tender and violent. Here is their searching portrait of our chaotic times. The haunting, lonely world of the child, the brutality of manhood forged in the hell of war. The restless search for love, the burning surge of lust. This is America . . ."

"The Last Christmas" fit aptly within this collection. Tellingly, his "bio" at the back of *New Voices: American Writing Today* hints at a novel in progress:

Mario Puzo was born in October, 1920. He served in the Army for three and a half years, in Europe. After the war, he worked for eighteen months as a War Department civilian in Germany. He has attended writing classes at City College, Columbia, and the New School. The writers he admires and who may have influenced him are Hemingway, Farrell, Celine, Maugham, Sherwood Anderson and Dostoievski. At present he is working on a novel dealing with postwar Germany, and also on a set of eight related short stories, of which "The Last Christmas" is a part. Mr. Puzo is writing a remarkable first novel about postwar Germany.

He was doing that all right. And more. Much more. By this time— as 1950 was drawing to a close—Mario was deep into a pattern that would define the next two decades of his life. His pay as a low-level government clerk (he continued in his civil-service capacity at an armory in New York) had to be supplemented. Overtime hours were necessary (yet didn't help enough), and working extra-overtime when possible was also essential. But with two children, a wife, and soon another baby on the way, there was a chronic money shortage distressing Puzo, along with lack of time to focus on his writing. It was at this time that he began to keep a journal, which he commenced just prior to New Year's Eve in 1950:

"Really, I should wait until the New Year to begin a journal, that would be psychologically correct. But I feel like beginning it now," he noted on December 29, 1950. Then he confessed the truth of his situation to himself.

"This is the end of a bad year," he admitted. "Two short stories and hardly anything on the novel. If I keep this up, I might as well forget about writing or becoming a writer." Puzo then goes on to weigh the issues of his writer's quest.

He muses:

"I've given it more thought, more reasoning than any time in my life—more analysis. I think I can truthfully say it's the most important thing in my life, more real than what I experience. Then why have I turned out so few pieces of work? I think or rather I hope that it was a serious internal preparation ... nearly every moment of the day I am thinking consciously of the work I am trying to do ... A year free just to write. I think I'm ready, but it's impossible and I'll have to do without it."

Then: Mario alters his opinion and suddenly the year just past—as writing goes—does not seem so dismal after all: "I feel that no matter what happens, I'll produce the work this [forthcoming] year. And last year wasn't too bad. Two good stories ... nearly 150 pages of the novel." That immediate change of opinion indicated how helpful it was merely to write in the diary and record his feelings. In the course of one long paragraph he moved from chiding himself to affirming that a significant chunk of work *had* been done.

That first entry in Mario's new journal as 1950 ended also charted the course he hoped his life as an author might take: "I would like to write five really good novels in my lifetime," he specifically declared, recognizing how "that would be twenty-five years in which to do it" on the assumption that he would "give five years to each."

The hopeful confidence inherent in such projections is stirring in the light of how much he was trying to balance. In the prior few years, Puzo had married his German war bride and together they started a family almost immediately. Moving back to America late in the 1940s ensured that Mario and his new family collided with the chronic housing shortages and the exceedingly limited employment options that plagued the many millions of postwar veterans who struggled to find their footing in the first decade after the war. Although he took advantage of the GI Bill in order to enroll in varied courses (and receive a stipend) at the best schools in Manhattan for writing classes, Puzo was too busy trying to also earn a living and support a family of four (soon to be five) to enjoy the distinction of acquiring a college degree. Nonetheless, his first short story had been handsomely introduced in *American Vanguard* and he was committed to completing his debut novel. The problem, in his estimation, was that the first novel was not taking shape as he wanted it to.

"So far *The Enemy* [his working title for what was later published as *The Dark Arena*] has taken me two years and it might eventually qualify as one of the worst novels ever written, " Puzo wrote toward the end of his new journal's first entry. "The whole damn thing is out of focus, like one of those blurred photos ... And yet I can't believe that it's completely without merit. That's why I go on with it. That and stubbornness and inability to let go, and this is a contradiction to the way I act in every other thing in my life."

Mario concluded the year 1950 by summing up in his journal what amounts to a self-assessment of sorts:

> *I am ready to relinquish my hold on anything—money, friends, my wife and children . . . with all these I am passive . . . Though I love my wife and children (how queer these words sound and how meaningless and insincere), if my wife were to come to me and say she was in doubt about staying with me, I would not try to keep her with me. If retaining friendship with any of the people I know and admire required any special effort, I could not make that effort . . . Money is another thing that I make no effort to keep and surprisingly enough that doesn't worry me perhaps because I haven't enough to worry about.*

And so, 1950 concluded for Puzo with a proclamation made in the pages of his personal journal: "The only thing I can take seriously is writing, no matter how justifiably ridiculous this is to people who are not writers or do not wish to write."

Thus began 1951.

The good news was that Mario could not only hold a job, but he could always work overtime, too. His years of experience navigating the varied bureaucracies of all those military government assignments during the war—plus his more recent years of experience as an expert paper-shuffler in his postwar civil-service appointment in Occupied Germany—generated appreciation for his skills in Manhattan's white-collar milieu of offices and file cabinets.

Mario and his growing family now lived in a low-income housing project apartment in the Bronx, but daily commutes to Manhattan were status quo. The sour news, of course, was that clerical work not only paid little but it was boring. Not just dull and repetitious, but stultifying. However, it didn't demand physical labor and though tedious, there was one distinct advantage to being employed in a low-level position as a clerk in any office: If the work could be done on automatic pilot, so to speak, it was then possible to day-dream and still get the job done.

Puzo had plenty to daydream about, with his novel in progress, along with the cycle of eight interrelated short stories he envisioned as a unified book-length work. "I'm beginning to be a bit more hopeful," he highlights in his journal early in 1951: "Thought of another story for the collection . . . really anxious to get to these stories before they fade out." Time flew.

Mario also acknowledged (in a diary passage dated January 7, 1951) that making any progress at all with his writing guaranteed that he was much easier to live with and more pleasant to be around: "What a nice guy I am when I get some writing done," he exulted, "and what a feeling of contentment . . . I played with Tony and enjoyed it, made E[rika] a little supper and sent her to the movies with my blessing. Sundays usually get on my nerves but not today . . . It's an obvious thing and yet really unexplainable. So I'll try to explain. Everyday life has such poverty . . . with writing or another art, you have a shield against life as well as an integrating force."

The bad news was that time after time, he received one rejection after another with the new short stories that he submitted to the leading magazines in New York. With each story's submission, after all the writing and rewriting, all the revising and his careful editing, followed by the final typing, proofreading, and then mailing off the polished work (all on his own of course, because to hire a secretary was out of the question), there was for Puzo a brief period of exalted hopefulness.

Maybe this time, after single-handedly making a comprehensive effort to create a worthy story that would galvanize a discerning editor and induce serious interest—yes, indeed, maybe *this* time there would follow a phone call from an esteemed personage with the power to publish a short story in the likes of *Harper's* magazine or the *New Yorker*.

And then, as Puzo doubtless knew, anything was possible. In recent decades, writers as well known as F. Scott Fitzgerald (whose posthumous reputation was now undergoing a fierce revival in the early 1950s) or John O'Hara, Irwin Shaw and more recently J. D. Salinger had all had their careers as novelists jump-started by the great successes they enjoyed with short stories published in the best magazines. All of those writers who were now household names had endured plenty of rejections.

Now it was Puzo's turn. "Got the blood bank story back from *Harper's*," he tersely noted in his journal on January 9, 1951. But at the end of the month, on January 28, he acknowledged in his diary that the commitment to his first novel was intact: "Starting to type up what I have of the novel. Doesn't read too badly, but it's pretty thin stuff. Hope it thickens itself in the typing. In any case it's obvious that the whole thing has to be rewritten."

Ten months later, toward the end of 1951, the workmanlike diligence possessed by Puzo (along with his ability to absorb rejections and keep on submitting his work, despite all doubts) is on display in the journal entry he wrote on November 12:

> I received a sign, a small sign, but one that really gave me a lift. I got the blood bank story back from the New Yorker. I sent it out to them even though I knew it wasn't their kind of story. The New Yorker is God as far as accepting material goes. Reading it as a kid, I learned a great deal about writing . . . Anyway, they sent me a form rejection slip. I expected it . . . didn't feel disappointed . . . I really didn't. And then I noticed on the bottom of the slip, with its cold and formal printed dismissal, somebody had written "Sorry and Thanks."
>
> I'll never know who the guy was, but he couldn't know how that phrase came at a time when the author of the story was really desperate, really needed something like that. I say to myself, "A guy on the New Yorker likes me, likes my writing. Maybe he even voted to take the story. I build fantasy on fantasy . . . though . . . maybe it was the office boy who happened to read the story while he was putting [in] the rejection slip . . . But it doesn't matter. If I ever get to know the guy who wrote it, he'll be my buddy for life no matter how big a prick he is . . . and [I] feel this way because I'm no longer sure of myself or my talent."

At such times, when Puzo felt his confidence slipping and when lamenting his lack of progress in regard to publishing in general and his first novel in particular, he was not able to draw strength from a community of like-minded fellow scribes.

Once he began juggling a second job with his full-time work schedule, the writing classes that he had attended at the New School and Columbia and City College quickly receded into a past that soon seemed as remote as his years in uniform.

Compounding the need for Mario to hold two jobs to support a growing family was the newest growth element herself: In September 1951, a second daughter was born to Erika Puzo. Now Mario and his wife welcomed Virginia into the family.

As if emerging together out of a continental wasteland resulting from a world war and marrying a "war bride" who had recently been part of a populace classified as "the enemy" and then moving to a country where she barely spoke the language weren't challenges sufficient enough to exhaust the young couple, they'd also committed to parenthood and now had a family of three small children, all born between 1947 and 1951. Quite a large agenda.

Meantime, as the weeks and months and years rolled by, Puzo always had one eye on the news of the day. In his journal from the early 1950s, he highlights in one Sunday entry that he's looking over the *New York Times*. That guaranteed that he had the weekly Book Review to add to his stress factors.

During those years, the *New York Times Book Review* included with each Sunday edition was replete with coverage of rising young stars in the literary world. Many of the new authors who were highlighted in the *Times* were veterans. Oftentimes they were still in their twenties (usually their late twenties) as their debut novels or their first short-story collections were issued by Random House or Rinehart or Harper & Brothers. It could not have been easy for Mario Puzo to be poring over the weekly Book Review in the "newspaper of record," when every Sunday issue shone a light on some other young man whose completed book was now out there for all the world to see.

And the end of 1951 had to be particularly difficult, because that was the peak season for James Jones's newly published novel *From Here to Eternity* (which was a blockbuster success from the get-go, enjoying enormous attention and selling in vast numbers since it first appeared in February of that year). But the staggering success of *From Here to Eternity* was unusual in every respect. Even Norman Mailer's 1948 debut (*The Naked and the Dead*), which had been a much-heralded best seller, was dwarfed by the immensity of Jones's achievement (in terms of size and sales).

More troubling to Puzo was that one after another, there seemed to be a non-stop array of compelling new narratives launching the literary careers of other young men his age; almost all of them were veterans and some of them were also married. Yet, in whatever way that they had to function in order to get their books finished, they had done so. The handsome dust-jackets and the authors' photos and the well-stitched bindings and abundant reviews were the proof. The weeks, months, and years rolled by.

To be an aspiring writer in those years was to have at least some sense of being at the red-hot center of a vibrant, important, national culture. Regardless of whatever struggles had accompanied anyone's quest to become a published author, it was clear in season after season that strong talents could be rewarded and superlative works were able to make it through the pipeline of the publishing industry.

In the recent years since Puzo had returned from Europe and settled again in New York, it wasn't just Mailer and Jones who had made a big splash. There was also John Horne Burns, who had seemingly come out of nowhere in 1947 with a deft, uniquely formatted novel titled *The Gallery*, which wasn't a novel in any traditional sense but rather a volume of seventeen interlinked chapters (both fiction and nonfiction) unified by Naples, Italy in August 1944 as the integrative element in the text. It was well-received by critics and enjoyed tremendous sales. Only two years later, Burns' second novel was published and by the end of 1952 he had completed and published his third book. In the meantime, during those same years, Irwin Shaw had made the leap from being a playwright and a short-story master (his *New Yorker* stories were the stuff of legend) to being a novelist, and *The Young Lions* had been another one of 1948's major successes.

One of Puzo's fellow ex-GI acquaintances was George Mandel (who later became a cherished lifelong friend), and Mandel's first novel, *Flee the Angry Strangers*, made for a rock-solid debut success in 1952. Mario had to know that Mandel's lengthy, densely textured first novel was wrapped up and contracted for publication at some point in 1951. And the kicker was that George Mandel was a combat veteran on full disability, getting on in life with a steel plate in his head (due to injuries suffered in the Battle of the Bulge). All around Puzo was the proof that much was possible.

As if further proof were needed in terms of his own peers riding high in the world of books, the National Book Award nominees for Fiction for 1951 included James Jones (*From Here to Eternity*), J. D. Salinger (*The Catcher in the Rye*) and Herman Wouk for *The Caine Mutiny* (Wouk was a bit older, but still a World War Two veteran).

When the ceremony was held on January 29, 1952 (Jones won the prize), the National Book Award again shone a light on a brand new rising star in the literary firmament. The same attention enjoyed by Jones as he collected his prize had been enjoyed by novelist Nelson Algren two years earlier, when he won the award for *The Man with the Golden Arm*. And the same praise and prestige would be lavished upon Ralph Ellison later in 1953, when *Invisible Man* won the National Book Award.

Mario Puzo himself felt like an invisible man in those years. And his observations and insights tell us why.

He finished typing a full draft of his first novel and its working title remained *The Enemy*. Although he wasn't finding it impossible to get readings from the premier publishing houses in New York (with Puzo's recent background as a creative writing student whose work had appeared in *American Vanguard*, he was taken seriously), he quickly ascertained that a whole new level of struggle had begun.

"The novel [is] finished and out to the publishers for the last two months," he wrote in his journal. "Publishers don't give a damn," he added. Then: "Never send out a piece of work that is not completely finished even if it means a great delay in publishing."

As 1952 loomed, such words clearly evinced Mario's intuitive conclusion that his first novel was not fated for a swift or easy ride to publication. He was right about that. And he was also right about his fiscal troubles. "Seems like I'll never get out of debt," he confided to his diary. The stress of money worries made everything worse.

Most of all, as 1951 segued to 1952, what plagued Puzo was the difficulty of managing his time in a way that allowed for episodes of real focus on his writing.

"Figuring out my free time to write," he noted one day, quickly adding, "it's tough with the overtime I have to earn to keep the family going. Have to do it, that's all . . . Saturated by my job and Sunday afternoon goes to the family, which is important. Leaves Sunday morning and Sunday night and maybe a couple of nights in that off week when we're not too busy (job)."

A particular problem created by the lack of time to focus exclusively on his writing was that Mario's concentration fizzled on the cycle of eight short stories that were intended to be an interlinked collection. One day he looked over his "notes of the stories I planned to write. Some gone soft and mushy like rotten fruit . . . [I] outgrew them."

Issues of growth, personal maturation, and the troubles involved in trying to find balance in his life were never too far from Puzo's mind at this time. And what he showed to the outside world often had little do with the distress he harbored within.

"This morning I got up and read the Sunday *Times*," he recorded on November 4, 1951, also noting that he "helped E[rika], played with the kids." And yet, he also acknowledged that "all the time [I was] thinking: I'm going under. Thinking it dispassionately as a matter of judgment as if it were someone else."

With his 31st birthday just behind him and 1952 on the horizon, Mario Puzo's ultimate priorities were simple to tally up. He had three children and a wife to support on the small pay of a low-level government clerk; his first novel was in circulation but in his heart he knew that it wasn't yet quite what it needed to be; and he had to carry on despite the escalating financial distress now drowning him.

There was no question in Puzo's mind that "money is really killing everything." He was working overtime for an average of 20 hours per week, thus clocking 60 hours per week at work. And yet, to support his family of five it was simply not enough. On top of which he realized: "I'm too tired to do any writing . . . [with] kids running around . . . [and] no place to work . . . Time, money, emotional stability . . . Right now it seems to be all gone." Years were dissolving.

Unlike many of his peers in the realm of writers and writing, Puzo did not turn to drink to try to lift his spirits, buoy his ego, or drown his sorrows. In a postwar culture that was then transforming America into Cocktail Nation (Manhattan's literary and social landscape in those years was thoroughly soaked in alcohol) it's really quite stunning that Puzo steered clear of booze as a palliative. By the time they were thirty years old, his fellow young writers à la Mailer, William Styron, James Jones, Vance Bourjaily, and myriad others drank heavily each night.

Of course, in some cases, Scotch or expensive whiskies were luxuries those fellows could afford. Mailer's smash-hit debut novel earned him big money that was wisely invested; in Styron's case, he went from being an only child generously supported by his loyal father to being the young husband of a wealthy heiress. Save for a brief stint as a slush-pile reader in a publishing house, Styron never worked at anything but his writing. Puzo could only dream of such privilege.

Nobody questioned the drinking culture out loud. Hefty boozing was the reward for a good day's writing or for at least being consumed by the ambition to write. The mystique of the hard-drinking author was at its peak and heavyweight iconic writers like Hemingway and

F. Scott Fitzgerald were not seen as cautionary tales, but, instead, as exemplars of lives devoted to booze and to books.

Not drowning himself in alcohol had much to do with Puzo's admirable ability to stay the course with his newfound responsibilities and to remain aware of the need to not let his discontent ruin his children's environment: " . . . if I do go under . . . live a life of 'quiet desperation,' I'll do everything to hide that from them," he vowed.

Nonetheless, every week was a struggle to make it through yet another month.

"I think I'll always remember [that] it was on a Sunday in the afternoon when I accepted and said it was me," he gloomily observed in his personal diary: "That I'm drowning and I really think I won't win the battles and that it's me, really me. I get a terrible feeling . . . I want to . . . tell somebody I care about how I feel and how there's nobody I can tell." Very much a man of his times, the notion of sharing his internal distress in conversations was not feasible to Puzo, even though he yearned to do just that.

Mario relented at one point and finally asked one of his older brothers to sign a note at a local bank, so that a personal loan could be acquired. It wasn't for selfish reasons or anything indulgent. His brother was "signing a note for me tomorrow so I can buy a bedroom set" for the children, and the emotional knots conjured up by such a situation were not lost on Puzo. "This humiliates me but it humiliates him even more," he pondered in his journal. "It makes him ashamed and angry with me that I lack the pride not to ask and lack the character to foresee [such needs] . . ."

Puzo did not shy away from admitting that he was financially a bust: "And here there is no question that I am incompetent. Monetarily insane."

Whatever Mario may have lacked in the world of personal financial acumen, he more than made up for in the realm of narrative integrity. As he continued to write and rewrite, revise and reconfigure his manuscript, he eventually found not just the form required to make his first novel work—he also found the leitmotifs that set his work apart in the overpopulated world of first-time novelists who were veterans.

Puzo had a real problem on his hands. The war had ended in 1945. And by the time the documents of unconditional surrender were signed (first by Germany, then by Japan), new novels were already coming out of the war, along with millions of GIs who couldn't wait to get their discharges, toss their uniforms, and start life anew.

Inevitably, there would be a surfeit of war novels. But, just as inevitably, there would be a discernible sense of civilian combat fatigue. Having been hammered for years with war news, innumerable radio reports, the endless newsreels from all the combative quarters of the world, and having had their own lives altered, disrupted, delayed, or sometimes dramatically or tragically affected by the war, the vast majority of Americans wanted nothing more than to start life over, move on, and in the parlance of the day "put the war behind them." It was an understandable urge.

It was also an impossible dream. No matter how strenuously anyone tried, the power of all the overlapping wartime changes, personal crucibles, experiences, and milestones ensured that in body, mind, soul, or psyche, most individuals had been so affected by the war's power to change human lives (internally and externally) that the idea of turning on a dime and simply resuming civilian life was not feasible. And yet, making the effort to do just that was by and large the one option available. Very few of the millions of men and women who'd served as civilian-soldiers during the war opted to stay in uniform. An effort to "forget the war" en masse was underway.

Nonetheless, in the first decade after World War Two had ended, there did gradually assemble a superlative cadre of fresh (and mostly younger) authors whose newly minted reputations rested on the public's strong reaction (or the critics' approval) in relation to a book revealing something unique about the war.

It didn't take too long for one aspect or another of the American experience in the Second World War to be embraced so effectively by a particular author that by the early 1950s a new challenge was presented to hopeful, unpublished writers. The challenge boiled down to the need to write about some part of the war that others had *not* yet addressed. It wasn't an easy task, considering how much ground was already covered in debut novels that were published between 1944 and 1951.

In that seven-year period, the agonies of the Italian Campaign had been anatomized in the much-heralded novels of Harry Brown (*A Walk in the Sun*) and John Hersey (*A Bell for Adano*), and the equally well-received fiction of Robert Lowry (*Casualty* and *The Wolf that Fed Us*) and Alfred Hayes (*All Thy Conquests* and *The Girl on the Via Flaminia*). As regards the post-combat occupation crises in Italy, everyone seemed to agree that *The Gallery* by John Horne Burns was the ultimate narrative triumph.

As for the war against the Japanese out in the Pacific, it appeared that Norman Mailer's *The Naked and the Dead* had a patent on that. In 1951, *From Here to Eternity* by James Jones was without a doubt the supreme evocation in new fiction in terms of summoning the long-lost world of the old-time, pre-war regular army, whose identity was upended after Pearl Harbor was attacked and millions of American civilians joined the ranks. Were publishers willing to consider another panoramic novel about the wartime exploits of GIs en route from America to France and then into Germany? After Irwin Shaw's *The Young Lions*, it was even harder to cover that terrain.

Equally abundant were Navy-based chronicles and novels or story collections revolving around the men at sea. Between *Mister Roberts* (by Robert Heggen) and James A. Michener's Pulitzer Prize-winning *Tales of the South Pacific* and then Herman Wouk's best-seller, *The Caine Mutiny*, the editors and the publishers in the early 1950s had already witnessed a surplus of successful navy fiction material.

Fortunately, it was possible for Mario Puzo to chart a new course. His own unusual postwar experience (staying in Europe and working side by side with occupation Armypersonnel, but doing so in a civilian capacity) blended with one specific theme that no other novelist was exclusively identified with: namely, the parallel universe of Occupation Duty amid postwar Germany's ruins. In any novel set in Germany just after the war, not only were flashbacks to the war years a distinct possibility, but there was also the horrendous fact that the war's worst revelations regarding the concentration camps would be an integral part of the narrative. How could it be otherwise? No matter how much people tried to ignore the topic (the subject of the Holocaust would not become mainstream until decades after the war), the lingering shock and the pulverizing impact of the newsreels and photographs from Dachau, Bergen-Belsen, and Buchenwald and other hellholes still haunted the world.

Unfortunately for Puzo, in the dark news days of the early 1950s, as the Korean War blasted its way into the lives of shell-shocked Americans, who were stunned to find their country at war again less than a decade after 1945 (and with the dread atmosphere of domestic suspicions, a manifest fear of Communism, and all the distrustful and varied political detestations now driven to new heights as Sen. Joseph McCarthy fanned the flames of a disorienting Red Scare), there would be a tough sell involved when it came to the novel Mario now re-titled *The Dark Arena*.

Puzo had a new title for his novel, but he had an old problem on his hands. The book was still engaging editors who expressed great interest at first, and then genuine admiration for the bulk of the work. Except the ending. The novel still did not resolve in a way that compelled a publisher to offer a contract. Of course, there was the other old problem: Money. At the end of 1951, the first of these conjoined troubles was briefly addressed in Mario's year-end journal entries: "Got the book back from Scribner's as I expected," he wrote on December 9. "Just have to do it over. Hope I get [a] month off. Met [another publisher] and he told me he was still interested in the book."

And then on December 30, he again turned to his diary and literally wrote off the year 1951: "I guess this will close out the year. Proved I'm not lazy about work. Averaged nearly sixty hours a week at the job . . . Program for the new year. Finish old book and start new one. Finish at least two new stories . . . quit my job if I can swing it . . . [this was a] lousy year."

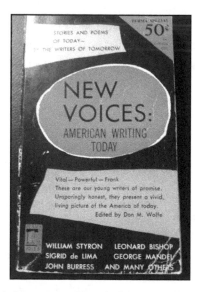

This 1953 anthology reprinted Puzo's short story "The Last Christmas," which first appeared in AMERICAN VANGUARD 1950

4

Up the Ante

Once as an adolescent, beset with guilt and feelings of unworthiness, hopelessly at odds with the world, I stumbled across the Dostoevsky novel *The Brothers Karamazov*. That book changed my life. It gave me strength. It made me see the vulnerable beauty of all people no matter how despicable they might outwardly seem. And I always remembered the day I took it back to the library . . . I had a feeling of grace . . . And so all I wished for was to write a book that would make people feel as I felt that day.

~~~ Mario Puzo, *Fools Die*

Almost one year later, in November 1952, there was a temporary surge of hope. Ultra temporary. Betting on major league sports events, a lucky winning streak allowed Mario to believe that he could afford to quit his job and focus wholly on writing. He committed to a new approach. At age 32, he now had for the first time a room of his own in which to think, read, and write. He rented the room. It cost him eleven dollars a week, and was furnished with a couple of chairs, a table, and a bed, plus "a window that looks out into a stone garden." His plan was to isolate himself and work on his book for three solid months in this rented space.

"I don't have to worry about working," he acknowledged in his journal. "I have this room alone where I can write in peace and quiet. And yet I feel desolate."

That immediate paradox should not have surprised him. Even though he'd won enough money to compensate for the loss of his usual salary for a brief period, no real cushion was in hand. "The problem of money [is] causing a terrific strain," he admitted, "however unpoetic that may be. And I have the nerve to quit my job."

In one word scribbled to conclude a diary entry, Puzo summed up: "Desperation."

It was a short-lived fantasy, and Mario realized things were not as they appeared.

"About quitting," he confessed to himself in his journal: "People . . . all say, 'Boy, you sure have a lot of courage, a lot of guts,' complimenting me and I play up to it. But on both sides there is something false."

He analyzed the unstated subtext that he detected in the air: "I sense in them an embarrassment at my ego," he wrote one day, "a slight contempt that I should believe so strongly in my talent (which I don't) and that pity you see for someone ridiculously deluding himself . . . On my side it is unhappiness . . . impossible to go on in a rut. I can last three months, finish [rewriting] the book, that lousy fuckin' book. If no money comes [it's] back to the coal mines."

He wrote those words on November 10, 1952.

In a startling turnaround and doubtless also to save forty-four dollars per month, Puzo decided only four days later to leave the rented room and go back to writing at home. Much to his own surprise—although hardly a happy surprise—he discovered that being alone was not at all his métier. A few insights about this were recorded in his diary on November 14: "Gave up trying to work in the room and moved [my] stuff home . . . inability to be alone . . . to isolate myself with my work . . . bad sign."

It may have been a bad sign, but only if one buys the notion that working in solitude is the sole way for an artist to function. There are, of course, numerous examples of the opposite truth. Composer and bandleader Duke Ellington, author Jack London, and filmmaker Oliver Stone are but a few of the creative innovators who always thrived in the midst of chaotic, distracting circumstances. In Puzo's case, one revelation was clear: "At home I'm happier." He had neither the time, the money, nor the ego required to wallow in any posing as The Solitary Artist.

Over the course of his first weekend back at home, after having packed his materials and left the room he'd rented, a contradictory array of moods and thoughts arose.

On Saturday, November 15, 1952, Puzo calmly noted: "Yesterday, everything fine. Read the book over, played with the kids, spent a quiet evening with Erika. Really enjoyed it. Now why? Another day exactly similar would drive me crazy . . . The ending of the book is still lousy. But maybe I know what to do with it."

The next night, when wrapping up his journal entry for Sunday, November 16, 1952, Mario reflected on how less than a week earlier, a striving fellow author had pleaded for his opinion in regard to a work in progress: "Late [last] Thursday [he] asked me, 'Tell me the truth, is my novel confused [?] . . . tell me the truth' . . . I've said the same thing to other writers . . . 'Tell me the truth, is it really good?' OK. No one is going to tell the complete truth . . . You can only say to yourself, 'Tell me the truth' . . . go over the manuscript . . . strike out what is false . . . never mind anyone else."

If anything, telling the truth would be one of the elements in *The Dark Arena* that inevitably made it a tough sell. Not only was its primary locale exceedingly dark in the most literal sense—postwar Germany had an ambience of shadowy, death-haunted, murky grimness—but its protagonist, Walter Mosca, was in almost every way the antithesis of America's image of GI jauntiness and youthful heroism. In an effort to tell the truth within the framework of a well-crafted novel, Puzo presented Walter Mosca as a rounded human being with qualities both positive and negative.

But readers learned in a hurry that the negative often outweighed everything else. After being saturated throughout the war and then for several years after 1945 with hundreds of high-profile movies, magazine articles, news reports, and LIFE photo-essays spotlighting the wholesome well-being of the "boys" who had won the war, it came as a bit of a shock when one writer or another managed to get into print with a novel that evoked the agonies of a returning veteran and his sense of disorientation. The inability to quickly "adjust" to postwar civilian living, with a job in the city and a house in the suburbs and soon enough children playing behind a white picket fence. That homogenized mass-media image of the newly married, happily productive, postwar GI now suited up in his civvies and seemingly unaffected by the war . . . well, to say it was fantasia is to be too polite. And Mario Puzo knew it was bunk.

A handful of published authors had succeeded in presenting maladjusted ex-GIs as protagonists in their novels. For example, in *Lucifer with a Book* (John Horne Burns' second novel, a not-well-received follow-up to *The Gallery*), there was Guy Hudson, whose effort to resume his career teaching at a boys' prep school in New England is doomed, because after the war he's unable to accommodate that milieu.

A far more popular narrative presenting a disgruntled, distressed, out-of-sorts ex-GI was Sloan Wilson's *The Man in the Gray Flannel Suit*, which for varied reasons caught on much more successfully with the mass public. In Wilson's novel (made into a popular film starring Gregory Peck), the ex-GI wins the sympathy of the viewers of the movie or the readers of the novel, thanks to his manifest effort to try to adjust to marriage, fatherhood, career struggles, and civilian life.

Contrarily, Puzo's evolving novel conveyed through the character of Walter Mosca almost complete disinterest in marriage, fatherhood, career struggles, and civilian life. He's a profile in Post-Traumatic Stress Disorder.

In *The Dark Arena*, there is in the first chapter a lengthy flashback to Walter Mosca's return to America after World War Two. With Puzo's autobiographical blueprint serving as a model, Mosca comes to life as a soldier who survived the war in Europe and who is now welcomed back to his New York environs by a mother and a brother who expect him to be thrilled that his ⊡girl⊡ is also there waiting to receive him. All⊡s not well, however, in the mind of Walter Mosca. Quickly he apprehends that he wants little to do with being ⊡at home⊡ again, because America in all of its postwar frenzy does not feel like home. And the prospect of hiring on with whatever job is available and soon marrying the girlfriend left behind when he was inducted distresses him. It soon becomes clear that all Walter Mosca wants to do is be left alone most of the time, unless his presumed fiancée feels like spending time with him in bed. If not, what Mosca desires is a trip to the movies. What about planning for their future? That⊠s what she hopes will be their mutual priority. But it's not going to happen.

Mosca is not interested in mapping out the next phase of his life —not if it means marrying, going back to work, and preparing to raise a family. The reader is bluntly informed, through dialogue and narrative detail, that prior to Mosca going overseas, he and his girlfriend had been lovers. Now, though, she refuses his advances and insists that they not resume their sexual relationship until they're married. Mosca shrugs off her new controlling restraint, and makes it clear that he is disengaging.

Not only does Puzo's protagonist disconnect himself from the "girl" he's expected to marry (a bright, attractive, young woman who has gone without dates for years while awaiting Walter's homecoming), but he also boldly informs both his mother and his brother that he wants next to nothing to do with family ties as well. Then: To the shock of all, Mosca accepts a contract offer to return to Germany and to work alongside Army Occupation forces in the vanquished land where he recently fought.

By the second chapter, Puzo immerses his readers in the devastated atmosphere of postwar Germany. None of his characters or scenes resemble in any way the mass media's relentless presentation of American soldiers or ex-GIs as Boy Scouts. Quite the other way. In *The Dark Arena*, what Puzo presents is a textured, richly detailed, narrative equivalent to the *film noir* cinema that so effectively countered Hollywood in the late 1940s and the early 1950s. And just as in *film noir* narratives, wherein seemingly regular (or "normal") people get swept up in dire circumstances that are sure to lead to personal ruin, *The Dark Arena* lures Walter Mosca to his fate.

By the time 1952 drew to a close, Puzo knew that his own fate was enmeshed with his first novel. The completion of the book continued to cause him great stress. But nothing proved more stressful than finances. Daily pressures of the most basic sort were now compounded by a cascading series of notices, memos, reminders, and legal threats from those to whom Mario owed various sums. He had chosen the wrong time to suspend his income.

Puzo was on the verge of despair shortly before Christmas in 1952.

"So I quit a good job to be a writer," he lamented in his journal, "and in these few weeks I realized I'd written a hopeless book. A hell of a thing to find out . . . I have to give up. After New Year's I'll look for a new job."

Then, two weeks before Christmas, the boom was lowered by a series of threatening letters in the mail. Mario had fallen too far behind on the monthly payback for a $1,000 personal loan. The bank called in his loan. Immediately. *Now.*

Mario grimly recorded: "A letter from the bank that it will be necessary for me to report to their Central Office because I can't pay the $1,000." He was startled by the severity of the institutional tone. At first, he reacted with a sense of resignation: "Paralyzed by this being in debt . . . Letter from bank about loan," he confided to himself in his diary. "It looks as if I have to go back to work in January."

Again and again, with Christmas only two weeks away, the pressure on Puzo over his debts translated into repeatedly recording the opening line of a bank notice in his diary. The formality of the bank's intimidation congealed in its opening line: *"It will be necessary to report to our Central Office immediately on receipt of this letter."*

Self-deprecating humor came to the fore as Mario wondered: "Christ, are they going to shoot me? Torture me? Send me to prison? Take my bed and tables and, thank God, my typewriter?"

But then some of the balls-out confidence that doubtless sustained him when he did his duty with the 4th Armored Division less than a decade earlier also emerged: "Well, fuck you," he decided. "I got the letter Thursday and I'm not going until Monday. You can't scare me."

Yet, there was plenty to be scared about. As the end of the year closed in, the holidays were of paramount importance, not only to Mario's new family with Erika and the children but also to his mother and his siblings. It was the worst possible time to be caught short financially and then to be overwhelmed with nasty memos.

"Friday the letter from Gimbels [came], Saturday the letter from the housing project and the insurance company . . . interest on the loan, the yearly premium. It really scares me."

Even by the economic measures of 1952, the sums were not huge. But to Puzo they were enormous. He desperately needed a lump-sum windfall that he had assumed would come in the form of a decent advance for the sale of his first novel. And he was right—in theory. Had the novel been successfully sold at the end of 1952, for example, and had it sold for as little as $4,000, then Puzo's many IOUs would have been settled overnight.

"What does it come to?" he asked himself. "A paltry $2,000 or less. Is this a cause for despair, for pulling out my hair . . . tacking a false ending to the falseness of three false endings (to my book) . . . is that reason [enough], this lousy $2,000?"

Money, however, was not the only issue. And Puzo knew it. There was a slew of secondary issues that all revolved around the weird power of money and how it coagulates in relation to emotions, trust, family dynamics, and the all-important fact of how one is perceived by others in the day-to-day world of practical living.

Mario knew full well that "it goes beyond" the basic business of daily cash flow or the almighty pride that many took to heart with their superior self-regard, when they were able to balance their checkbooks without stress.

To Puzo, even worse than not being able to join the crowd that loved to boast about paying their bills on the first of the month was the problem of "living [amid] people who do not understand what you love. It comes of years of swallowing pride and bending to work I hated . . . my own great flaw in discipline."

His willingness to acknowledge a lack "in discipline" dovetailed with his own awareness that poor planning had also hurt his prospects. Too many bills to pay, three children now, borrowing from cold-blooded institutions instead of yielding to the need to ask family members for help (again), it all led to a state of anger and angst and worst of all a sense of hopelessness about how to finish his novel. Puzo had an epiphany that he summed up in seven words in his journal one night, as he pondered the prospects before him: "Achieving your dream can destroy your talent."

The winter of 1953 was rough on Mario. Yet weather was not the key issue. His novel was. Puzo had blitzed on the finale and by January 17 the book was "finished and up at the publishers. With the worst possible ending, murder and suicide."

Less than one week later came devastating news, when he "got [a] letter from [the] publisher turning down the book . . . Back to work grinding on a steady job. What else? Nothing."

Two months later, the month of March ended on an equally blue note: "Sweating out [the] answer on [the] book from Bobbs-Merrill.

The last hope really. I've borrowed and chiseled to last till now. E[rika] very hurt that I can't give her money for [the] family's Easter clothes. Haven't got."

The chronic stress about fiscal matters and the grueling episodes of waiting for publishers' verdicts combined to induce another epiphany for Puzo: "What is hardest to bear is that in those people nearest to me I do not inspire confidence, or love, or trust, or faith, or respect . . . I think I tried, I tried as hard as I could."

But he knew in his bones that any insights that bordered on self-pity had to be checked. He was in a situation of his own making. This was his quest. He had chosen it. One diary entry boldly confronts this head-on: "The self-pity in all the previous pages would be inexcusable if it were expressed openly to the people involved. I write it here to get rid of it as a health measure. Because the sad fact is that everyone is caught in his own little trap of hopes; they resent me as I resent them. I disappoint them as they disappoint me. And really it's not anyone else's fault. Accept."

His pattern of submissions and rejections continued, and Puzo kept the faith.

Yet he struggled not to give in to impulses that would compromise his visions of narrative or personal integrity. He made the effort to write "a trashy potboiler" on the assumption that it could be completed in a hurry and turn a quick buck; then decided that he "had to give it up." Sounding a lofty note (and doubtless aware that he could scarcely afford such exalted principles), Mario soon branded the effort as "immoral and uninteresting."

It wasn't until the following year (after further revisions) that he sold his novel.

Random House, the largest and at that time the most prestigious American publisher, bought *The Dark Arena* on January 20, 1954. They paid a tiny sum in the form of an advance, and by this time Mario was again working full-time at a Civil Service job. The most important thing was to breach the high-walled fortress of the publishing world in New York City. Thus a first novel to be published by Random House qualified as a coup. Fatigue diminished the hopeful joy caused by the sale.

Wheels turn with excruciating slowness in book publishing, though. They always have. *The Dark Arena* would not appear until one year later, in February of 1955.

It didn't catch on or catch fire. The reviews that praised *The Dark Arena* were sincere and Puzo was welcomed to the club of new postwar American novelists. A particularly positive review, by esteemed critic Maxwell Geismar, appeared in the *Saturday Review of Literature*, which was then a highly influential weekly periodical that had much to do with launching the careers of John Horne Burns and James Jones. In both cases, those authors and their debut novels were featured on the cover of the magazine. Not so with Puzo. The affirmative review penned by Geismar was tucked deep inside. Still, though, Geismar's long, thoughtful review served as a fine counterweight to a short, unfriendly critique in *Commentary*. Side by side, those two reviews more or less summed up the highs and lows that other critics noted.

Equally telling was the public's general indifference. When *The Dark Arena* appeared in the winter of 1955, the tenth anniversary of the end of the Second World War in Europe was coming up. There was no interest whatsoever in any national commemorations. American life at that time was consumed by the power of America's roaring postwar economy; the surplus of new children to be raised as the Baby Boom reached an all-time-high; and the degree to which television was now conquering not just the national culture but almost every living room in homes from coast to coast. The timing of the publication of Puzo's novel was unhelpful.

But it wasn't just the timing that made for trouble. The novel itself is a gripping, often mesmerizing reading experience—provided one enjoys densely textured pages full of reminders about the self-centered, seemingly amoral, and most of all selfish preoccupations of American characters who, even in the midst of others' desolation, are forever trying to hustle, make a deal, and in effect put the screws to someone else for the sake of a tidy profit. The novel's *film noir* elements appear on just about every page. Shadows abound. The ruins of postwar Germany are not just omnipresent externally, but serve as metaphors for the internal wreckage in the hearts, minds, and souls of the characters. And the primary characters are wholly at odds with the idealized portrait of American military personnel illustrated in the media (from Hollywood to the *Saturday Evening Post*, the GI as an unimpeachable archetype of The Good Guy was unassailable).

By telling the story of Walter Mosca and his inability to

accommodate civilian life back home in triumphant America, the novel begins on a note of discontent that contradicts the tone of buoyant optimism that supposedly was embraced by all "the boys" who returned from the war. And as soon as Walter Mosca's back in Germany as a civilian employee of the U.S. War Department, the novel's chapters illuminate and illustrate the fact that human nature dictates—long after battles have been won and the enemy defeated—that the joy of victory is fleeting, self-interest rules, and a view of life as one cynical transaction after another is for many the only way to live.

In *The Dark Arena*, the main story of Walter Mosca (who searches out and finally locates his former German lover, Hella, with whom he soon shares a billet—against Army regulations—and plans to wed, once the ban on marrying *Frauleins* is lifted) is complemented by an array of characters whose bartering schemes are constant. Anything can be had in exchange for cartons of cigarettes, chocolate bars, or other items that the PX furnishes at drastic discounts on the American military base. It's a world of victors and vanquished. What makes Puzo's novel different from, say, John Horne Burns's *The Gallery* (which also anatomized a panorama of conflicts between the powerful and the weak in the realm of shattered Naples, Italy, after the Allies set up occupation headquarters there) is that in *The Dark Arena* the principal story of one man and one woman (Walter Mosca and Hella) predominates, with the subplots revealing the travails and the subterfuge of others blending in.

Money is a significant theme in the novel. The most dangerous of the schemes conjured up by a handful of occupation troops with whom Walter Mosca finds himself enmeshed is an adroit plan to get their hands on a massive cache of military currency (known as "scrip") and exchange it for cash (and fat profits) with the German civilians. It's a shady, knotty, doomed enterprise. But as a leitmotif, it makes complete sense. The whole novel is an evocation of murk and conniving.

The only remotely hopeful notes are sounded by Hella, the German woman who soon enough is pregnant with Mosca's child. She is a stalwart, tough survivor. And it's only when he is in her company— especially in her arms—that Mosca drops his guard, softens up a bit, and allows his basic human decency to be on full display. But their relationship—truly the cornerstone of the narrative—ensured that Hollywood would not come calling to purchase the film rights to *The Dark Arena*. Not only does Puzo's main protagonist have premarital sex with one of "the enemy," but they enjoy it a great deal whenever possible and they're happily looking forward to the birth of their child, even though they're not yet married. No such story was going to find its way to the silver screen in the 1950s, when the Production Code was entrenched.

And then there was the issue of the Holocaust.

At the time, that subject was largely taboo. It was scarcely broached in academe. Rarely did any movie, novel, or play come close to hinting at it.

Although there were hundreds of new films and books and articles about the war in Europe that were widely seen or read in the decade after World War Two, hardly any confronted the issue of the Holocaust, which would not be commonly referred to by that term (with the "h" in "holocaust"—defined by Webster's as "to be consumed by a large fire"—always capitalized) until decades later.

Figuratively speaking, the mass media and the public at large had buried those issues of *LIFE* magazine (and the concomitant newsreels) from 1945, and a definite policy of willful amnesia was invoked. Thus it was unusual and brave of Puzo to create in *The Dark Arena* the character of Leo. He is a secondary character in the novel, but in certain chapters and throughout critical scenes, his presence is vital. And his words are crucial. As a survivor of Buchenwald who is open to answering rudimentary questions about the concentration camps when he's conversing with Walter Mosca or a handful of the occupation troops with whom Mosca surrounds himself, Leo and his thoughts carry a great deal of weight.

Not only was Buchenwald one of the camps that American Army soldiers liberated in April 1945, it was also one of the camps that by name and also by a surfeit of horrific newsreel images had infiltrated the American psyche. Legendary radio newscaster Edward R. Murrow was at Buchenwald shortly after its liberation, and he broadcast a special radio program heard nationwide, describing in detail the ghastly netherworld discovered by the GIs.

The U.S. Army Signal Corps had filmed a tremendous amount of what was found at Buchenwald: skeletal survivors in unspeakable distress; corpses piled high and left to rot; the crematoria. And photos in *LIFE* magazine had been so graphic that many subscribers hid the magazine from their children when "those pictures" were published. But every now and then, in the first decade after the Second World War, a grim reminder emerged in the culture.

In 1948, when author Irwin Shaw published *The Young Lions* (a panoramic novel of the war in Europe from the perspective of two exceedingly different American GIs and one German *Wehrmacht* officer) there was, toward the novel's end, a re-creation in fiction of a camp liberation. Irwin Shaw had served in the Army and was part of the Signal Corps filmmaking outfit helmed by the highly regarded Hollywood director George Stevens. The color footage shot by Stevens's unit at Dachau still retains the power to shock. But in Shaw's novel, the concentration camp scenes were limited to part of one chapter. Similarly, when *The Young Lions* was made into a movie in 1958, the brief scene near the end when the GIs enter a nameless camp barely hinted at the extremities of what the troops witnessed back in 1945.

Nonetheless, Shaw's novel shone a light on the war's darkest corner.

So did a singular work of nonfiction that became a best seller for a brief time circa 1950: *The Theory and Practice of Hell* (by Eugen Kogon) was a unique book that explicated not only how Buchenwald had functioned and "worked" as a concentration camp, but also educated Americans (and all other readers) by reminding them that the site was a labor camp for political prisoners before the war began, and then evolved (like Dachau) into a more nefarious abyss of torture, slave labor, medical experiments, and murder by the time the war peaked in 1944-1945.

Buchenwald's lengthy history was also alluded to in Puzo's novel, time after time, when either Walter Mosca or Leo (the camp survivor) reminds others that Leo had spent eight years incarcerated there. Those "eight years" stressed in the novel correctly define the chronological history of Buchenwald, which operated near Weimar between 1937 and 1945—in full view of the local townspeople, of course, which was another aspect of Buchenwald's history that Puzo raised in *The Dark Arena*.

The most important aspect of Leo's role in the story is his discerning intelligence. In the novel, he is admired for his willingness and ability to go testify against former German officers at the Nuremburg trials.

Leo is not presented as a stock sympathetic character nor as a pathetic victim, although it's made clear that his experience sets him apart from the others. Without invoking flashbacks to the atrocities of the concentration camps, it's still ascertained that even compared to the combat-hardened background of some of the other characters, Leo is different. One night, in the company of Walter Mosca and a few others (where the beer is flowing), there's a flash of anger when Mosca says: "The guy was in the camp for a long time. Don't you know what that means, for Christ's sake?"

Puzo's choice to specify Buchenwald and to have the name repeated in the novel was provocative in the 1950s. It was also a choice rooted in Puzo's wartime past. One other reason that the 4th Armored Division was a standout juggernaut in the final months of World War Two in Europe is that the 4th AD was the first American Army unit to discover and to liberate a concentration camp. On April 4, 1945, at a slave-labor camp called Ohrdruf, soldiers of the 4th AD were filmed in the company of Generals Eisenhower, Patton, and Bradley, all three of whom toured the grounds of Ohrdruf, which was a sub-camp of Buchenwald. Although obscure and small, the human detritus and grotesque evidence at Ohrdruf were grim enough to instantly galvanize Eisenhower, who ordered the U.S. Army Signal Corps to film everything. Not just at Ohrdruf, but wherever such camps were found. One week later, not far from Ohrdruf, the larger and even more disorienting Buchenwald was liberated.

That name alone had come to symbolize the unspeakable for many Americans.

It's now quite impossible, though, to convey how quickly the topic of the camps was erased from the public's mind in the years after the war. The vivid newsreels were archived. The magazines were bound and stacked on dusty library shelves. There was a universal resistance in all the media—films, books, radio, and plays—to any evocation of the memories sure to be revived by any story or any image recalling the striped uniforms or the piles of corpses; the barbed wire, ovens, and smoke. One book in particular was barely able to get published.

In the early 1950s *The Diary of Anne Frank* was rejected by American publishers all across the board, until Judith Jones at Doubleday saw its value. Otherwise, the coming-of-age chronicle left behind by the teenage Jewish girl hiding in the attic (and who was doomed to be discovered by the Nazis, sent to Auschwitz and then Bergen-Belsen, where she died) was a literary document that caused publishers to recoil and refuse it outright. One senior editor at Vanguard summed up as follows: "Under the present frame of mind of the American public, you cannot publish a book with war as a background." And another editor at Alfred A. Knopf rejected *The*

Diary of Anne Frank with this brush-off: "Even if the work had come to light five years ago, when the subject was timely . . . I don't see that there would have been a chance for it." This postwar state of denial and the suppression of bad memories (which invite such denial) were succinctly expressed by another editor's observation that *The Wall*, a new novel by John Hersey based on the 1943 uprising in the Warsaw Ghetto, wasn't "doing as well as expected." And one of that editor's colleagues spoke for an industry-wide policy when explaining that readers would "avert their eyes from so painful a story which would bring back to them all the evil events that occurred during the war."

This makes Puzo's accomplishment even more admirable. To crack the wall of such resistance in New York publishing was no small feat. But, like it or not, *The Dark Arena* invariably conjured up "all the evil events that occurred during the war."

Tellingly, the epigram chosen by Puzo for *The Dark Arena* was a passage from Dostoevski. Having read and reread *The Brothers Karamazov* since first discovering that novel in his mid–teens, Mario made use not just of the oft-quoted apercu—"*Fathers and teachers, I ponder, 'What is hell?' I maintain that it is the suffering of being unable to love*"—for his debut novel's sole epigram, but the next words too:

> "*Oh, there are some who remain proud and fierce even in hell, in spite of their certain knowledge and contemplation of the absolute truth; there are some fearful ones who have given themselves over to Satan and his proud spirit entirely. For such, hell is voluntary and ever consuming; they are tortured by their own choice. For they have cursed themselves, cursing God and life. They live upon their vindictive pride like a starving man in the desert sucking blood out of his own body. But they are never satisfied, and they refuse forgiveness, they curse God Who calls them. They cannot behold the living God without hatred, and they cry out that the God of life should be annihilated, that God should destroy Himself and His own creation. And they will burn in the fire of their own wrath forever and yearn for death and annihilation. But they will not attain to death . . .*"

Critiques of *The Dark Arena* ranged from laudatory and welcoming to dismissive and downright insulting. The novel provoked serious reactions, one way or the other.

Unfortunately, one of the most negative write-ups was seen early on in *Kirkus Reviews*, which had been a powerful force in the world of books since 1933.

Featuring brief summaries and seemingly definitive critical verdicts (although one never knew who was writing the review; they were unsigned), the anonymous write-ups in *Kirkus Reviews* were usually the first to be quoted elsewhere; and the helpful or harmful assessments were taken seriously by bookstore merchandisers, book club mavens, librarians, and other tastemakers affecting the national culture.

Even now, well over a half-century since it first appeared, the critique of *The Dark Arena* in *Kirkus Reviews* stings with its relentless negativity:

"A book that shocks one to the fibre of one's being. Did it have to be written? Or if written published?" Right off the bat, this exceedingly influential media organ was more or less suggesting that *The Dark Arena* never should have seen the light of day.

"In comparison," *Kirkus Reviews* went on, "the shock techniques of *The Naked and the Dead* and *From Here to Eternity* seem pallid." No specifics are offered. There's not one salient detail provided to support such a claim. Instead, there's nothing but a fleeting allusion to Mailer and Jones's controversial debut novels. But the insight is neither representative nor comprehensive. It's a subjective opinion, one with little basis in the text itself. True, there are passages and even scenes in *The Dark Arena* that illustrate greed, unethical choices, bad behavior, and the awkward and awful impulses that humans are prone to (from the way men behave in a strip club to the infinite transactional interactions between the victors and the defeated).

Also there are scenes harking back to the damages wrought by the war: Damage to the spirits of women and men, as well as to the landscape of Europe and the physical infrastructure of German cities, which lay in ruins. The narrative is steeped in ashes and rubble.

Yet, the critic at *Kirkus Reviews* took umbrage in a tone of high dudgeon that echoed some Park Avenue matron: "In *The Dark Arena* the picture of occupation forces, military and civilian, seems to indicate that all are tarred with the brush of self seeking, cruelty, barbarity, indifference to human suffering, the vices of the conquerors, the cupidity of the thwarted, the sadism of those whom suffering has scarred." The launch of Puzo's first novel had to be harmed by a *Kirkus* piece that concluded that "the sneering characterization at every level, the filthy language, the presumption that there is no decency anywhere (except perhaps in Hella, the German girl), leaves a bad taste—a sense of profound shock."

One could never guess from such denunciations that textured, subtle, eloquent passages were in each chapter and on every page of *The Dark Arena*. Its gruff lyricism is a match for its distressed themes. But Puzo's writing still glows:

> *Mosca woke. The room was shot through with shadows, the last ghosts of night, and he could make out a vague outline of the wardrobe. The air was cold, but the fever and chill had left his body. He felt a gentle tiredness that was pleasant. He was very hungry, and he thought for a moment how good breakfast would taste later in the morning. He reached out and felt Hella's sleeping body. Knowing that she had never left him, he put his cheek against her warm back and fell asleep.*

And one would never know from *Kirkus Reviews* that Puzo had opted to restrain his use of profanities (his characters do curse and cuss at times, but compared to the first novels of Jones or Mailer, *The Dark Arena* is not replete with vulgarisms). In fact, Puzo's restraint in regard to language indicated that he was highly aware that years earlier other authors (especially Jones) had already broken those barriers.

Fortunately, the takedown in *Kirkus Reviews* appeared on February 1, 1955, more than three weeks before Random House published the book on February 23.

Even more fortunately, the very week that the novel appeared it was cheered in the *Saturday Review of Literature* (in its issue dated February 26, 1955). The widely respected literary critic Maxwell Geismar signed his name to an essay that wholly countered the prim denunciations of others.

Declared Geismar: "I should add that the book is written in the only new language to emerge in our literature since the stylistic innovations of Hemingway. The folk language of the G.I.'s may be shocking, but it is a remarkably colorful, open, and pungent form of speech, which is recorded here with great fidelity. 'The Dark Arena' is impressive and illuminating."

In *Commentary*, though, fellow novelist (and occasional critic) Chandler Brossard gave Puzo the back of his hand. Lumping *The*

Dark Arena together with four other new novels in a composite review that barely had two paragraphs to spare for each book, Brossard accused Puzo of writing "a bleak homage to every literary and middlebrow cliché imaginable."

Brossard then tipped his hand and inadvertently paid Mario an enormous compliment by comparing his work to that of a quartet of literary innovators. Brossard meant to be pejorative, but the passage of time has transformed his cheap shot into an accidental affirmation any writer would die for. He likened the text of *The Dark Arena* to "an example of automatic group writing, with the participants—Alfred Hayes, Hemingway, Remarque, Irwin Shaw—dreamily pouring out their simplest and cheapest images of pseudo-experience." It's telling that Brossard dropped those four names. His envy and chagrin were on display. The two authors associated with World War One (Hemingway and Remarque) were so iconic that only last names were required. As for Hayes and Shaw, they'd both recently enjoyed huge critical and commercial success, whereas Brossard was a published novelist who had to write book reviews for pocket money. Chandler had issues.

As comparisons go, no words could have been more treasured than those of Maxwell Geismar, who began his critique in the *Saturday Review of Literature* by lamenting that "very few good novels were published in 1954 [the prior year]." He then mused that he and others were "beginning to look back upon the work of James Jones, Norman Mailer, William Styron, and John H. Griffin with something like nostalgia."

And then Geismar let the trumpet sound: "I am not sure that Mario Puzo's 'Dark Arena' quite comes up to the level of this earlier group of new writers. But it is a very good novel indeed, and one reads it with the sense of discovery and pleasure that a new talent evokes. Mr. Puzo has brought some excitement to the opening months of the new year." In *The Nation* magazine, another critic flat-out insisted that *The Dark Arena* was "one of the finest works of fiction to come out of this country's occupation of Germany," while fellow New York author Seymour Krim commented: "I knew what a human furnace Mario was inside . . . from *The Dark Arena*, that grim and hopeless picture of what we American slobs were really like in postwar occupied Germany."

Puzo waited. Nothing happened. His phone did not ring off the wall. There were no inquiries about interviewing the author. Hollywood did not call to express any interest in the film rights. The days and weeks and the months rolled by. And nothing happened. In Mario's day-to-day life situation, his entire focus remained—as it had to— on the patching together of enough income to support his expanded family. On the book jacket of *The Dark Arena*, the biographical blurb on Puzo concluded by saying: "He is married and has four children." In addition to his wife Erika, the basic (and always increasing) needs of Anthony, Dorothy, Virginia, and now Eugene were priorities.

Puzo's debut novel sold in low numbers (like most first novels), and by year's end it was clear that the glorious burst of sudden fame and new fortune enjoyed by a select few other first novelists was simply not in the cards. Instead, Mario got sick.

Not with a head cold or a sick stomach. But really ill. Sick enough to find himself falling out of a taxi on Christmas Eve, after he went alone to the VA hospital on 23rd Street in desperate need of a gall bladder operation. So much for the year 1955.

For the next ten years, with two significant and noteworthy exceptions (one positive, the other negative), the general pattern of Puzo's life remained the same.

Unfortunately, that meant that his continuous small-time betting on sports ruled (and often ruined) his weekly finances. Decades later, Mario was upfront and blunt about those years: "In the late 1950s, I was a sports addict gambler," he admitted. "I bet baseball, I bet basketball, and I bet football." Those were the main events. At that time, neither golf nor tennis had any real presence on television, and though he dabbled now and then in horse racing, Puzo really didn't care for playing the ponies. He also once wryly commented: "I wasn't rich enough to play the stock market."

The truth was, he was not solvent enough to bet the sums that he risked. But on the off chance that something went right, his quest for a lucky streak continued.

In those years, Mario earned $120 per week in his position as a government clerk. His immediate superior also gambled on sports, and they became a duo. Together, they "bet at last $50 a day, every day, on one sporting event or another. We averaged $300 a week or at least $15,000 a year in bets," Puzo later recounted.

That ensured that Mario's cash flow would often be negative, which ensured that he'd have to reach out again and again to finance companies or banks for personal loans. In a crunch, he knew he could always count on borrowing from his older brother. A cycle of constantly "borrowing from Peter to pay Paul" (as the old saying goes) was fully in play. "Of course we didn't lose all that money—sometimes we won," he recalled. Nonetheless, it was a cycle that guaranteed frantic behavior.

As Mario once said, "sports betting makes for a hectic day." He further explained:

> *In the morning at work I picked afternoon baseball bets. During lunch hour I ran uptown to see the bookmaker. During the afternoon I picked night bets and before I went home to supper I dropped in to see my Shylock if I had been a loser in the afternoon. Then I went to see the bookmaker. Sometimes I went to the night harness racing. It was exhausting.*

Now and then, however, something went right. Periodically, there was a windfall. Decades after one special Sunday, Puzo still rejoiced while recollecting "one of the great days of my life, one that I will never forget." Here is what happened:

> *I took my oldest kid to the Polo Grounds to watch the Giants play the Dodgers. The Giants won and my son and I were both overjoyed. My emotion was less pure than his. I had the Giants bet in a three-way parlay and as we walked on the deep green playing field toward the exit, part of a happy throng, I looked up at the scoreboard and saw that all of my bets had won. I picked every game right that day. It was a Sunday, no night games. The amplifying system played a glorious victory march and I was rich. I had made nearly a thousand dollars, a fortune for me in the 1950s. I would not have to borrow money to buy clothes for my kids when they started school in the autumn. I did not gamble that money away. I was not a degenerate gambler.*

Sometimes an equally well-timed victory came in smaller numbers, but the win was no less critical. Summing up living on the edge, Mario once told this story: "I had to move my family to the Bronx into a new housing project. I only had $20. I bet the $20 on a baseball parlay taking two underdogs with big odds. I won. I didn't have to borrow the money. I kept my pride." Supporting his family came before all else, and while Puzo eventually began to work and make slow progress on a second novel, which he composed with the same loving care for language and the same literary integrity achieved in *The Dark Arena*, it would not be until 1965 that *The Fortunate Pilgrim* was published. When it did appear, Puzo was a forty-five year old man with five children to support. Mario and Erika's youngest child, Joseph, would be born in 1960, the same year that two other life-transforming situations (one good and one bad) challenged him. Threatened him—that's putting it more accurately.

Years later, in his most transparently autobiographical novel *(Fools Die)*, Puzo recapitulated his struggles as an impecunious, married, stressed-out young novelist whose day job as a government clerk for the Army Reserves carried over into the 1960s.

> . . . *[and then] the Berlin crisis, which made President Kennedy decide to call up hundreds of thousands of Reserve troops. Which proved to be very unlucky.*

> *The Armory became a madhouse when the news came out that our Reserve units were being called into the Army for a year's active duty. The draft dodgers who had connived and paid to get into the six months' program went crazy. They were enraged. What hurt the worst was that here they were, the shrewdest young men in the country, budding lawyers, successful Wall Street operators, advertising geniuses, and they had been outwitted by that dumbest of all creatures, the United States Army. They had been bamboozled with the six months' program, tricked, conned, sold, never paying attention to the one little catch. That they could be called up to active duty and be back in the Army again. City clickers being taken by the hicks . . . I never realized that this would bring on the catastrophe I had long foreseen. I was too busy processing the enormous paperwork involved to get my units officially on active duty.*

> *There were supplies and uniforms to be requisitioned, all kinds of training orders to be issued. And then there was the wild stampede to get out of the one-year recall. Everybody knew the Army had regulations for hardship cases. Those that had been in the Reserve program for the last three or four years and had nearly finished their enlistment were especially stunned. During those years their careers had prospered, they had gotten married, they made kids. They had the military lords of America beat. And then it all became an illusion.*

As America transitioned into the 1960s, Mario Puzo segued into his forties.

5

Side Game

At the office the FBI agents dropped by a couple of times a week, usually with some young guy that they were obviously identifying me to. I figured it was some reservist who had paid his way into the six months' program . . . Every time the doorbell to my apartment rang at an unusual time my heart really jumped. I thought it was the cops or the FBI.

~~~ Mario Puzo, *Fools Die*

First Novel, 1955

SecondNovel, 1965

For many Americans—both famous and anonymous—the year 1960 launched the best of times. Excitement was in the air for citizens who lived and breathed national politics, because the imminent presidential election in November heralded a new generation of leadership, which for the G. I. Generation signified that their time had come. Both presidential candidates were veterans of World War Two.

It was also the first American presidential election in which the two candidates were both born in the 20th century. Senator John F. Kennedy and Vice President Richard Nixon ran vigorous, compelling campaigns and their televised debates were milestones in media history (the martyrdom that followed JFK's tragic demise has since given his campaign an invincibility it didn't enjoy throughout that year).

But if one did not thrive on political discourse, there were other reasons for optimism and a sense of excitement. Fans of rock 'n' roll music jumped for joy when Elvis Presley was honorably discharged from the Unites States Army in March 1960. Presley then rapidly conquered pop culture anew by appearing (for a record-breaking fee) on a Frank Sinatra television special; recording a heavily blues-inflected new album (*Elvis is Back!*); and starring in the movie musical *G. I. Blues*.

For all the fans of folk music, with its themes of social justice, yearning for brotherhood, and varied lamentations, the rise of the Sit-In movement in 1960 was a clarion call. Joan Baez had released her first album. Soon she'd be touting a new voice wheezing from the scruffy form of diminutive, lyrically brilliant Bob Dylan.

Fifteen years had passed since the end of World War Two. On the campaign trail, JFK declared: "It's time to get this country moving again!" Despite occasional bouts of short-term recession, the economy roared as the postwar Baby Boom reached its finale with the children born between 1960-1964.

During that same period—beginning in 1961 and not concluding until 1965—there was in the life of Mario Puzo more stress, fear, worry, and panic than he'd endured in the past, because throughout the first half of the 1960s, Puzo was the subject of an ongoing FBI investigation about alleged bribery and Army Reserve enlistments.

Before that quasi-nightmare began, however, there was a higher and happier note on which to ring in the new decade. Not only was a fifth child (Joseph) born to Erika and Mario in 1960, but, for the first time in his life Mario was hired in a freelance capacity that eventually led to a salaried position requiring one thing only: Writing.

It marked the beginning of a sinecure around which his life would be organized until the end of the 1960s. For reasons involving the FBI investigation that shadowed Puzo throughout the first half of the 1960s, his years of government clerking would finally end in 1962. However, before that investigation had even commenced, Mario was moonlighting throughout 1960 and 1961, writing magazine adventure stories for so-called "men's magazines" published by Martin Goodman, who ruled the roost at Magazine Management Company in New York City. "I was working on a string of adventure magazines," Mario later said, "writing free-lance stories and being treated by the publisher, Martin Goodman, better than any other publisher I had ever had."

Magazine Management Company published a monthly tonnage of print material to stock the newsstands and drug-store racks all across America. The magazines that were published weekly and monthly by Martin Goodman's corporation did not have the polish of the *New Yorker* or the authority of *Time* and *Newsweek*. Nor did they have the royal budgets allowing both *LIFE* and its offshoot, *Look* magazine, to offer readers an extraordinary array of world-class photos with each new issue.

One of Puzo's colleagues was novelist, playwright, and short-story writer Bruce Jay Friedman, who had gone to work for Martin Goodman starting in 1954. In his literary memoir, *Lucky Bruce*, the less-than-glittering atmosphere of Mario's new realm is concisely detailed. "Magazine Management people," Friedman recalled, "seemed not so much to have been hired as to have washed ashore at the company like driftwood. We were all slightly 'broken' people. A few had gifts, but we were 'rejects' all, having clearly been unable to cut the mustard at the Luce and Hearst empires." Friedman eventually became the executive editor for three of the most popular Martin Goodman publications: *Men, Male,* and *Man's World*.

From their one-word titles (*Stag, Male, Men,* and so forth) to the promises implicit in two-word titles like *True Action, Man's Life, Man's World,* and *Man's Conquest* (one popular weekly was titled *Mr. America*), the periodicals cranked out by Magazine Management

Company satisfied the ravenous male hunger in postwar America for content-driven, boldly illustrated magazines that promised an array of wartime flashbacks, aggressively proactive soldier-of-fortune adventures set in the present time, and of course an abundance of sexy female protagonists. There were even three-word titles like *World of Men* and *Men in Conflict* on the agenda.

These were all "pulp fiction" periodicals. And Mario was conscripted primarily to write highly fictionalized accounts of World War Two-era battles, skirmishes, and tantalizing lurid encounters. Everything was exaggerated. Fantasies were the prime element in the material that readers devoured in these periodicals. Combat fantasies, presented as true accounts, and sexual fantasies satisfying every day-dream were the glue holding the thoroughly fabricated stories together.

Certain recurring topics and themes were all too obvious, especially when enhanced by the illustrations that were drawn to push all the hot buttons. There was no shortage of cleavage-baring women being subjugated by Nazi SS officers or other archetypes of evil. Tellingly, the story titles and the graphic art illustrations often presented an equal balance between stories of WW II and newer conflicts in hotspots all over the world. One April issue of *Man's World* in the early 1960s offered up a title that highlighted the derring-do of President Kennedy's newly created American warriors: "8 Green Berets Trapped . . . Outnumbered . . . Marked for Death." America was now increasing its military role in Vietnam, and the "pulps" seized on the mystique of the Green Berets, who were boldly pitched as the New Frontiers sequel to Darby's Rangers or Merrill's Marauders in World War Two.

The titles of the features in any random "pulps" from Magazine Management Company ranged from "Sergeant Lewis and His Squad of Girl Guerillas" or "Vile Secrets of the Nazis' Cult of Horror" to "Sin Happy Co-Eds" and "I Was an Office 'Passion Lottery' Girl." In addition to all the battle-driven, guerilla-laden tall tales of invincible American he-men, there was a surfeit of domestic stories promising tell-all exposes of easy women and endless sex. The "pulps" served up a rougher, raw, B-movie type of variation on the sophisticated A-list fantasia published monthly in Hugh Hefner's *Playboy*. Sometimes the illustrations in the Magazine Management Company stories were more provocative than the coy, airbrushed topless "girls" on Planet Hefner. True, one could see bare breasts in *Playboy*, but in many of "the pulps" the illustrators often got away with placing grasping male hands atop female chests as a heroic rescue (or some dastardly Nazi humiliation) was underway.

What Mario Puzo had to do was write fast and write to order. Pages had to be filled. Reams of copy were required. And flights of impure fiction were called for. Hyperbole ruled. Exaggeration was the status quo.

"I became an ace pulp writer," Mario once said: "I wiped out whole armies. I wrote a story about an invasion in which I killed 100,000 men and then later read the statistics. There were only 7,000 killed. But in the process I became an expert on World War II. I knew more than anybody [at Magazine Management Company] because I read all the books."

The "postwar pulps" were magazines that no married man would wish to subscribe to, because the last thing he'd want was his wife to see a cover that was strewn with illustrations of half-clad women in damsels-of-distress postures, with slavering evil Nazis or sex-mad Commies threatening their virtue. The titillating men's adventure magazines published by Magazine Management Company were marketed to be bought off the rack. Many of the buyers might have subscribed to *Argosy* or *Field & Stream*, but those were Boy Scout manuals compared to *Man's Story* or *Man's Life*.

The lurid fantasia at the core of the magazines' content always tapped into putative "real accounts" of sexual excess in some remote place or another, whether it was a faraway island in wartime or a suburban enclave in time present. As often as possible, the "postwar pulps" used the words nymph, nympho, or nymphos (plural, the better to imagine orgies) on their covers. Examples abound: "The Embattled Yank and the Nymph of the Fifteen Islands"; and then there was "The Nympho Castaway and Her Crew of Five."

When nymphomania was not deployed as a title tactic, a few suggestive words put the same message across, always feeding on chronic sexual cravings and visions of priapic indulgence that had none of the urbane, big-city polish of stories in *Playboy*. "Tahiti: Lusty Island of Untamed Women" and "Nudist Paradise on the Riviera" and "Torture in Darkest Africa: Trapped by Mau Mau Terror" were all emblazoned on one magazine cover, dominated by an illustration of a half-naked sex siren. Oftentimes, the ravished woman was supine or on her knees.

All of the "postwar pulps" were intended for the diversionary entertainment of blue-collar, working class, non-college educated guys who would have gladly stared at the *Playboy* centerfolds, but didn't give a damn about Hugh Hefner's fey, pithy commentaries on being "sophisticated." Martin Goodman's men's magazines piled up in barbershops and VFW halls. They were sold by the ton in train stations and at drug stores. Nobody ever complained (and no one had to ask why) if a guy left such periodicals behind at his neighborhood tavern. It was understood that this stuff was not for the Mrs. to see.

Unless, of course, some poor schnook actually thought that his wife might benefit from stories titled "10 Ways to Train a Dame" or "Secret Sex Orgies of the Khama Kall," not to mention "San Diego: Passion Port of the Pacific" or "American Men Are Unfit for Married Love." Sexual insecurity was a recurring theme, with oscillating stories about the rampant erotic travails of women and men. Such as: "Masculine Inadequacies Drive Women Nuts!" and "Jealous Husbands and Chastity Girdles" and "The Stewardess 'Call Girl Slave' Ring." Most content was aimed below the belt.

The image of "jolly, rotund Mario Puzo" that Bruce Jay Friedman always retained from this period is that of a corpulent wordsmith "leaning back in his chair, a large cigar in his mouth, reading six books at once, three in each arm, like he was tasting food." By now, Puzo was carrying slightly over 200 pounds on his five-foot-six-inch frame, and his newly expanded income dovetailed with his enlarged belly. He looked like a shorter, darker version of Jackie Gleason, with a "Ralph Kramden" girth on display, along with his daily supply of eight-inch cigars. Puzo's appetite for rich Italian or Chinese foods was matched by his perennial appreciation for the finest of cigars. Most of all, however, he appreciated the chance to generate more income as a writer for hire. It may have been true that Magazine Management Company was populated by a staff full of bruised and distressed individuals: "There was an astronomically high divorce rate," as Bruce Jay Friedman remembered, and he also noted that "now and then, an editor who found life intolerable would run head first into a water cooler and have to be carried off to a rest home, never to be seen again."

The vagaries of the writing life were often on full display, even in unexpected ways. "The novelist Richard Yates turned up one day," Bruce Jay Friedman later wrote: "[Yates] sat down behind an empty desk as if he worked on the magazines and hung around for weeks. It was difficult to know what to do with him. He was a disheveled-looking man with a handsomely ruined face . . . I knew of his quality . . . I had read *Revolutionary Road* and the word-perfect *Eleven Kinds of Loneliness* . . . He just wanted to sit there, as if we were operating a shelter of some kind."

For Mario Puzo, it was a haven. In no way was he bummed out because "the fates had consigned him to be trapped in a magazine *purgatorio*, and a down-market one as well," Friedman noted. Mario gloried in his ability to do what so most writers cannot do: Constantly produce. Puzo understood that the kind of writing required to fill Martin Goodman's magazines had nothing to do with literary virtuosity or exquisite effects. Those qualities were reserved for his second novel, which he now progressed on. Mario's serious fiction was a third-shift endeavor. Being something of an insomniac as well as a moderate drinker who didn't routinely go to bed drunk made it possible for Puzo to work on his literary manuscript in the wee small hours.

"Puzo took to the job at Magazine Management Company with great enthusiasm and cheerfully pumped out stories by the dozen," said Bruce Jay Friedman. Many years later, in the only novel Puzo ever wrote that featured a first-person narrator for the bulk of the book, transparently autobiographical riffs reiterated the point:

> *Much to my surprise . . . I turned out to be a hell of a magazine writer. I could write the pulp and adventure war stories. I could write the soft porn love stories for the top-of-the-line magazine. I never signed my real name to any of this stuff. But I wasn't ashamed of it. I knew it was schlock, but still I loved it. I loved it because all my life I never had a skill to be proud of. I had been a lousy soldier, a losing gambler. I had no hobby, no mechanical skills. I couldn't fix a car. I couldn't grow a plant. I was a lousy typist, and not a really first-rate bribe taker government clerk. Sure, I was an artist, but that's nothing to brag about. That's just a religion or a hobby. But now I really had a skill. I was an expert schlock writer, and loved it. Especially since for the first time in my life I was making a good living. Legitimately.*

Then the FBI pounced.

According to a declassified FBI report dictated on January 19, 1962, Mario Puzo was "interviewed under oath" three days earlier on January 16th. The interview was conducted at the Armory in

Manhattan where Puzo had worked as a clerk for years. In addition to noting his work address (529 West 42nd Street), the report that was sent on to FBI headquarters (to the "Director," of course, thus ensuring that J. Edgar Hoover had another batch of papers to file in his cavernous archives) made note of some basic facts, official figures, and unflattering observations about Mario.

The facts and figures were simple enough: Puzo was described as a white male, age 41, living in the Bronx at 27-45 Samson Avenue, Apartment 3A. His date of birth (October 15, 1920) and place of birth (New York City) were duly noted, as were his height (5' 6"), his weight (200 pounds), and the color of his eyes and hair (brown). A "Medium" complexion was cited, in addition to the fact that the subject was one who "wears glasses." His occupation was listed as "Government employee," and as for any arrest record, the best possible word appeared: "None." He was designated as "Married" with five children.

About the personal observations: J. Edgar Hoover's legendary obsessions with others' appearances (and the image projected by his agents) were in effect. All FBI agents were held to rigorous standards regarding their weight—lean and fit, their attire (dark suits, white dress shirts, plain ties, polished shoes, and most important of all—one had to wear a conservative hat), and deportment. That's why Mario's lack of concern with self-presentation certainly caught their attention. Puzo was bluntly described in the report as not just "obese," but also as "sloppy."

In the dry tone of official bureaucratese, the following summary was dictated:

PUZO stated that he is a unit aid [sic], Department of Defense, United States Army, and a GS 5. He stated that he has been with the Department of Defense of 17 years. He said the units for whom he does the paperwork in his capacity as a unit aide are . . .

The Special Agent in Charge then dictated a list of six Quartermaster Corps by their official numerical designations, before finally getting to the essence of the interview, which was conducted as part of a continuing investigation:

PUZO denied ever receiving any money from anyone to effect their enlistment or anyone's enlistment in any of the reserve units with which he worked.

That was the meat of the matter. The investigation harked back to allegations of a bribery scheme allowing draft-age young men facing two years of active duty (the peacetime draft was in full force) to acquire a slot in the Army Reserves instead, provided they pay a bribe. Waiting lists to get into the Reserves were long and unpredictable, and spots were limited. Oftentimes a guy on a waiting list for the Army Reserves (which required six months' active duty, followed by an exceedingly light schedule of weekend meetings and two-week summertime maneuvers for six years, as opposed to a full-time two-year hitch) ended up being drafted while he waited in vain (always hoping).

With no major "hot wars" involving Americans at this time (Vietnam was a little-known country where only "military advisors" were being deployed), there was a colossal interest in the Army Reserves as an option for draft-eligible young men.

A month earlier, one man who had landed a spot in the Reserves gave what the FBI report defines as a "voluntarily issued statement." The statement was taken during the first phase of the investigation, which unfolded over a three-week period between December 1st and December 21st in 1961. The name of the individual who apparently first cited Mario Puzo in relation to this mess is continuously blacked out, as is the name of a colleague of Puzo's at the enlistment center on 42nd Street.

What seems clear now is that one of Puzo's administrative superiors was under investigation, and when certain individuals in the Reserves were interviewed by the FBI it came to light that a pattern of favoritism and preferential treatment had been in play at the Armory office where Puzo worked as a GS 5 clerk for years. The investigation began as 1961 tipped into 1962.

Two key paragraphs in the report dictated on December 22, 1961, spelled it out:

[Name of FBI Agent Blacked Out] advised that on December 14, 1961, [Name Blacked Out] of the 411th Quartermaster Company furnished in the form of a sworn voluntarily issued statement that in or about December, 1958, or January, 1959, a [Name Blacked Out] contacted him, with a proposition that [he] join the Reserves. [Name Blacked Out] advised . . . that he could join the reserves for $225 and . . . believing the reserve program was closed to enlistments as of that time and knowing that he would be otherwise drafted and required to serve two years active duty, [he] contacted MARIO PUZO at the suggestion of [Name Blacked Out] and paid PUZO $225 to get into the Reserves as PUZO was employed at the Reserve Center at 529 West 42nd Street, New York City.

[Name Blacked Out] advised that after returning from six months active duty he was assigned to the 411ᵗʰ Quartermaster Company and he attended weekly [meetings] and summer camp in 1960 until he found out that for a sum of money he could remain away from these meetings and still get credit for attending them.

By the time the FBI conducted its first interview with Mario in mid–January of 1961, they had already completed over 100 interviews with men in the Army Reserves. It was a wide-ranging investigation that would not conclude until the end of 1965.

Meantime, the cultural maelstrom engulfing America in the 1960s was rampant.

As an avid moviegoer all of his life (and as a man whose worldly perspectives were in large part formed by the cinematic experiences he was immersed in as a boy in the 1930s, when a ten-cent ticket bought a day's worth of Hollywood films), Puzo required no Communication Arts professor to explain to him that a sea change was affecting American culture. In 1961, he saw the artfully bleak and psychologically probing film based on Arthur Miller's story *The Misfits*, featuring Clark Gable and Marilyn Monroe transcending all of their stereotypical roles and co-creating (along with Montgomery Clift, Eli Wallach, Thelma Ritter, and director John Huston) a new breakthrough in adult drama.

A few years later, in 1965, the release of *The Pawnbroker* (with Rod Steiger in the lead role) marked the first time that a widely seen American film confronted a Holocaust story (the movie was based on E. L. Wallant's novel). It also explored themes of racism and class bigotry in modern-day America. There were gripping flashbacks to a concentration camp in *The Pawnbroker*, along with a distressing evocation of ethnic conflict in New York City, evoked most tellingly between the Jewish European refugee played by Steiger and the Puerto Rican employee with whom he's always interacting at the pawnshop that serves as the story's base.

Although the world of television and cinema would be colorized by the end of 1965 (two months after the Beatles taped their final in-person appearance on *The Ed Sullivan Show* in August 1965, the Sullivan show began broadcasting in color), films like *The Misfits* and *The Pawnbroker* were in black and white, just as the prose and the tone and the mood of Mario's new book were steeped in past shadows.

Throughout these years, Puzo continued to make slow but steady progress on his second novel. Titled *The Fortunate Pilgrim*, it was later described as "a small classic" by a critic at the *New York Times*, and near the end of his life Puzo called it "my best novel and my most personal one."

As he worked on *The Fortunate Pilgrim* during the first half of the 1960s, though, the Hell's Kitchen setting of the novel (back in the 1920s and 1930s) and its narrative recapitulations of the Southern Italian immigrant struggles meticulously re-created in Puzo's heartrending fiction were at odds with the world that was exploding all around him in post-1960 America. In the JFK years, the 1930s seemed like eons ago. Looking back was not in vogue. "New" was the coin of the realm.

The first half of the 1960s in America, when seen through the aperture of the network television programs emanating from the antenna-controlled tube that dominated most living rooms in this peak period of the postwar epoch, weirdly includes beloved characters from *The Dick Van Dyke Show* and *Leave It to Beaver* with junk by the ton (necessary to keep the TVs glowing almost 24 hours per day), complemented by startling news reports about intense violence at sit-ins in the South, as well as international conflicts that reached boiling points at Cuba's Bay of Pigs in 1961 and once again during the Cuban Missile Crisis in 1962.

In the nerve-wracking shadows of the FBI's investigation of the Army Reserves, the writing of *The Fortunate Pilgrim* must have been a comforting, soothing, perhaps therapeutic act of self-preservation for Puzo, because as he composed his second novel—surely the most literary of his works—he continually returned in the privacy of his mind to his childhood memories, his early youth on the Lower East Side, and the domestic world that once was defined by his mother's indomitable love for her family and, ultimately, her will to survive against all odds.

The realm of *The Fortunate Pilgrim* was merely a few decades gone by, but it could have been set in another century compared to the world of Mario's children, the oldest of whom were now in their teens as America tumbled through the 1960s.

There were no fancy family vacations, and a new car in those years was not a luxury that Puzo could afford. Nonetheless, when observed by Erica Heller, the daughter of novelist Joseph Heller (to whom Mario had been introduced years earlier by writer George Mandel), the image of Puzo that emerges is a picture of convivial domestic vitality, especially when he was immersed in a beloved diversion with his buddies. Erica describes a pivotal memory:

Sometime in the early 1960s, Dad [Joseph Heller], George Mandel, and Mario Puzo started meeting, usually at our apartment, to develop and play a horse racing board game that they'd invented called Horses. I remember nights when the living room was thick with cigar and cigarette smoke and ashtrays spilled over with empty red pistachio nut shells. When a game of horses was in progress, the apartment was under siege . . . since they were playing for money, they were savagely competitive. According to Tony Puzo, Mario's oldest child, the only time they cheated was if someone's kid was playing. Then they fixed it so that the kid would win.

Also, like the vast majority of Americans, Mario and his family began absorbing the maelstrom of the 1960s through the medium of television. The pageantry of John F. Kennedy's 1961 presidential inauguration was a national viewing experience that induced ratings even higher than the Kennedy-Nixon debates had drawn four months earlier.

Soon enough there would be equally compelling news footage pouring forth from television screens, illustrating for all Americans the violent depths of racism in the land, as the Freedom Riders in 1961 became the talk of the nation.

In their crusade to test the Jim Crow laws that still affected interstate transportation routes throughout the Deep South, the Freedom Riders and their Greyhound Bus journeys triggered the worst elements of violent resistance to integration in the South. Busses were firebombed. Freedom Riders were attacked and viciously beaten. During the Mother's Day weekend of 1961, as the mayhem reached its apex in Anniston, Alabama, it fell to President Kennedy and his younger brother, Attorney General Robert F. Kennedy, to dispatch dozens and then hundreds of Federal Marshals to Alabama in an effort to protect the Freedom Riders, quell violence, and prevent the possibility of any deaths.

One year later, in the realm of TV news, the early summer of 1962 sizzled with a dramatic confrontation between the Kennedy Administration and the State of Alabama. That showdown was personified by the grating voice and scowling face of Governor George C. Wallace, whose bold vow to "stand in the schoolhouse door" to prevent the federally sponsored integration of the University of Alabama brought forth the full weight of federal intervention.

Once again, with television cameras capturing the hour-by-hour drama of it all, the precarious and potentially violent situation impelled President Kennedy and Attorney General Robert F. Kennedy to send a huge contingent of Federal Marshals to enforce the laws that the Supreme Court had sanctioned back in 1954 with its unanimous desegregation decisions.

In the autumn of 1962, the national drama of the emergent Civil Rights Movement was superseded (for thirteen days in October) by the international threat presented by the Cuban Missile Crisis. Like most other American parents, Mario and Erika sat before the television set at varied times during that ghastly fortnight, wondering if their children would have any future at all. When that crisis resolved at month's end, the Kennedy Administration enjoyed a political victory. The midterm elections of November 1962 swung in favor of the Democrats, and the youngest Kennedy brother (Edward, who was usually called Ted or Teddy) joined his older brother the President and his other older brother (the Attorney General) in Washington, D. C.

For most of 1963, *LIFE* magazine and other media outlets had a field day with the ultra-photogenic First Family and its ever-growing presence in national life. Seeds of a major theme were planted at this time, because in no way would it have escaped Puzo's attention that the mystique of the Kennedys was defined by the story of an all-powerful, elusive, king-like patriarch (Joseph P. Kennedy, Sr.), and three sons.

A traditional high school odyssey for young Americans occurs over a four-year span of time. That's forty-eight months. Or 208 weeks. Put another way, it's 1,460 days.

Four years: Freshman. Sophomore. Junior. Senior. (Add in all the summertime months.) That length of time illustrates one way to understand the stress under which Mario had to function as the FBI's investigation carried on for the same amount of time that a regular high school career demands: 1,460 days. In a row. His anxiety had to be off the charts.

For four whole years (1962, 1963, 1964 and 1965), the FBI had an open and active case that generated periodic questioning, and chronic worry. One of Puzo's senior colleagues was found guilty of taking bribes to ensure the enlistment of young men in the Army

Reserves, and he was sentenced to a two-year prison term. What would happen to Puzo's family if he suffered such an unlucky fate?

Mario dug in his heels.

By the middle of 1962, Puzo quietly resigned from his government job as a GS 5 clerk at the enlistment center in Manhattan. Just as quietly, he shifted from working as a freelance writer at the Magazine Management Company to being a full-time staff member with a weekly salary of $150. To supplement that income, Mario wrote a slew of extra-long stories for Martin Goodman's varied magazines. Heralded on the magazine covers as "A Book Bonus Feature," such extra-long tall tales ran to tens of thousands of words; they read like short novels in comparison to the average articles or stories.

Once again, the friendly and supportive relationship that Puzo enjoyed with Bruce Jay Friedman (who was now billed on the masthead as Editorial Director) came to the fore. Friedman had his own literary aspirations to tend to after hours (by the late 1960s he would be celebrated as both a novelist and as a playwright).

To make a living in the early-to-mid 1960s, though, Magazine Management Company remained Friedman's base. In his memoir, he highlights the Book Bonus element: "The fee for a 30,000 word Book Bonus had stood resolutely for years at five hundred dollars. I became Puzo's hero when I insisted that Martin Goodman raise his figure to seven-fifty."

The problem, of course, was that such periodic supplements to Mario's income were already spent by the time he was paid. True, his annual salary of $7,200 per year was only slightly below average in the early 1960s. But in addition to having a wife and five children to support, Puzo also had a folder chock-full of monthly bills, grim statements, and the occasional threatening letter (or letters) from creditors, loan officers, and finance companies.

His old pattern of borrowing to stay afloat ensured that big chunks of his "Book Bonus" windfalls had to go to service debts. Especially his credit card debts. The wildly popular postwar surge in the use of credit cards was, for Puzo (and doubtless innumerable others), both a blessing and a curse. He relied on such cards, racked up high balances, and then had to lop off big chunks of any paychecks in order not to lose the cards.

There were so many IOUs dogging Puzo that Jules Siegel, a fellow writer and friend who also had a job at Magazine Management Company remembered this: "He kept his accounts in a legal size manila folder with lines and lines of different payments. He said that just the postage for sending in the payments was a significant expense. "

It speaks volumes that Mario "never added it all up," according to Siegel, "because he was afraid to see how much it all amounted to."

Nonetheless, in addition to the constant financial pressures that were compounded by the worrisome FBI probe that had to be on the edge of his consciousness at all times, Puzo kept on plowing forward. "Mario worked harder than any writer I knew," Jules Siegel recalled. "He used to turn out a minimum of 30-40 thousand words a month under [pen names] at Magazine Management Company, then go home and work on [his] novel or [a] major magazine assignment." Siegel was well placed to witness such prodigious word counts.

"We were more than acquaintances," Jules Siegel once explained: "We worked at adjoining desks at Magazine Management Company in 1964-65."

Elsewhere, at other adjoining desks, FBI agents working on the case concerning alleged bribery schemes and the Army Reserves continued to compare notes. One aspect of the whole process that surely made Puzo's head spin was that as the mid–1960s unfolded, the details of the FBI's investigation went back nearly a decade.

A former Reservist offering a statement to the FBI specified this: "My first contact with Mario Puzo was, to the best of my recollection, in September 1957."

To put historical bookends on this span of time, it helps to recall that September in 1957 was the month of the crisis at Little Rock High School, when President Eisenhower finally chose to send units of the 101st Airborne Division to Little Rock, Arkansas, to resolve the ongoing public protests that had shut down the public high school in the wake of its integration efforts.

Seven years later, in September of 1964, as the FBI probe continued, it must have been dizzying to Puzo to contemplate that he was being grilled about issues that harked back to the high-water mark of the Eisenhower years. Meanwhile, America in the early autumn of 1964 was still getting its bearings in the aftermath of President Kennedy's murder one year earlier.

By year's end in 1964, Mario's second novel was in production. *The Fortunate Pilgrim* was scheduled for publication in January of 1965. High hopes abounded.

Such high hopes were justified. Puzo had labored over each sentence in his second novel. The world of long-ago New York City was vividly brought to life. There was a classical narrative of immigrant struggle, assimilation, and family lore.

In *The Fortunate Pilgrim*, the towering presence—the commanding, all-embracing omnipresence—of its matriarchal hero, Lucia Santa, was derived from the larger-than-life figure of Mario's own mother. A radiant autobiographical aura emanated from the book. And, once again, Mario selected one profound passage by a writer he revered to serve as an epigram. The writer was Frenchwoman Simone Weil (1909-1943), whose life had been defined by political activism, philosophy, and Christian mysticism. Albert Camus had once called her "the only great spirit of our times." Simone Weil's words, setting the epigrammatic tone, were these:

> At the bottom of the heart of every human being from earliest infancy until the tomb there is something that goes on indomitably expecting—in the teeth of all the crimes committed, suffered, and witnessed—that good and not evil will be done to him. It is this above all that is sacred in every human being.

When published in January 1965, the novel received the praise all writers long for. On January 23, 1965, in the *Saturday Review of Literature*, an appreciative critic comprehensively summarized not only the quality of the new novel, but also many of its particularly strong literary elements, which other reviews echoed. To shine a light on how Puzo's second novel was then exalted by some of the most discerning arbiters of new literature, it helps to quote the *Saturday Review* critique at length:

> An evocative and fluent prose unmarred by mannerisms, a sensitivity to the quality of relationships between individuals within a family, an authentic knowledge of milieu, and a gusto exhibited both in hilariously comic and laceratingly painful scenes—these are among the gifts manifest in Mario Puzo's second novel. The narrative moves simultaneously on two levels. First, it chronicles fifteen years in the life of an immigrant family living in lower Manhattan, and on this level Mr. Puzo incisively conveys the emotional undercurrents surging beneath the tempestuous and often crude day-to-day experience of poor folk whose prime concern is survival, and after that, if possible, respectability. Second, the writer renders with fidelity the lifestyle of an Italian-American community in which Old Country values of propriety, order, and obedience to established authority collide with New World ambition, initiative, and disdain for tradition.

Able as is its treatment of an environment, the novel derives its urgency and excellence mainly from the portrayal of the Angeluzzi-Corbo family, and especially from its luminously visualized matriarch, Lucia Santa, whose love and strength bring her children through death, madness, adversity, sickness, pain, and her own sins of the heart. In searching for an analogue, we are reminded of Hemingway's Pilar in For Whom the Bell Tolls, *although Lucia Santa might best be compared to those fierce, tender, unlettered, cunning and wise immigrant mothers we know from reality.*

Mr. Puzo sketches in minor characters with broad, sure strokes. Dr. Barbato, living testimony to the efficacy of the bootstrap, and Mr. La Fortezza, the shyly larcenous social worker, are done with striking vividness. A solid work of realism, this novel imparts much of the texture of life and something of life's unpredictability.

What then? Anemic sales. A punishing example of life's "unpredictability" hit Mario sideways when even in the aftermath of a *New York Times* review that sang his praises in a major way—"Puzo has written a chronicle of Italian immigrant life which is a small classic . . . [the] novel is lifted into literature by its highly charged language, its penetrating insights and its mixture of tenderness and rage"—the novel did not sell. *The Fortunate Pilgrim*, at that time, did not even merit the most common of fates for new books: a paperback sale. Instead, it simply disappeared.

It wasn't only Mario's second novel that, in a way, proved evanescent. There was a Hollywood producer who had expressed interest in *The Fortunate Pilgrim*, and he performed a disappearing act worthy of Houdini. Puzo considered this episode to be his initial "enlightening experience with Hollywood movie producers."

Due to the exceedingly strong reviews that appeared all over the country, inquiries were made to the agent who represented Mario at the William Morris Agency. One day he called Mario to request that Puzo meet for lunch with John Foreman, whom the agent described as "a big wheel" (Foreman had produced a number of Paul Newman's films). The agent insisted that Puzo take the meeting. He did so—with abundant hopefulness.

"John Foreman was dynamic," Mario recalled. He remembered it clearly: "For three hours he talked about my book, how he loved it, how he was determined to do it as a movie. He quoted all the best parts. He liked all the right things. I was thrilled and impressed. The movie was definitely on. As he left, he said he would call my agent the next day and arrange the financial details of the contract. Nobody ever heard from him again."

The self-deprecating humor of that anecdote masked a smoldering fury that now affected Mario's well-being. His weight had continued to increase throughout the 1960s, due to lack of exercise and his love of certain foods (especially Italian and Chinese, with midnight forays to the fridge being routine for second—or third—suppers consisting of his beloved pasta and "spaghetti smothered in butter sauce").

Heavy cigar smoking remained his standard daily vice. Diabetes became an issue. Age and stress were colluding against him. And money was now an embarrassment.

As 1965 came to an end, Puzo began to reassess his journey as a man and as a writer. He was not pleased at all, but his sense of humor saved him from plunging into despair. Still, in reflecting on the prior decade and his career as a literary novelist, he succinctly tallied up the disappointing issues and most of all the devastating sums that wounded his pride.

"My first novel, *The Dark Arena*," he recounted, beginning his reassessment with the pivotal event in his life as a writer back in 1955, "received mostly very good reviews saying I was a writer to watch. Naturally I thought I was going to be rich and famous. The book netted me $3,500."

Then: Leaping forward ten years to his most recent book's publication, he noted that, "My second novel, *The Fortunate Pilgrim* . . . netted me $3,000. I was going downhill fast. Yet the book received some extraordinarily fine reviews. The *New York Times* called it a 'small classic.' I . . . immodestly think of it as art."

With both novels, however, Mario endured a lamentable lack of continued interest from his publishers. After *The Dark Arena* had fizzled back in the 1950s, Random House showed no further interest in him. A prestigious new company, Atheneum Books, contracted for *The Fortunate Pilgrim* later on.

Because they were "known as a classy publishing house more interested in belles-lettres than money," Mario assumed that all the sterling reviews made him "a hero."

On that assumption, Puzo "asked them for an advance to start on my next book . . . and the editors were cool. They were courteous. They were kind. The showed me the door."

That was a devastating blow. Being dumped by two major

publishers (ten years apart) smacked of disinterest. If he did not know better, Puzo would have been justified in thinking that his writer's quest was the folly of a delusional man. "I couldn't believe it," he later said. And with good reasons, once he "went back and read all the reviews on [the] first two books. I was acknowledged as a real talent at least . . . two acclaimed novels behind me, every word in them sweated over and all mine. No help from anybody. It couldn't be true that my publisher would not give me an advance for another novel."

It was true.

Nonetheless, there was another meeting with the Atheneum editors, who were not responsive to the elements of the new novel that Mario had in mind. "It sounded like another loser," Puzo once said, summing up the editors' indifference.

Yet, one man set off a chain reaction. At an awkward moment during the meeting, when silence filled the air, Mario recalled that a certain Atheneum editor "wistfully remarked that if *Fortunate Pilgrim* had only had a little more of the Mafia stuff in it the book would have made money. (One of the minor characters was a mob chief.)"

The passage of time had not dimmed America's perennial fascination with gangster tales. Especially when the stories emerged from the news of the day, instead of a Warner Brothers back lot.

Back in the early 1950s, the televised Kefauver Hearings (a Senate investigating committee helmed by Sen. Ernest Kefauver of Tennessee was looking into a spate of corruption issues involving "organized crime" in America) had scored extraordinary ratings at the dawn of the television era. Later in the 1950s, similar congressional hearings under the gavel of Arkansas Senator John McClellan made TV stars out of two brothers whose careers in the nation's capital were fast rising.

The so-called McClellan Hearings riveted the nation, as chief counsel Robert F. Kennedy exchanged heated remarks with Teamsters president Jimmy Hoffa. And sitting center-stage at the McClellan Hearings, as a member of the investigating committee, was the chief counsel's older brother: Senator John F. Kennedy. For both brothers, this putative crusade against "organized crime" (J. Edgar Hoover and his FBI men refused to acknowledge the existence of any "Mafia") was a gambit very much intended to enhance JFK's imminent 1960 run for the presidency.

Another televised spectacle occurred in the early 1960s when the hearings that were highlighted by the testimony of Joseph Valachi became a sensation. It was Valachi (a lifelong criminal with deep roots in the Sicilian-based East Coast mob network) who explained in his testimony what Cosa Nostra ("this thing of ours") was all about, along with many of its code expressions ("omerta" for silence, and so forth).

One of the major priorities of the Kennedy Administration between 1961 and 1963 (when former chief counsel Robert F. Kennedy served as Attorney General in JFK's presidential Cabinet) was to drastically increase prosecutions against major and minor figures in the realm of "organized crime." When Americans were not tuned into a beloved TV show like *The Untouchables* (with its retro-exploration of FBI crime-fighting back in the 1930s), all they had to do was pick up a newspaper and they'd likely find new stories about the ongoing "vendetta" between Attorney General Robert F. Kennedy and Jimmy Hoffa, whose Teamsters Union pension funds seemed to be a chronic source of dispute in relation to vast schemes of bribery, vice, and varied modes of corruption from coast to coast. It was a vivid morality play.

Meantime, in the pages of the men's magazines that Mario continued to write for at Magazine Management Company in the mid–1960s, there was an occasional story highlighted by a title with the word "Mob" in it, or the expression "The Syndicate."

But the bulk of their content continued to be adventure stories about soldiers of fortune on faraway islands that were teeming with scantily clad "wild women" or more of the highly exaggerated, largely fictionalized accounts of clashes during World War Two (always with barely dressed women in the illustrations always seen in brassieres and garters, somehow enmeshed with the derring-do all around them). Puzo once recalled that for a magazine story he wrote that was set against the Allied debacle in Holland in 1944 (the ill-fated "Bridge Too Far" endeavor), he rewrote the history of Operation Market-Garden so that in his version it was a German defeat and an Allied triumph—totally the opposite of how it actually unfolded in 1944.

Nobody complained. No one cared. The magazines were selling macho fantasy.

For Mario Puzo, the paramount question was this: Could he sell another novel? He was at a crossroads. And he knew it.

"I was forty-five years old and tired of being an artist," Puzo explained. "Besides, I owed $20,000 to relatives, finance companies, banks, and assorted bookmakers and shylocks." This was at a time when $20,000 could buy two new homes in a middle-class neighborhood in most parts of America. It was a daunting sum, and equally daunting was the prospect of having no publisher behind him.

The one ray of light was the Atheneum editor's remark about "a little more of that Mafia stuff" and how such material might make for a book that succeeded in the marketplace. "So I told my editors," Puzo recalled, "I'll write a book about the Mafia, just give me some money to get started. They said no money until we see a hundred pages. I compromised, I wrote a ten-page outline. They showed me the door again."

For Puzo, 1965 crawled to a close. He had labored for years on a second literary novel, somehow never allowing the tropes and the narrative clichés of the pulp magazine stories he wrote, strictly for a paycheck, to harm or affect the exquisite prose of *The Fortunate Pilgrim*—and though his new novel had heralded a new year when it was published in January, the book remained largely unknown to the public.

Now Thanksgiving and Christmas were on the horizon, and clearly Atheneum would not once again gamble on him.

In a fascinating variation on the theme of the embittered artist, he later admitted: "I was furious, but only at myself." Whereas other writers might rant and rave about the stupidity of the masses or the inability of readers to appreciate the essence of a certain work they'd completed, Puzo put a different spin on matters as he continued to re-evaluate his postwar writer's quest. "I rethought my whole life," he once said.

And he confronted himself with a series of tough-minded questions: "Why should the public care that I put so much of myself into that book, so much care into each sentence? Why should my family care about my [literary] writing when it didn't earn my daily bread? Why should they indulge my eccentricity? And the public, why should they care about tragedies that didn't reflect their own experience?"

All this came to a head as Mario reckoned with the corner he had written himself into. "I came to the point where I was terribly angry at my wife, at my brothers and sisters, at my mother," and also at fate in general, he recalled.

In his view, "nobody was on my side in this struggle. They were perfectly right in the way they felt, and I was perfectly right in the way that I felt."

But there is no doubt that Mario was facing a crisis. Rejection is the primary reason that so many writers forfeit any effort to seriously pursue a career as an author, opting instead to hide in classrooms or sometimes abandon the profession.

Rejection early on is often enough to obliterate one's desire to persist. But this was different. Puzo's crisis was due to the overlapping rejections he endured in 1965, when rejection came his way from the reading public and his publishers.

Sadly, few books ever turn profits and it has always been thus. Yet, even as the 1960s tipped into their second half, there were entrenched patterns in the world of "gentleman's publishing" and one of those patterns was that if sales were weak but reviews were strong, a serious writer could still be buoyed. Given another chance.

"I received marvelous reviews," Mario recalled. Atheneum Books still cut him loose. He later summarized how badly this hit him: "There is no way to explain the terrible feeling of rejection, the damage, the depression and weakening of will such manipulation does to a writer. But this incident also enlightened me."

The reality check that Mario finally yielded to was this: Publishing was a business and his two literary novels (unlike the fiction of more fortunate authors) had not succeeded as commodities. They had been, by and large, very well reviewed and were admired (by an elite minority) as works of art.

But, by his own admission, Puzo realized something: "I had been naïve enough to believe that publishers cared about art. They didn't. They wanted to make money. (Please don't say, 'No kidding.') They were in business. They had a capital investment and payrolls to meet. If some lunatic wanted to create a work of art, let him do it on his own time."

A shift in Puzo's thinking now occurred. The key issue was to let go of his lifelong devotion to the idea of artistic purity. This was no small matter. Since his teenage years, Mario had beheld the notion that nothing mattered more than making art: "I didn't believe in religion . . . I didn't believe in society or philosophy. But I believed in art for forty-five years." However, in his mid–forties he had to surrender such lofty ideas.

"All young writers dream of immortality," he once explained. Writers dream "that hundreds of years in the future the new generations will read their books and find their lives changed, as my life was after reading *The Brothers Karamazov* at the age of fifteen."

This lifetime conviction was an article of faith, rooted in the fact that for Puzo (who had no traditional religious faith or training) art was, indeed, sacred.

"I had been a true believer in art," he once averred. "It gave me a comfort I found in no other place." Nonetheless, commitment to artistic purity was unaffordable.

And to make matters worse, a dread fear was manifest in Puzo's mind. "I knew I'd never be able to write another book if the next one wasn't a success. The psychological and economic pressure would be too much."

In this state of uncertainty (and with the ongoing FBI investigation still shadowing him), he continued to pump out adventure stories to ensure his paychecks from Magazine Management Company, and he brooded—cigar locked between grinding teeth—about his predicament: "I was willing, I had a ten-page outline—but nobody would take me. Months went by."

Months, indeed. Long months.

For an insecure writer just past his forty-fifth birthday (who was also a novelist recently dumped by a respected publisher), a long season with no new contract, no new novel underway, a mountain of debts, and the nagging worry brought about by an unresolved FBI investigation, created inner, private torment. America's literary history is replete with authors who quit under far less pressure.

For the first time in his life, Mario Puzo seriously considered throwing in the towel. "I was ready to forget about novels except maybe as a puttering hobby for my old age," he once said.

In the back of his mind, however, there lurked one improbable conviction. For an author whose two novels had failed to find a wide audience (despite strong reviews all over the country), it was not just an improbable conviction—it bordered on the irrational. Still, Mario harbored a bedrock belief about one option he had yet to try as a novelist. When despair threatened to do him in, he articulated his belief.

"I could write a best-selling commercial novel whenever I chose to do so," he insisted to everyone in his life. Years later, when looking back on this tipping point, he recalled that there was a consensus of reaction: "My writing friends, my family, my children and my creditors all assured me now was the time to put up or shut up."

One day at the Magazine Management Company, during that season of uncertainty, it was fellow writer Jules Siegel (who aptly described the company's output as "the kind of pulps with covers of eight girls in bikinis with machineguns storming out of black helicopters") who made a gesture in support of Mario's languishing ten-page outline. "I gave him some research materials on the Mafia in Sicily," Jules Siegel said: "Norman Lewis's book, *The Honored Society*, among other items."

Around the same time, a pivotal encounter occurred. "A writer friend dropped into my magazine office," Mario recounted. In a gesture of appreciation for the visit, Puzo handed his visitor a gift copy of *The Fortunate Pilgrim*. One week later, the two men had lunch and Puzo was moved and gratified by the man's effusive praise.

"He thought I was a great writer. I bought him a magnificent lunch," is how Mario later summed up their get-together. But there was more. Apparently, it was during that long lunch that Puzo riffed impromptu, entertaining his admiring colleague with "some funny Mafia stories," as well as details from his ten-page outline.

Something clicked. One thing led to another. Soon thereafter, at the behest of the fellow author, a meeting was arranged with a cadre of top guns at one of New York's leading publishing houses: G. P. Putnam's Sons. The informal session suited Puzo.

Editor-in-Chief William Targ leaned in and listened intently with his rapt colleagues.

"The editors just sat around for an hour, listening to my Mafia tales, and said go ahead," Puzo later explained. They also offered him a $5,000 advance.

The advance, however, would be paid in a series of three installments. Up front, Mario received far less than $2,000. Still, it was a breakthrough.

But then, another break came in the form of the best possible Christmas present for a man with five children, a worried wife, and other high-stress factors in his life.

During Christmas week in 1965, an official decision was reached regarding the FBI's probe into bribery schemes and the Army Reserve office at the Enlistment Center in Manhattan, where Mario had shuffled papers all those years ago.

The decision was made on December 20, 1965, and a single-paragraph report was sent to J. Edgar Hoover's office on December 22nd, ending 1965 with these words:

DETAILS: On December 20, 1965, Assistant United States Attorney, BERNARD W. NUSSBAUM, Southern District of New York, advised he has conferred with Chief of Criminal Division, Southern District of

New York, in reference to this matter. He advised that as a result of this conference a decision has been made to decline prosecution as to the remaining subjects in this case, as it is felt that the facts of this matter would not lend themselves to a successful prosecution as to the remaining subjects.

As one of those "remaining subjects," Mario Puzo exulted. He was off the hook.

On that note, 1966 began quite nicely.

Mario Puzo (left) with colleague, friend, and fellow author Bruce Jay Friedman; photographer unknown

6

All In

I had contracted for Mario's novel from a verbal run-through; there was no outline, no synopsis or sample chapter to read, as has been reported by one or two motion picture executives. Of course I had read Mario's two previous novels. They were first-rate books, though commercial failures. He had been introduced to me by a friend of his who told me that Mario was broke. Puzo and I met; I liked him. We talked; I wanted him for Putnam's and we gave him a contract for $5,000, with a $1,250 down payment.

~~~ Publisher and Editor William Targ, *Indecent Pleasures*

The bullpen we worked in reeked of cigar smoke and there was Mario—overweight, rumpled, slightly sweaty—pounding away on his portable typewriter. He wrote furiously and well—that's how he mastered his craft. He was also a gambler, and he owed a lot of money, which is why he batted out so many stories at Magazine Management . . . [but] he was never too busy to advise us younger writers. He kept saying: "Write, write, write! You only know what you think when it's on the page." Mary Bringle [was] also an editor at Magazine Management . . . Mario really encouraged her.

~~~ Biographer and Memoirist Patricia Bosworth

 In the life of Mario Puzo, a new pattern commenced in 1966. For the next three years, all he did was write daily, write nightly, and write in the wee small hours.

But for a while, it was not his new novel that commanded the bulk of his attention.

Though he was happy to receive the backing of Putnam's editors, there was no getting around how carefully they were hedging their bets. No author with five children to feed and a wife and a home to support could wallow in literary brooding simply by getting his hands on a fraction of a $5,000 advance. And so, with a portion of the advance, and with his head full of sketchy ideas and echoes of old-time stories of "hoods" in New York City, there now occurred . . . something of a grand pause on his novel with the working title of *Mafia*.

Years later, Puzo reflected on this transitional time: "As soon as I got my hands on the Putnam money," he recalled, "I naturally didn't work on the book." A galvanizing motivation, though, was that Putnam's standard agreement was in effect, whereby the advance was paid out incrementally. As Mario later noted, the key issue was that "part of the advance was payable on the handing in of the complete manuscript."

He later admitted (in a bemused way) that if it weren't for that stipulation, "I would never have finished it." And Mario later conceded, when looking back, that lurking in his imagination was "another novel I wanted to write. (I never did and now I never will. Subject matter rots like everything else.)"

Puzo's comrades offered mighty encouragement regarding his new contract with Putnam's. In the offices of Magazine Management Company, hopes were high. "All my fellow [writers and the] editors on the adventure magazine told me to get cracking on the book," Mario said. "They all were sure it would make my fortune. I had all the good stories, it was writing to my strength."

Meantime, while Putnam's waited to see the first complete chapters of Puzo's so-called "Mafia novel" and as an array of freelance pieces were written to generate income, a unique diversion led to a different kind of book publication in 1966: "I sneaked in a children's book," he once said. Today it would be positioned as a Young Adult novel, and this work led to "a rave review from *The New Yorker* magazine," which was, Mario curtly observed, "the first time they knew I was alive."

A small New York-based company (Platt & Munk) published *The Runaway Summer of Davie Shaw* in 1966. Although defined by Puzo (and marketed back then) as "a children's book," it was no minor offering. At 186 pages, the text exceeds a great many short novels that have been published as single volumes.

The Runaway Summer of Davie Shaw is an engaging, highly readable narrative that tells the tale of a thirteen-year-old boy's journey across America, from California to New York. It's a clever variation on the national theme of "Go West, young man!"

In this case, it's "Go East!" Davie Shaw is a willing traveler.

He yearns for adventure. In his royal and highly active imagination, he feels that his life is stunted by his parents. When they decide to celebrate their sixteenth wedding anniversary by embarking on an around-the-world cruise, Davie Shaw is expected to stay with his grandparents and also to visit his Uncle Bernardo. Way leads on to way, however, and soon enough "DavieShaw (that is how everybody pronounced his name, all run together") is en route from the West Coast to the East.

Along the way, he listens raptly and learns much from varied short-term mentors: The Old Guru offers sage advice and imparts secrets about avoiding conflicts; and The Man Who Lived in the Exact Middle of the United States helps him along, as does Eunice Rill, Herpetologist (her information on snakes is crucial, to say the least).

The primary theme in *The Runaway Summer of Davie Shaw* is the hunger for independence. The deep need to be free. As the publishers highlighted on the book's dust jacket: "Mr. Puzo knows that in the order of boyhood dreams the very first one is a wild urge to be on your own. Answering the call of the open road, Davie Shaw engages life just over the horizon as every boy wishes he could."

Below an author's photo that showed a smiling, portly, well-dressed Puzo (wearing a dark suit, a tie, and a white dress shirt), the publishers made sure to shine a light on what a family man Mario happened to be.

His biography on the dust jacket informed readers: "[Puzo's] oldest child is in college and his youngest in kindergarten, a fact which, as he says, 'gives me a fairly broad view of what American children are thinking about.'"

Fittingly and tellingly, the dedication page of *The Runaway Summer of Davie Shaw* was devoted to Mario's own kids: "For Joey, Virginia, Eugene, Dorothy and Tony."

By listing his children in reverse chronological order (Joey being the youngest and Tony being the oldest), Puzo was reminded that as of 1966, he'd been a father for nearly twenty years.

Those two decades of paternal commitment provided him with a storehouse of emotions and ideas to draw from as a writer. And when he did finally dig in and immerse himself in the writing of the first part of his "Mafia novel," Mario made a choice that determined every aspect of the novel and automatically set it apart from all the usual images, clichés, and expectations associated with Mob narratives.

A father figure would be at the center of his story. An Old World patriarch who functioned as a protector, a mentor, and a benevolent source of justice for those who had been wronged and who endured contempt and indifference in courts of law . . . such beleaguered and humiliated individuals would know that this one man was the figure of authority to whom they could turn in their times of trouble. And, if this man had to make use of the violent force at his disposal, so be it. He would be a man who always preferred to reason with others, as opposed to ordering any beatings, bloodshed, or worse. However, if reason failed, force was inevitable.

Everything about Mario Puzo's new novel reinvented Mob stereotypes.

After decades of gangster films chronicling everything from the Roaring Twenties and Prohibition to cinematic biographies of celebrity renegades like John Dillinger, Al Capone, Baby Face Nelson, and Pretty Boy Floyd, not to mention the national memory of hundreds of televised hours of congressional hearings devoted to often dramatic testimony about racketeering, labor union corruption, and all sorts of crime syndicate rumors and revelations—all that ensured certain expectations.

It was assumed that any narrative highlighting Mafia characters would be dominated by uncouth, slick, violently unpredictable, and quick-to-kill one-dimensional figures. Mobsters à la Hollywood. Unsympathetic figures. Goons and goombahs. The last thing anyone was expecting was a compassionate man who also possessed an Old World code of ethics and behavior sanctioning occasional murder.

One after another, there are three characters in a state of personal crisis introduced in the novel's opening pages. In a New York courtroom, we meet Amerigo Bonasera (that's Italian for *America Goodnight*), whose daughter lingers in a hospital after two all-American college-age louts beat her in the aftermath of their effort to sexually assault her. The would-be rapists are sons of well-to-do Americans. Bonasera, an Italian immigrant, is duly shocked by his humiliation as a judge hands down a suspended sentence to the grinning young men who attacked his daughter. Realizing that putting his faith in the American justice system was folly, Bonasera tells his wife: "For justice we must go on our knees to Don Corleone."

There's a quick transition to a hotel suite in Los Angeles. Readers are introduced to Johnny Fontane, a popular singing sensation whose personal life is in disarray (his wife is flagrantly cheating on him) as his career begins to capsize. Fontane is caught between his helplessness in Hollywood (he's unable to land a role in a big new film that might restore his faltering status in show business) and the nasty taunting and ridicule that his wife heaps upon him: "You poor silly bastard . . . Ah, Johnny, you always will be a dumb romantic guinea, you even make love like a kid. You still think screwing is really like those dopey songs you used to sing." Fontane's epiphany comes in a flash of awareness: "There was one person who could save him. He would go back to New York. He would go back to the one man with the power, the wisdom he needed and a love he still trusted. His Godfather Corleone."

Then there's Nazorine the Baker. He's desperate to get a problem resolved. The problem is that his daughter is in love with an ex-soldier from the Italian army, who is now a prisoner of war in America: "One of the many thousands of Italian Army prisoners paroled daily to work in the American economy, he lived in constant fear of that parole being revoked." It's clear to Nazorine, who has allowed Enzo (the POW) to work in his bakery that "Enzo must be kept in America and be made an American citizen. And there was only one man who could arrange such an affair. The Godfather. Don Corleone."

Thus the reader realizes that the story is set in a time long past. The narrative immediately connects all of these disparate characters with a sweeping flourish:

All of these people and many others received engraved invitations to the wedding of Miss Constanzia Corleone, to be celebrated on the last Saturday in August 1945. The father of the bride, Don Vito Corleone, never forgot his old friends and neighbors, though he himself now lived in a huge house on Long Island. The reception would be held in that house and the festivities would go on all day. There was no doubt it would be a momentous occasion. The war with the Japanese had just ended so there would not be any nagging fear for their sons fighting in the Army to cloud these festivities. A wedding was just what people needed to show their joy.

What follows is a first chapter offering sixty-four pages blending pulp ingredients with serious fiction. Conflicts are revealed, discussed, dramatized, and detailed as the festivities unfold throughout the day of the wedding reception. It's within the context of the wedding reception that the reader meets each of the three sons of Don Vito Corleone. There's the edgily aggressive Santino, who is almost always called Sonny; then the sympathetic but feckless Fredo; and, finally, Michael, the Don's youngest son, who broke ranks with the family to enlist—against his father's wishes—in the Marine Corps and who has now returned home as a war hero. There's also an adopted son, Tom Hagen (he kept his original surname by the Don's decree, so as not to dishonor his family of origin); and he's a law school graduate serving as Don Vito Corleone's special advisor: the *Consigliere*.

A parallel universe of authority, power, hierarchy, patriarchy, family structure, and social status is illustrated and illuminated. Each of the three individuals (Amerigo Bonasera, Johnny Fontane, and Nazorine the Baker) whose crises were sketched in the opening pages eventually appear again, as their problems are further delineated and their requests for help are granted in turn. Much of the afternoon finds the Don in his cavernous home office on Long Island, compelled by Sicilian tradition to receive these cries for help and always roping his *Consigliere* to tend to the resolutions. As Tom Hagen explains to his annoyed wife (who has no choice but to sit alone for most of the party), it's a matter of honor wherein "no Sicilian can refuse any request on his daughter's wedding day." The name Corleone comes from a small, remote town in Sicily.

Soon enough, as the narrative expands and the personal problems of three individual characters give way to larger issues, challenges, and confrontations ranging from the grim manipulations of a Hollywood film producer (who's also a pederast) to the drug-trafficking plans of Virgil Sollozzo, whose plan to import heroin for mass distribution in American cities is rejected out of hand by the Don, the reader is drawn into a world as far removed from the late 1960s as possible.

Absurd though it now sounds (and ridiculous though it was then), the fact is Mario Puzo made a radical choice when he chose to anchor his novel's storyline more than twenty years in the past, and to create *dramatis personae* rooted in Old World mores and family fealty. In short, he was working against the Zeitgeist of the late 1960s.

Between the years 1966 and 1969, every aspect of American culture was affected by the worldwide mass media's utter devotion to the youth market. Rapid changes in every realm—music, clothes, films, and theater were seemingly being recycled and revolutionized every season—were compounded by the rising tensions and the explosively agitated national mood as the Civil Rights Movement shifted from "We Shall Overcome" to "Black Power!" Similarly, the tone and mood of the protest movement against the escalating war in Vietnam switched from "Bring the Troops Home" to "Hey, Hey, LBJ: How Many Kids Did You Kill Today?" or the even more in-your-face "Up Against the Wall, Motherfuckers!" favored by the angriest dissenters.

There was a relentless fixation in 1966-1969 media (especially magazines, books, and television shows) about what was *new* and what was *next*. Looking backward was not just considered out of fashion; it was considered a commercial death wish. Almost everything in the culture of the late 1960s was pitched to the public as a cutting-edge departure from the past. There were rare exceptions, of course. In 1968, Barbra Streisand's film debut in the ultra-retro *Funny Girl* was a smash hit. But only because of Barbra, who had already enjoyed years of phenomenal success on television and Broadway, in clubs, and also on records. Later in 1969, the studio that financed the big-budget musical film version of *Hello, Dolly!* (also starring Streisand) discovered quickly that such material was doomed in an era dominated by Woodstock and the *White Album*.

More than anyone else, in fact, the Beatles and their ever-changing appearances and shape-shifting full-length albums signaled more changes in the culture than anyone could keep up with. It was nearly impossible to believe that the eight-by-ten glossy photos tucked inside the *White Album* for its Christmas 1968 release were pictures of the same four guys who had been cute mop-tops in matching suits with proper ties and clean white shirts on *The Ed Sullivan Show* only four years earlier. Now they were hippie *artistes*, mixing and matching bohemian and Edwardian fashions, sporting shoulder length hair, and creating studio-based music never intended to be performed on stage for concert audiences. By 1968 and 1969, the mid–decade explosion of Beatlemania highlighted in America by the band's multiple appearances on *The Ed Sullivan Show* in 1964 and 1965 already seemed quaint.

The talk of the nation was about the so-called Generation Gap. Everything from the mass marketing of the Pill in the mid–1960s to the onset of the first co-ed dorms in colleges and universities in the late 1960s suggested that traditional values were under siege in the era of the putative Sexual Revolution. Meantime, the war in Vietnam became increasingly divisive and America's racial tensions skyrocketed. Authority everywhere was challenged, from draft boards to Columbia University, where dissident students shut down the school and occupied the president's office.

Yet, in these same years, Puzo's new novel unfolded against the backdrop of 1945 through 1955. Ironically, there is a major aspect of Mario's narrative that was as current as the nightly news: Regardless of how the Corleone Family was rooted in what now seemed a distant past, the key element is that the Don, as an overlord of one of the Mafia's pivotal Five Families in New York, is more than a renegade. He is a law unto himself, and his influence is so vast that he commandeers a fraternity of judges and lawyers, not the other around. When Don Vito Corleone stated, "Lawyers can steal more money with a briefcase than a thousand men with guns and masks," he was shown by Puzo to be an authentic anti-Establishment maverick—and far more titanic a force than any hippie, Yippie, or ranting, bedraggled college radical.

American society underwent jolting transformations between 1966 and 1969. No one who voted for either presidential candidate in 1960 would ever have believed, back then, that only eight years later there would be riots in the streets of Chicago when the Democratic Party convened there in 1968 or, for that matter, that popular singers defined by the likes—and the looks—of Elvis, Fabian, and Bobby Darin were now overrun on the Top 40 charts in 1968 by bushy-haired, costumed, surly-posing psychedelic marauders bearing odd names à la Jefferson Airplane and Cream.

In the latter years of the Sixties, everything that had appeared to be settled, assured, and reliably popular and desirable as the Eisenhower Fifties gave way to the JFK era in the first few years of the 1960s —everything now seemed to be in turmoil, under siege, or in a state of agitated transition. Two of the most popular new slogans that suddenly manifested on posters, buttons, bumper stickers, placards, and of course in the magazine articles that chronicled the curdling national mood were "Question Authority" and "Don't Trust Anyone Over 30." The notion that conformity was ideal was not just questioned, it was ridiculed as the YouthQuake caused cultural tremors.

In varied realms, the goal of burning away the past was encapsulated in particular slogans that mainstream Americans of Mario Puzo's generation now found startling.

Adults of Puzo's own demographic (those who had been children of the Twenties, who had come of age in the Thirties and endured not just the Great Depression but also World War Two in the first half of the 1940s, and who struggled in the two decades since to provide for their own kids and families a modicum of safety and security that was unattainable in the past) were not just startled but often shocked by the febrile intensity of the rhetoric blaring from their TVs and radios or appearing in newspapers: "Burn Your Draft Card!" was a declaration some citizens considered tantamount to treason. And "Burn Your Bra!" foretold a new wave of feminism that traditionalists were convinced would drown the values and verities of proper family hierarchies. And then there was "Burn, Baby, Burn!" That was the most disorienting of proclamations because in its alliterative glory it tried to suggest that the best solution to America's racial crisis was to commit arson on grand scales. The long, hot summers were underway with a vengeance, and the ghastly riots and horrendous fires in Watts, Newark, Harlem, Detroit, Chicago, Baltimore, and other major cities were beyond shocking. Seen on TV, they were terrifying and surreal.

It was against this backdrop of myriad national convulsions that Mario Puzo made slow but steady progress on his new novel. "It took me three years to finish," he once noted. "During that time I wrote three adventure stories a month for Martin Goodman [at Magazine Management Company] on a free-lance basis." Indeed, as a way of spurring himself on and to ensure no slacking off on his novel-in-progress, Puzo had made a bold decision: He quit his salaried position with Martin Goodman's company, opting instead to submit monthly pieces for one-shot stipends instead of drawing a weekly salary. To compensate for the loss of the predictable income of a weekly salary, Mario took on other freelance assignments: "I wrote a lot of book reviews," he once said, adding that he also pumped out "magazine pieces, two of which were for the *New York Times Sunday Magazine*, who, though they do not stuff your pockets with gold, treat your work with enormous respect."

That's more than he could say for *TIME* magazine. Unsigned book reviews written by Puzo appeared in *TIME*, but in Mario's opinion they constituted "lousy work." Like anyone being published in Henry Luce's pages in those years, Puzo's words were endlessly altered and revised by the cadre of editors and rewrite minions who inevitably transformed all copy into depersonalized, monotonic *TIME*-speak.

However, the stipend for a single book review was $300, which was a fat sum in the late 1960s. Mario cashed the checks and forgot about those reviews.

Matters were entirely different when in came to publishing reviews for *BOOK WORLD*, a prominent weekly periodical edited by a trailblazing polymath named Byron Dobell. The reviews were signed in *BOOK WORLD*, and as an editor Dobell was willing to allow his writers a wide berth. It was here that Mario Puzo's powerful critical intelligence and discerning taste were given a new platform.

BOOK WORLD was neither a skimpy nor a minor publication. Edited out of Byron Dobell's office at the *New York Herald-Tribune* in Manhattan, the Sunday periodical devoted entirely to reviews of new books, literary columns, and authors' interviews was a substantial, much-admired weekly compendium of opinions. It appeared as a Sunday supplement in the *Washington Post* and the *Chicago Tribune*, as well as in the *New York Herald-Tribune*. Its circulation was in the millions.

On Sunday, October 29, 1967, the first review that Mario ever wrote for editor Byron Dobell was published. Not only did Puzo think that Dobell "was the only guy that would have printed it," but also that "certainly [he was] the only editor who would have given it a front page."

The piece was written as a critique of *Writers at Work: The Paris Review Interviews*. This was the third volume of collected interviews culled from the literary quarterly that had been co-founded in Paris in 1953 by short-term expatriates George Plimpton, William Styron, Peter Matthiessen, Harold "Doc" Humes, and others.

The Paris Review had morphed into a remarkably consistent, esteemed literary quarterly with an emphasis on publishing new short stories and poems by writers who were then gradually building their careers. The new poems and stories in each issue were placed before and after what soon became the magazine's signature feature: the lengthy interviews with prominently published authors, under varied rubrics: "The Art of Fiction," "The Art of Poetry," "The Art of Theater," and so on.

Although the poems and stories published in *The Paris Review* were new, and usually by younger writers, the interviews featured an admixture of scribes considered the younger authors of the day (Saul Bellow, James Jones, Arthur Miller) plus those considered to be old masters (Hemingway, Faulkner, Robert Frost). To make Vol. 3 of the *Writers at Work* series even more formidable, an introduction by Alfred Kazin was solicited. At that time, Kazin was a feared and respected critic.

Literary politics, anxiety about making waves, and the understandable urge to kiss the rumps of those who had "made it" would have caused most book reviewers to tread lightly, perhaps hoping to ingratiate themselves with the literati. Just the opposite happened with Puzo. And his intelligence and wit had a writer's field day.

Instead of a typical review in straight-ahead paragraphs, highlighted by selected quotations from the book at issue, Mario's review adopted the form and the format of the interviews for which *The Paris Review* was most famous. The piece begins with a disclaimer making it clear that this unusual approach is Puzo's doing.

Casual readers likely didn't make much of this, but for those in the know—that is, the ever-competitive and highly attentive careerists in what Gore Vidal referred to as the Land of Book Chat—it's safe to say that eyebrows (or hackles) were raised. If anyone's eyes shot to the attribute at the end of the review, the reminder that Puzo was a published author was off-set by the fact that neither of his two novels had been been a big success. And yet, here he was, jabbing, tweaking, and zinging away.

Perhaps editor Byron Dobell was delighted to publish a review that visually startled readers for a change. An exceedingly visual person, Dobell's passion for painting eventually led to a second flourishing career. Three of his portraits now hang in the Smithsonian's National Portrait Gallery and he has enjoyed tremendous success with ten Manhattan solo exhibitions of his portraiture.

The book review that Puzo designed in the form of a faux-interview was unlike anything readers had ever seen in *BOOK WORLD*. Most surprising was that from the get-go Mario's sharp insights were balanced with his sly humor. This guaranteed that certain egomaniacs who thought of themselves as "big" (either the writers who were interviewed or those asking them questions) were going to be taken down a peg. Puzo's refusal to court collective egos was bold.

Here's how the review began on Page One of *BOOK WORLD*:

Writers, Talent, Money, and Class: AN IRREVERENT INTERVIEW

Rather than write a formal criticism of this collection, Mr. Puzo invited the editors of *The Paris Review* to interview him as they would any eminent author. However, it must be understood that Mr. Puzo is responsible for all that follows.

INTERVIEWER
Did you like the book? Do you think it was a good job?

PUZO
A wonderful job. And the whole idea is so respectful of the writer, just letting him ramble on. Who the hell ever listens to him? And all your interviewers keep themselves in the background. They know their place. They know they are not important.

INTERVIEWER
Thank you.

PUZO
And you never try to booby-trap the writer or put him down. I get the feeling *The Paris Review* is *for* the writer all the way. However, I don't think this Third Series is as interesting as the first two. But I wish you'd collect all three in one volume. It would be the perfect gift to anyone interested in literature, a must for every writer's library.

INTERVIEWER
You don't seem to have a library.

PUZO
Neither does Nelson Algren. That's how you can tell an honest writer. No, don't write that down. I'm kidding. I'm just sensitive about money. How come you people never ask writers about money? You ask them if they use a typewriter or a pen, how many pages they write a day, all kinds of personal sex things. How come you never ask them how much they got for their paperback rights?

INTERVIEWER
We feel our readers are not interested in that sort of information.

PUZO
That's because you already have money. I hear *The Paris Review* crowd are all a bunch of rich kids. No, don't get mad. I believe in money and I believe in rich people. They can *afford* to be honest, truthful and discriminating.

In the middle of his review-in-the-form-of-an-interview (with himself), Puzo serves up a chart that lists the fourteen writers whose *Paris Review* colloquies are included in this third *Writers at Work* volume. His chart separately rates both the quality of the interviews as well as how he values their work.

The fourteen writers listed are: Louis Ferdinand-Celine, Lillian Hellman, Allen Ginsberg, Saul Bellow, Blaise Cendrars, James Jones, Evelyn Waugh, Harold Pinter, Jean Cocteau, Arthur Miller, William Burroughs, Norman Mailer, Edward Albee, and William Carlos Williams.

And the piece at large is peppered with Mario's stinging observations: "Coupling novelists with playwrights is a form of intellectual bestiality. Theater writing today is not literature. The best dramatist doesn't have a quarter the artistic brainpower of a third-rate novelist."

Yet, there's also an undercurrent of respect throughout: "Ginsberg! He comes over like a real *mensch*. I never expected that." About Saul Bellow: "He's so damn smart, he believes, and he's been faithful to art in his fashion." Then there's Lillian Hellman: "A real womanly

woman despite her tough mind. Too bad she became a playwright."
As for James Jones, he's dubbed a "Regular Guy," and Harold Pinter is
defined as a "Modest Englishman." In the case of poet William Carlos
Williams, there's a corrective jab: "*Paris Review's* fault. He's a better
guy than this."

The ultimate takeaway from this idiosyncratic debut by Puzo in
BOOK WORLD was his assessment of Norman Mailer, whose career
was enjoying a renaissance due largely to his latter-day plunge into
nonfiction writing.

INTERVIEWER
Do you know Mailer's work?

PUZO
I know *that* work all right. He was an honest, believing writer
until the publishers worked him over when he was trying to peddle
The Deer Park. Now he's a crook, his last two novels dastardly crimes
committed in cold blood and in full view of the public. And that's
OK, but he shouldn't attack straight writers like Faulkner, [William]
Styron and [James] Jones as a cover. He should just scoop up his loot
and make his getaway fast. No fellow novelist will reproach him. It's
embarrassing to his friends when Mailer puts Faulkner down as a
person. Because quite simply, Faulkner's career is every writer's
dream, Mailer's is every writer's nightmare.

That paragraph alone was sure to get tongues wagging. Those who
could read between the lines knew that Puzo was saying in print
what many had chosen to whisper off the record: Mailer's "last two
novels" were *Why Are We in Vietnam?* (a short novel published one
month earlier in September 1967; considered a Joycean tour de
force by some but branded by others as a meandering scatological
mess), preceded by *An American Dream* (written on monthly serial
deadlines for *Esquire* magazine as a highly publicized stunt in 1964
and published in book form in 1965).

Mario Puzo using the phrase "in cold blood" was the kind of
admiring allusion to Truman Capote's smash-hit magnum opus that
was sure to set Mailer's teeth on edge, just as Norman himself had
set others' teeth on edge when publishing essays that condemned
William Styron as "a fat, spoiled rich boy," whose *Set This House on*

Fire was "a bad, maggoty novel," while also being sure to assert that James Jones "has sold out badly over the years." It had become a blood sport for Mailer to publicly ridicule most of his peers, sometimes challenging them physically with his booze-fueled mania for arm-wrestling, boxing, and head-butting competitions. "A good novelist can do without everything but the remnant of his balls," Norman once declaimed.

Pointing out that Puzo was hardly as well-known or as "successful" as Mailer or Capote would have been feckless, because in his *faux-*interview with an imaginary *Paris Review* interviewer, Mario had already highlighted his own obscurity: "I've written better novels than some of these guys in your collection and you people never came around to see me. I got asked to sign a Vietnam war protest ad but that's all." To which the rejoinder is: "You're not quite well known enough. Frankly we never heard of you."

Nobody anywhere (including Puzo) would have believed how dramatically that would change. And Norman Mailer's balls would have shrunk to the size of Chiclets had he known that two years hence, Mario's third book (with its working title, *Mafia*, changed to *The Godfather*) would be the fastest-selling novel in publishing history.

In the meantime, 1967 drew to a violent, chaotic close. The country was teetering on the edge of a national nervous breakdown after a year of catastrophic inner-city riots, massive antiwar demonstrations, and further escalation of the Vietnam War.

However, on a quieter note altogether, the fact that Mario had changed the working title of his developing novel did not necessarily mean that his theme was altered or that the structure of his story was reconfigured.

If anything, calling the novel *The Godfather* instead of *Mafia* shone a light on the transfer of power within the Corleone family, which is at the heart of the story.

As readers would see upon the novel's publication, the looming presence of the aging patriarch in Puzo's narrative is superseded by another man's captivating, charismatic rise to power, thanks to Mario's storytelling sleight of hand.

After a failed assassination attempt against the Don occurs less than one third of the way into the book, the story's weight falls squarely onto the shoulders of the Don's youngest son, Michael. Step by step, incrementally, with reticence at first and then with tentative confidence and finally with a mythic phoenix-like reinvention of himself, the odyssey of Michael Corleone's life becomes the most gripping aspect in the arc of the Corleone's myth.

But it's certainly not a one-man show.

All along the way, as Michael Corleone sheds his military uniform and his pre-war Ivy League accomplishments, he is surrounded by a chorus of supportive, comforting, stalwart figures: his mother, Mama Corleone, and his brothers Sonny, Fredo, and Tom Hagen. There are also the two *caporegimes* (Salvatore Tessio and Peter Clemenza) who have served Don Vito so loyally, and who just as faithfully shift their allegiance to Michael after his return from enforced exile in Sicily.

Michael has to flee to Sicily to be protected and hidden by a family ally, after successfully executing Virgil Sollozzo, the man who masterminded the attempt on his father's life. In the company of Sollozzo was a bodyguard who was also a New York policeman, the thoroughly corrupt and odious Captain McCluskey. After Michael guns down both men in a public execution that becomes the stuff of legend, his exile in Sicily is followed by a return to America and his own ascension to the role of being the Don.

Its crime angles aside, *The Godfather* is still Mario's magnum opus about a family.

One week after New Year's Day 1968, the readers of the nationally distributed BOOK WORLD found Mario Puzo writing about another kind of patriarch for another kind of "Family." Norman Podhoretz's first memoir, *Making It*, had just been published by Random House. Although ten years younger than Puzo, the trajectory of the career of Norman Podhoretz was dramatically different in comparison to Mario's own long and winding road. So different, in fact, that by the age of thirty, "Poddy" (as his closest friends called him) was appointed editor in chief at *Commentary* magazine, one of America's premier intellectual journals. He would go on to hold that position for more than three decades.

In *Making It*, the first of a handful of memoirs Podhoretz published, he used the term "The Family" to describe the elite, highly educated, royal coterie of esteemed critics and cultural commentators whose bylines appeared perennially in periodicals like *Commentary*, the *Partisan Review* (not to be confused with *The Paris Review*), *Dissent*, and others. Except for *The New Yorker*, subscription levels were not large (the subscribership to the *Partisan Review* never approached twenty thousand) and the readership consisted primarily of professors in the Liberal Arts and Humanities, but such journals of opinion and literary criticism had enormous influence in those years.

More than one generation of rising American academics aspired to have an article published in any of the "little magazines" that prominently featured "pieces" by the exalted critics who were dubbed "The Family" by Podhoretz. Their clique included Lionel and Diana Trilling (the First Couple of New York's intelligentsia), plus Irving Howe, Hannah Arendt, Philip Rahv, Mary McCarthy, Alfred Kazin, Edmund Wilson, and a conclave of others. In fear of any future critical retaliation, a novelist or a poet would never be chided for declining the invitation to review a book-length work by the likes of Norman Podhoretz, whose reputation as a fierce critic was entrenched long before the 1960s. In the late 1950s, in fact, with his blatant denunciation of Jack Kerouac's *On the Road* in tandem with Allen Ginsberg's edgy poetry and other writings of the newly emerging Beat Generation (a Podhoretz essay titled "The Know-Nothing Bohemians" dismembered Kerouac and his cohort), "Poddy" made his mark as a younger critic defending older forms; a critic who not only disliked but detested most new trends.

So, what did Mario do with this assignment? He chomped on one of his eight-inch cigars, exercised his own first-rate critical thinking skills, and put on boxing gloves.

Puzo's review of Norman Podhoretz's *Making It* was titled "Big Literary Gun Aims at Self and Misses."

The lead paragraph set quite a tone: "As Roman gladiators once dreamed of watching Nero fight in the arena, so do novelists pray for a critic to publish a work of some artistic pretension. And for the same reason. To see the congenital thumbs-down s.o.b. get killed." Then Puzo quickly admits: "Such an attitude is, of course, completely indefensible, petty, and unliterary. But it is all too human . . ."

And that's just the opening. Knowing full well that the vast majority of Americans who were likely to read a Sunday supplement like *BOOK WORLD* had never heard of Norman Podhoretz (many a Manhattan literary star remains unknown outside of New York City), the next paragraphs humorously clarified some of the basic issues:

> *Norman Podhoretz's* Making It, *a memoir, will most certainly be greeted by the same savage shouts of joy that once welcomed Louis XVI's tumbrel to the guillotine; and it is especially difficult to resist joining the mob in this case. For Mr. Podhoretz is not only one of the double-0-numbered, licensed-to-kill literary Bonds but a federalized intellectual who gets invited to the White House—and goes. More. He danced at Truman Capote's famous masked ball, he is the powerful editor of* Commentary *magazine, and wantonly, in a dark moment of his soul, he made the infamous suggestion that the magazine article might be equal to the novel as art.*

> *To counter the mob, and to be fair, let's quickly say that there is nothing wrong with his being a tough critic; that's his job. And as Podhoretz himself points out, it shows his respect for literature. (Besides, he's not always that tough. Read him on [James] Baldwin and [Norman] Mailer.)*

> *As for attending White House barbecues and Capote's ball: No writer's wife would permit her husband to turn down such invitations.*

The bulk of Puzo's review of *Making It* summarizes the memoir's content and at the same time offers up pertinent, astute, discerning judgments: First, it's a "literary-intellectual autobiography in which we get very little of the author's emotional life"; the author "was singled out and befriended by a female teacher who spotted his brilliant mind" and "he won scholarships like crazy, went to Columbia and studied under the great Lionel Trilling"; then "we see Podhoretz in his early twenties, writing book reviews for *The New Yorker* and *Partisan Review*"; and soon enough Norman Podhoretz "becomes chief editor of *Commentary*, before his thirtieth birthday."

Smack dab in the middle of the review, Puzo strikes:

> *And that's it. For the rest of the time you are in the mind of Norman Podhoretz as he discovers how important fame is, how important money is, and how he comes to realize that the cultural indoctrination by American colleges makes you lose sight of those things. There are no sexy stories in this book, no inner-circle gossip. He is too hung up*

*on the "dirty little secret," as he calls it, complaining that nobody
told him that success, money, fame and power are worth having, the
hungered-for prizes everybody sneakily aspires to. Never realizing
that the reason nobody told him is the same reason nobody told him
why men go dancing with girls. Everybody knows. What's to tell?*

Although there are complimentary lines ("he is a good critic . . .
one of the few who nailed *Augie March* as a phony book"; "he is a
man who loves literature and to read him stripping down a book . . .
is to enjoy a master craftsman with an impeccable ear"), the ultimate
verdict is tough-minded and specific: "The prose in this book really
does not have the force Podhoretz generates in his essays. The
sentences have no ring to them. The paragraphs go mushy. He is at
his worst in the closing paragraphs when, to make sure we do not
hold his book cheap, he instructs us on its importance."

To lower the boom decisively, Mario then concluded: "With scarcely
a trace of human warmth, he has drawn the portrait of someone,
surely not himself, who is an intellectual *nebbish*."

Readers who needed to look up the definition of any Yiddish
words quickly learned that a *nebbish* is "a person, esp. a man, who is
regarded as pitifully ineffectual, timid or submissive."

With that book review, published on January 7, 1968, Mario Puzo
began what would turn out to be the most transformative year of his
life and career.

The quest to complete the writing of *The Godfather* now had new
momentum. The imminent summer of 1968 marked a milestone of
sorts for Mario and Erika Puzo. As of the middle of 1968, it would
be twenty years since they had left Germany as a young couple,
with their first child on the verge of toddlerhood. Twenty years
since Erika had seen her family. Two decades since the start of their
marriage. Mario made the promise that no matter what, this would
be the year to go back to Europe, even if he had to finance the trip
with credit cards and a personal loan. His promise to Erika was not
about a second honeymoon. (They'd never really had a first.) It was
a promise to take their whole family on a vacation that would finally
lead to a chance to meet with her family in what was then called

West Germany. A tall order.

Meantime, he made significant progress on the final portion of his new novel. The overlapping storylines in *The Godfather* were firmly under control: No matter what happened in the narrative, all roads led back to the Corleone compound on Long Island (modeled on the legend of the Kennedy compound at Hyannis Port). From there, as all the conflicts and confrontations in the narrative unfold, the gradual emergence of Michael Corleone as head of the Family dominates the tale.

The subplot involving Johnny Fontane out in Hollywood and Las Vegas (a variation on the legendary rise, fall, and renaissance in the career of Frank Sinatra in the early 1950s), as well as the subplot detailing Michael's exile in Sicily, which follows hefty background material on his father Vito's childhood in Sicily, never causes confusion. In fact, those Sicilian sequences and the flashbacks to Vito's childhood in Sicily effortlessly transition to the Don's rise to power on the Lower East Side in the Little Italy era of the First World War. Seamlessly, the story oscillates between times and places.

The structure and the clarity of *The Godfather* are remarkable. Equally remarkable is the balancing act that Puzo succeeded at regarding the novel's tone and mood. It is a textured, sometimes flamboyantly rhetorical novel that is also infused with the elements of "the postwar pulps" that Mario had written for throughout the 1960s. The writing never becomes tawdry or "dirty" simply for the sake of shock value, but time after time, at deliberate intervals, there are scenes of violence or sex that Puzo knew would keep any reader turning pages. And yet this was no mere potboiler.

Aside from its preponderant focus on family love and unconditional family loyalty, there's one theme that glues together the narrative architecture of *The Godfather*.

That theme can be stated in one word: *betrayal*. In some way, shape, or form, it is betrayal that serves as the defining factor in every major plot twist and in each transition of the story. From the lowliest underling to the most powerful of fellow Dons in the world of organized crime, there are acts of betrayal generating decisions that ensure that the members of the Corleone family meet their separate fates.

How does the theme of betrayal permeate the storyline? The heroin trafficking agenda relentlessly pushed by "the Turk," Virgil Sollozzo, betrays the Old World ethos that Don Corleone seeks to uphold, because inevitably such drug trafficking will poison the lives of children and families. Contrarily, the Don perceives the illegal activities of prostitution, gambling, and labor racketeering as vices that can be regulated honorably. No rejection will stop Virgil Sollozzo, however, and when Don Corleone refuses to finance Sollozzo's operations (or to grant "political protection" to "the Turk" by sharing the influence of lawyers and judges that Don Corleone "keeps in his pocket"), the attempt to kill the Don is Virgil Sollozzo's act of betrayal.

The assassination attempt against Don Vito Corleone is aided and abetted by the absence of Paulie Gatto, the Don's driver and bodyguard. Paulie fakes an illness and calls in sick on the day the Don is to be killed. That leaves Fredo, the Don's middle son, to substitute as driver and bodyguard. Fredo is weak in spirit and he is not that sharp in his thinking. In effect, he leaves his father wide open in a public space. The Don is shot five times, but manages to survive. Quickly, it is ascertained by Sonny Corleone that Paulie Gatto's illness was a ruse. There's no doubt in Sonny's mind that "Paulie sold out the old man," and has surely been recruited and paid by Sollozzo. Betrayal. Thus Sonny has Paulie Gatto eliminated.

When Michael Corleone agrees to meet with Virgil Sollozzo to negotiate a truce in the aftermath of the failed attempt to assassinate the Don, the key problem is that Sollozzo's bodyguard is New York police captain Mark McCluskey. He's a crooked cop being paid fat cash stipends to protect "the Turk." Betrayal. Captain McCluskey has betrayed his policeman's oath, his uniform and badge, and his fellow citizens. In a way, it's a moral victory when both Sollozzo and McCluskey are killed by Michael.

Unfortunately, that singular act is the ultimate act of self-betrayal. And yet, at the same time, it's the ultimate act of self-actualization. Either way, Michael is never the same again. After spending his young adulthood avoiding all aspects of the Family business (by attending Dartmouth, joining the Marines, planning to marry his non-Italian New England fiancée), he now steps onto a path that guarantees that due to one crisis after another, one year after another, his own humanity will be compromised.

From the first page of the novel, when Amerigo Bonasera realizes that he and his injured daughter have been betrayed by the police and the courts of law and that their only recourse is to beg Don Corleone for justice, to the paramount deceits and insidious treacheries climaxing the novel as Michael Corleone assumes the mantle of the

Don and not only faces the betrayals of competing crime lords but also has to outwit the enemies within—both his brother-in-law, Carlo Rizzi, and one of the Family's longtime *caporegimes,* Tessio, become traitors—the theme of betrayal is a constant thread.

It was a national theme as well. More and more and more, 1968 not only unfolded but detonated in a series of explosive events causing America at large to tremble with rancor and rebellion; a sense of betrayal abounded. At the end of January in 1968, on the eve of the Chinese New Year, the Tet Offensive erupted in South Vietnam. Out of nowhere, more than three dozen simultaneous attacks were launched against fortified American targets by the seemingly ubiquitous Viet Cong, who for a brief time occupied the U.S. Embassy in Saigon.

Americans at home were bewildered by the immensity of the coordinated surprise attacks, which indicated (among other things) an intelligence failure as prodigious as the one that preceded the Japanese attack on Pearl Harbor. After all, President Johnson and General Westmoreland had assured everyone at home that the U.S. and South Vietnam were winning; and that there was, indeed, "light at the end of the tunnel."

The month-long ravages of the Tet Offensive proved otherwise. This would be the fourth year of full-scale war in Vietnam for America, and a sense of betrayal swirled around one and all. The grunts in the field felt betrayed not just by the protesters at home, but also by the idiotic strategies of their obtuse commanders. Civilians at home felt betrayed by LBJ's hawkish administration, which they increasingly realized was not telling the truth about the war.

Those who supported the war (accepting it as a policy of resistance to Communist expansion in Southeast Asia) convinced themselves that their government was betraying the anti-Communist cause and the troops "in country" by holding back, not invading North Vietnam, refusing to wage all-out war.

And the youth who opposed the war felt betrayed by the pro-war Hawks, by their elders, and especially by those who clung to their Silent Generation reticence.

Now more than ever, television brought the war into American living rooms. The degree to which the Viet Cong had successfully infiltrated South Vietnam was not just stunning; it was revelatory. No such all-encompassing infiltration could have happened without the cooperation of untold numbers of South Vietnamese. When legendary newscaster Walter Cronkite dropped his mask of journalistic "objectivity" and concluded one broadcast by flat-out stating that it appeared that America simply could not win in Vietnam, he shocked viewers. After all, Walter Cronkite was no anti-Establishment rabble-rouser. For decades, he'd been a stalwart American voice and a reassuring television presence. "Uncle Walter" *was* the Establishment.

President Johnson was heard to say: "If I've lost Cronkite, then I've lost the country." Doubtless the famously profane Johnson said many other things that weren't fit to print. LBJ felt betrayed by the Cronkite proclamation, and soon thereafter made his historic speech about opting not "to seek another term as your president." When that speech was aired on Sunday night, March 31, 1968, it shook the nation. In the midst of a war that was going badly, the Commander in Chief was checking out. A great many American citizens felt betrayed not only by Johnson's abdication, but also the degree to which his Great Society programs were defunded to pay for the Vietnam War.

Some of the toxic tensions causing the nation to feel at war with itself had congealed at the massive antiwar protest event that came to be known as the March on the Pentagon. It occurred on October 21, 1967, and vivid news coverage was broadcast across America and the world. Between 50,000 and 75,000 varied demonstrators (young and old, black and white, male and female, all political stripes ranging from mainstream Democrats and Republicans to communists, anarchists, and apolitical Flower Power archetypes) chanted, marched, and to a limited extent tried to "storm the Pentagon." They were met by large numbers of soldiers, military policemen, and National Guard troops, as well as Washington, D.C.'s police.

That one-day event was given new life in a book-length work of memoir, reportage, and history published by Norman Mailer in the spring of 1968. Titled *The Armies of the Night: History as a Novel, the Novel as History*, it was embraced by almost all critics as Mailer's most important work since his debut novel twenty years earlier. For a slew of reasons, *The Armies of the Night* quickly caught on and reinvigorated Mailer's career in every way. He appeared on television talk shows relentlessly. His new chronicle was awarded the National Book Award and the Pulitzer Prize. In his own way,

Mailer had reinvented himself as a nonfiction-writing provocateur, and though he was in his mid-forties (considered old amid the "Don't Trust Anyone Over 30" demographic), he was fervently embraced by the antiwar legions on campuses. (For the record: Mario detested America's war in Vietnam.)

One of the only book reviews not expressing admiration for *The Armies of the Night* was written by Mario Puzo and published in *BOOK WORLD* in April 1968.

He pulled no punches. As a writer, as a critic, and as a man, Mario was appalled by the self-aggrandizing egocentricity of Mailer's latest work. All the elements causing others to wet themselves in praise of Mailer's new book struck Puzo as just another sign of how Mailer had (as far as Mario was concerned) betrayed his own gifts: "Mailer gives the impression of a writer so disoriented from his art that he is perhaps consciously writing the equivalent of Fitzgerald's *Crack-Up*; the idea being that if he shows his mind with complete honesty the public will understand why he cannot write the great novel that is expected of him."

The narrative point of view that swiftly became Mailer's signature style in his nonfiction for the next decade (that is, the use of his own persona, referred to in the third person, as a central player in the narrative at large) seemed cloying to Puzo, who summed up brusquely:

> *This book . . . includes the peace march to some extent. But it is primarily a character study of a literary general . . . it may be as such the most excruciating exhibition of pomposity available in our literature.*

> *Perhaps to lessen the awesome authority of a prose adorned with more gold braid than [General] MacArthur's hat, Mailer hits on the device of using the third person instead of the pronoun "I." And so we get this at the very beginning of the book: "Mailer had a complex mind . . . ." "Mailer was bitter about drugs . . . ." "Mailer was not in approval of drugs . . . ." "Mailer does not usually answer the phone himself . . ." followed by two pages of closely reasoned argument about why Mailer does not answer the phone himself.*

> *But we know that's Mailer saying Mailer. Gertrude Stein used the same technique—successfully—when she wrote* The Autobiography of Alice B. Toklas.

And Henry Adams had used the same narrative technique sixty years earlier, when he wrote and published *The Education of Henry Adams* in 1907. There was ample precedent for the rhetorical stunt that Mailer enthusiastically replicated.

Puzo's assessment of Mailer's new book invariably touched on a number of issues, because Mailer's chronic projections, boasts, grudges, and judgments about other writers and myriad literary feuds were woven into *The Armies of the Night*.

Part of the book is about the peace march. A sympathetic history. Mailer tries to inflate the event with an importance it simply did not have and to give the people in it a stature they do not have.

The prose ranges from the awful to brilliant.

The paradox is this. Mailer may very well have been the most gifted writer of our generation. If so, he has done less with his gifts than any other writer of comparable worth. He admits, in this book, that his work in the last few years has seemed too easy, has not extended him as it should, and he is puzzled because critics continue to praise him. He will be puzzled once again, and he will not be alone.

This must be said. Mailer calls John O'Hara a mere storyteller, but Mailer has not written anything so good as Appointment in Samarra. *Mailer showers condescension on his contemporaries, but he himself has not created one memorable character in his fiction. Though he is the darling of magazine editors and though book publishers fight for his work, I know of no working novelist who bothers to discuss his fiction or gives it the respectful attention shown Malamud, Styron and some lesser-known writers. [Mailer] has become what TV calls a "personality" rather than an artist. This book is written out of that personality.*

No one felt the loss of LBJ's Great Society efforts more than America's urban poor, many of whom were African-Americans crowded together in ghettos from coast to coast. Their lives were hamstrung by the endless collusions between realtors, banks and their loan officers, and other manipulative honchos who quite deliberately engineered and maintained the phenomenon of big-city

black ghettos, from Oakland to Baltimore. One of those ghettos was
in Memphis, Tennessee, and when the Rev. Dr. Martin Luther King
was shot and killed there at 6:01 p.m. on April 4, 1968 (only four
days after President Johnson threw in the towel on his own doomed,
failed administration), the United States imploded with more
riots, more violence, more arson, and larger outbursts of domestic
upheaval than it had seen at any time since the Civil War. More than
120 American cities were ablaze with catastrophic fires and deadly
violence in the ten days that followed Dr. King's assassination. To
supplement the National Guard regiments ordered into the raging
cauldrons of Los Angeles, Newark, Chicago, Detroit, and elsewhere,
President Johnson authorized the deployment of combat troops
returning from Vietnam to finish their tours of duty by patrolling the
America's major metropolitan areas, including the war-torn streets
of Washington, D.C.

All the hopes and dreams of the Civil Rights Movement died when
King's body lay in a crimson river of blood on that motel balcony in
Memphis, Tennessee.

The one large American city not besieged by arson and riots
after Dr. King's death was Indianapolis, Indiana, where presidential
candidate Sen. Robert F. Kennedy made an impromptu speech the
night that King was murdered. It was astounding. RFK's campaign
notes were thrown away and he delivered instead (to a primarily
African-American audience) the news about MLK, followed by a
spontaneous, heartfelt, riveting call for reconciliation and calm. RFK
expressed not only his grief over what had happened to Dr. King, but
also his continued grief over what had happened to his brother John
back in Dallas in 1963 (barely five years earlier).

Two months later, Robert F. Kennedy was murdered in Los
Angeles, after winning the crucial California primary in his quest for
the Democratic nomination in 1968's presidential race. The double-
assassinations of MLK and RFK pulverized America.

It was in this dreadful period of national turmoil that Mario
Puzo hunkered down in his writing den on Long Island. Through a
successful series of fiscal maneuvers, he had been able to purchase a
developer's model home several years earlier. Part of the deal insisted
on by Puzo was that the developer leave all of the furniture that was
on display in the Bay Shore house. Working at the office of Magazine
Management Company was not conducive to concentration. But
Mario made frequent trips into the city to deliver typescripts of
articles and book reviews. From his home office on Long Island,

using a 1949 manual Olympia typewriter that he considered his talisman, Mario pounded out more pages than ever before.

At the end of June 1968, as America remained stunned, distressed, and fearful about the recent double-assassinations as well as the dread possibility of another long, hot summer replete with big-city riots and more arson and mayhem, a critique that Mario published in the *New York Times Book Review* proved yet again that Puzo was not enthralled by authors who had become "celebrities" and he certainly did not hold back in fear of "weakening his position," as the cliché goes. Put crudely: Mario was no star fucker. And having already dressed down Mailer, he now expressed with precise, comprehensive opinions how off-key he thought James Baldwin was.

In his review of Baldwin's fourth novel, *Tell Me How Long the Train's Been Gone*, Mario evinced his awareness of the turmoil wracking America, and how such a febrile era was not just affecting but also afflicting author James Baldwin.

Tellingly, in this review, Puzo's literary sensibility shone vibrantly:

> *Tragedy calls out for a great artist, revolution for a true prophet. Six years ago, James Baldwin predicted the black revolution that is now changing our society. His new novel, "Tell Me How Long the Train's Been Gone," is his attempt to re-create, as an artist this time, the tragic condition of the Negro, in America. He has not been successful; this is a simpleminded, one-dimensional novel with mostly cardboard characters, a polemical rather narrative tone, weak invention and poor selection of incident. Individual scenes have people talking too much for what the author has to say and crucial events are "told" by one character to another rather than created. The construction of the novel is theatrical, tidily nailed into a predictable form.*

Once again, as had been the case with Mailer's *Armies of the Night*, the book's point of view became the locus of Puzo's discontent. And his astute observations were sharp:

> *"Tell Me How Long the Train's Been Gone" is written in the first-person singular, the "I" person, perhaps the misused, most misunderstood technique today, from its irrelevance in Mailer's "Deer Park" to its crippling effect on Styron's thought and style in*

"The Confessions of Nat Turner." It doesn't do Baldwin any good here, because the "I" person should never be used in a novel of social protest, which this is. Why? Because it doesn't work.

What the "I" person cannot be is a bore, or a moralist in a straight out polemic way. In Baldwin's book the "I" person hero is both. His name is Leo Proudhammer; he has risen from the slums of Harlem to become the most famous Negro actor in America and the opening chapter has him suffering a massive heart attack on stage. We get flashbacks covering his life while he is being given emergency first aid and then while he is recovering in the hospital. The flashbacks are done in thin theatrical fashion rather than novelistic technique, and this doesn't help.

Puzo's review of Baldwin's fourth novel is an illuminating essay in its own right. He cites James Baldwin's peerless talent for composing nonfiction ("his essays are as well written as any in our language; in them his thought and its utterance are nothing less than majestical"), and also lauds him for "the virtues of passion, serious intelligence and compassionate understanding of his fellow man." Yet, after a sweeping recapitulation of the new novel's plot and its cast of characters, Mario concludes that "Baldwin's greatest weakness as a novelist is his selection or creation of incident. Time and again, his conclusions are not justified by narrative action. Too many of his characters are mere cardboard. There are scenes that are simply echoes of the literature of the Thirties, and they were cornball even then."

Most startling of all is the roundabout way in which Puzo alludes to the imminent rise of the Women's Movement. He shines a light on a whole host of sex and gender issues with a long paragraph that deserves to be fully quoted because it illustrates the textured, astute, bold contrarian thinking that Puzo brought to his book reviews.

If this makes the book sound like soap opera, that's exactly right. White Barbara, white as snow, is right out of a slick magazine, flat as cardboard. At the end of the book Barbara tells Leo she has always loved him and will always continue to love him. Her lines are extravagant, theatrical; she will always come to him when he calls. Barbara gives this speech at the age of 39; she is rich, she is famous, she has been presented as a reasonably intelligent woman. She has known Leo for 20 years. And yet we are asked to believe that the only man in the

*whole world she can love forever is a Negro homosexual actor. This is
a romantic condescension equal to anything in "Gone With the Wind,"
in that Baldwin does not* recognize a parallel revolution, the feminine
against the masculine world (emphasis added).

By the time those words appeared in print on June 23, 1968,
television had already broadcast a great deal of "Live!" news
coverage regarding "a parallel revolution, the feminine against the
masculine world." In Atlantic City, New Jersey, a heady round of
protest actions against the protocols and the very premise of the
Miss America Contest had added yet another layer of activist dissent
to a year—in fact, to an era—that increasingly found one institution
after another being questioned or ridiculed. As passersby, observers,
and television crews looked on, a new wave of articulate and angry
women who called themselves "Women's Liberationists" went to
town. One of those activists was Robin Morgan, who forty years
later in a documentary titled *1968* (narrated by NBC's Tom Brokaw)
highlighted the fact that the women veered away from using the
word "feminists," opting for "Women's Liberationists," which echoed
the rhetoric of revolutionary zeal being heard throughout the world
in 1968.

At that event in Atlantic City, outside the auditorium where the Miss
America Contest was being held, several dozen feminist protesters
created a slew of brazen images (tossing their bras and girdles into
trash cans, declaring their goals about economic independence,
comparing the Miss America Contest to animal shows at county fairs)
suggesting that traditional models of womanhood, motherhood, and
domestic roles were under siege. The exponentially expanding protest
movements of the day had segued from the Civil Rights Movement
(challenging old, entrenched social norms) to the Antiwar Movement
(questioning patriotism, militarism, and the authority of government).

By now, the once-upon-a-time church-based Civil Rights Movement
seemed like a sepia-toned photograph framed by an integrated choir
singing "We Shall Overcome." As of the summer of 1968, however,
the American masses repeatedly witnessed (via television) not
just the riots, arson, and conflagrations erupting from the nation's
incendiary ghettos, but also the manifest ways in which the Black
Panther Party (with its thousands of members identically dressed
in their uniforms of black leather jackets, dark pants, sunglasses
indoors and out, and black berets) called for violent retaliation
against the police who harassed, harmed, or in any way threatened

black citizens. It appeared that American society was buckling.

And beneath the tremors and social convulsions, millions yearned for some kind of return to calm and order; they wanted an authority figure to fix the crises. Fast.

In the meantime, Mario Puzo had to complete *The Godfather*. Fast. As usual, the reason for such a big push was money. In addition to the writing of his adventure stories, feature articles, and book reviews that paid small stipends, a lump sum payment in excess of $1,000 awaited a full draft of his novel. And that lump sum was essential, if the Puzo family was finally going to enjoy a vacation.

Mario later recalled:

> *I finally had to finish* The Godfather *in July, 1968, because I needed the final $1,200 advance payment from Putnam to take my wife and kids to Europe. My wife had not seen her family for twenty years and I had promised her that this was the year. I had no money, but I had a great collection of credit cards. Still I needed that $1,200 in cash, so I handed in the rough manuscript. Before leaving for Europe, I told my publisher not to show the book to anybody; it had to be polished.*

Even with trans-Atlantic Pan Am airline prices that now seem like tiny sums (not to mention the moderate costs of food and rail travel), a vacation to Europe for a family of seven was no small feat. But it worked out. Thanks largely to the magic of plastic.

"My family had a good time in Europe," Mario recounted, because "American Express offices cash[ed] five-hundred-dollar checks against their credit cards."

Puzo spelled this out with his usual self-deprecating humor:

> *I used their offices in London, Cannes, Nice, and Wiesbaden. My children and I gambled in the poshest casinos on the French Riviera. If just one of us could have gotten lucky, I would have been able to cover those checks that American Express airmailed back to the United States. We all lost. I had failed as a father. When we finally got home, I owed the credit card companies $8,000. I wasn't worried. If worse came to worse we could always sell our house. Or I could go to jail. Hell, better writers had gone to jail. No sweat.*

It wasn't just credit card numbers that added up. Less than a year earlier, a segment of *The Godfather* had been plucked out of the unfinished manuscript, reconfigured as an adventure story, and presented as a factual article in one of the periodicals issued by Magazine Management Company. No one quibbled about the story being "presented as fact in the shamelessly corrupt policy of the company's products," said Mario's colleague Jules Siegel, especially after the excerpt "went through the roof on all the marketing survey categories—they read it, remembered it, liked it, and wanted more of the same."

Back home in Bay Shore, Long Island, at summer's end in 1968, Puzo headed one day "into New York to see my agent, Candida Donadio." Modestly hoping that "she'd pull a slick magazine assignment out of her sleeve and bail me out as she'd often done in the past," Mario made his way to his agent's office. His life changed. Fast. She had big news. Dizzying news. "She informed me," Puzo said, "that my publisher had just turned down $375,000 for the paperback rights to *The Godfather*."

By the end of the week, according to publisher and editor William Targ, a surreal triumph was at hand: " . . . our luncheon at the Algonquin in 1968, [that was] the day I invited [Puzo] to lunch in order to bring him some 'special news.' Mario was heavily in debt at the time, 'piss-poor.' I carefully spelled out the details of the paperback sale of *The Godfather* for $410,000. I explained to Mario that we now owed him not less than $205,000 in American dollars. He turned to me, paused, then said, 'I don't believe a fucking word you've told me.' And then he added, 'This must be some kind of Madison Avenue put-on.'"

Mario Puzo and Joseph Heller;
photographer unknown

7

Jackpot

Clyde Taylor was my strongest ally. It turned out to be the most profitable single novel ever published by Putnam's. At this writing [in 1975], it has sold around fifteen million copies in various editions in the United States alone. What it sold throughout the world I can't say, but it was definitely a bestseller everywhere. It has outsold all of the major bestselling novels of our time."

~~~ Publisher William Targ

No matter. The good times are beginning. I am another Italian success story. Not as great as DiMaggio or Sinatra but quite enough. It will serve. I have my retrospective falsification (how I love that phrase). I can dream now about how happy I was in my childhood, in my tenement, playing in those dirty but magical streets—living in the poverty that made my mother weep.

~~~ Mario Puzo, "Choosing a Dream"

H istory.

For the remainder of that life-transforming day when the paperback rights to *The Godfather* were ultimately sold for a record-breaking sum, Mario Puzo was either sitting or standing in the midst of history. Publishing history. Personal history.

Humid, late-summer weather suffocated New York City. It was the time of year when Manhattan's canyons of steel and glass and its crowded avenues of cars and pedestrians could set anyone's nerves on edge. By this time in his life, commuting from Long Island was no pleasure for Puzo, who freely admitted that he "hated the city" for its congestion, grime, noise, and stress. Yet, "this was no time to complain," he concluded, tweaking himself with the recollection that prior to leaving for Europe, he "had given strict orders" to his agent, Candida Donadio, about *The Godfather*: "it wasn't to be shown to even a paperback house," due to Mario's bedrock belief that the finished draft required serious polishing. After all, he had handed in the final chapters merely to collect the last $1,200 of his advance. Now he stood in Candida's office, and quickly absorbed information that seemed surreal.

Fortunately, by temperament and deportment, his agent was neither frantic nor rash. Any agent lined up for a commission on such a colossal deal would likely be bouncing off the ceiling. But not Candida Donadio. In a publishing business replete with hyper-competitive wheelers and dealers, her persona was unique. Mario's old friend and colleague Bruce Jay Friedman (who by this time had left his post as a top editor at Magazine Management Company, to emerge successfully as a novelist and playwright) was another of Candida's clients, and he always remembered her as "a small, plumpish woman with large black eyes, who seemed almost to be hiding behind her desk and melting away with shyness."

Donadio was a woman of Sicilian heritage, and her client list included Puzo and Friedman, along with Joseph Heller, Philip Roth, Robert Stone, and Thomas Pynchon.

According to Bruce Jay Friedman, one key element making Candida Donadio a magnetic power was not just her client list, but her voice: "Her voice wasn't everything, but it had a great deal to do with [her success] . . . it was the most beautiful voice I had ever heard. Rich, deep, womanly, reassuring, and then oddly hesitant and girlish . . . it was highly seductive . . . sometimes it was just gasps, faint sighs, a struggle to express wonderment or disbelief." She was also made of steel.

Both "wonderment" and "disbelief" were swirling all around *The Godfather* now.

From the office of Candida Donadio, a call was placed and Mario spoke with his editor at G. P. Putnam's Sons. His editor, William Targ, was a seasoned pro in the book business. Targ both confirmed and updated Donadio's information. By this time, the offer of $375,000 had increased. A staggering sum of $400,000 for the paperback rights to *The Godfather* was on the table. However, Targ informed Puzo that they were "holding out for $410,000 because $400,000 was some sort of record." This turned out to be a classic example of records existing to be broken.

Out of an admixture of panic and fear that the whole negotiation could collapse, another author might have insisted that they seal the deal right away. Instead, Mario stepped back; he did not interfere. When editor William Targ asked Puzo if he wished to speak with Clyde Taylor, the man adroitly conducting Putnam's sale of the paperback rights, Mario declined: "I said that I had absolute confidence in any man who could turn down $375,000."

Going home was impossible. Standing by and staying close to telephones now mattered most of all. New York City may well have been the capital of the world in 1968, but there were no cell phones and texting or emailing was light years away.

"I hung around New York," Mario recounted, "had a very late lunch with Targ, and over our coffee he got a call." Clearly a celebratory lunch was set (on the publisher's dime) at the upscale Algonquin, because Targ needed to know that a waiter could immediately bring a telephone to the table in the event of any important call.

What happened must have induced otherworldly feelings in Puzo, because he knew that in the publishing world this deal was a milestone. And yet, when recalling the revelatory moment, Mario kept it simple: "Ralph Daigh of Fawcett had bought the paperback rights for $410,000."

As if he was following a script about a Walter Mitty-ish character who had daydreamed his life away and suddenly hit it big, Mario instantly left his job.

"I went up to the adventure magazine office to quit my freelance job and tell all my friends there the good news. We had some drinks and then I decided to get home to Long Island."

Rectangular booths with pay phones used to stand on almost

every other corner in America's big cities. And pay telephones (or "coin phones" as they were also known, because the caller had to walk about with nickels, dimes, and quarters in order to make any calls) lined the walls of waiting areas in metropolitan parking garages. With his brain chemistry galvanized by a record-breaking book contract and a few cocktails, Mario made use of the nearest pay phone:

> While waiting for my car, I called my brother to tell him the good news. This brother had 10 percent of The Godfather because he supported me all my life and gave me a final chunk of money to complete the book. Through the years I'd call him up frantic for a few hundred bucks to pay the mortgage or buy the kids shoes. Then I'd arrive at his house in a taxi to pick up the money. In rain or snow, he never took a taxi, but he never complained. He always came through. So now I wanted him to know that since my half of the paperback rights came to $205,000 (the hard-cover publisher keeps half), he was in for a little over twenty grand.

No luck. Mario's older brother wasn't home. The irony hit Puzo right between the eyes. His older brother was "the kind of guy who [was] always home when I call[ed] to borrow money," but now in this moment of supreme triumph, he was gone. Or, as Mario perceived it: "Now that I had money to give back, he was naturally out."

Feeding coins into the pay phone, Mario succeeded at connecting with his eighty-year-old mother. Maria Le Conti Puzo had never become a reader, but she spoke a highly communicative "broken English" and understood the language well.

Her son the writer now explained that his new novel had just been sold as a paperback, in advance, for the record-breaking sum of $410,000. At this time, a brand new Cadillac cost far less than $10,000. At the other end of the retail scale, most new hardcover books were priced below five dollars, and a great many paperbacks still listed for ninety-five cents. The vote of confidence implicit in Fawcett's purchase of the paperback rights to The Godfather was monumental. The paperback publisher was willing to gamble $410,000 on one book's prospects.

And that gamble rested on the fortunes of a single novel written by the son of illiterate Southern Italian immigrants. This was a classic rags-to-riches tale.

Except for one thing: Mario's mother was pretending not to

understand. As Puzo recalled years later, her response to his phenomenal news was that she repeatedly asked, feigning confusion: "40,000?"

Time after time, he spelled out the truth: "I said no, it was $410,000. I told her three times," he later recalled. After his third reiteration, she consolidated eighty years of modesty, wisdom, and discerning peasant intelligence, and said: "Don't tell nobody."

Summertime traffic was heavy and Mario later remembered that "it took me over two hours to get home" to Bay Shore on Long Island. When he finally arrived at home, Erika was alone. All five of their children were out. And while Erika "was dozing over the TV," Puzo recounted, "I went over to my wife, kissed her on the cheek, and said, 'Honey, we don't have to worry about money anymore. I just sold my book for $410,000.'"

Erika was suspended in that state of oblivion somewhere between napping and deep slumber. "She smiled at me and kept dozing," Mario said. He let her doze on. In his home office, with his black manual 1949 Olympia typewriter at rest for a change, he called his other siblings: "The reason for this was because every Italian family has a 'chooch,' a donkey. That is, a family idiot everybody agrees will never be able to make a living and so has to be helped without rancor or reproach. I was the family 'chooch' and I just wanted to tell them I was abdicating the family role."

Mario put a call through to his older sister, the sibling who had been his mother's primary ally in the raising of the younger children. He asked her: "Did you hear?"

Once again: Disappointment. There was no big cheer. She did not yelp. It seemed as if everyone somehow failed to grasp the enormousness of the sale. "My sister's voice was pretty cool," Puzo recounted, and "I started getting annoyed. Nobody seemed to think this was a big deal. My whole life was going to change. I didn't have to worry about money. It was almost like not having to worry about dying."

Their conversation didn't heat up, yet Mario's older sister was no stranger to his travails. Or his timetable. She knew that he had worked for three years on his new novel. Adopting an almost matter-of-fact tone, she said: "You got $40,000 for the book. Mama called me."

Pro-rated over three years' time, that wasn't too much: A thousand per month, plus change. And of course there would be taxes and various deductions. No fortune.

"I was exasperated with my mother," he admitted, but Mario tamped down his frustration (he assumed that "she had gotten it all wrong" and as far as he was concerned "her eighty years were no excuse"). Then he clarified matters. "No," he quietly explained to his older sister: "it was $410,000."

Finally! There now erupted the response that conformed to Mario's daydreams. His fantasy of a big reaction: "There was a little scream over the phone and an excited minute of conversation."

Still, something gnawed at Puzo, who later remembered that he "had to get back to my mother. I called and said, 'Ma, how the hell could you get it wrong? I told you that it was $410,000 not $40,000. How could you make such a mistake?'"

Maria Le Conti Puzo said nothing. Silence ensued. It was clear to her that while her authorial son may have emerged as that rarest of creatures—a woolgathering writer who had finally made not just real money, but a small fortune—he was definitely more of an American than a traditional Southern Italian: He was actually, openly, telling others the news. Not practicing "omerta" at all.

Mario was then reminded about her strategic thinking: "There was a long silence," he later explained, and finally at long last Maria Le Conti Puzo "whispered over the phone, *'I no maka a mistake. I don't want to tell her.'*"

For the umpteenth time in his life (Mario's forty-eighth birthday was imminent), he learned a lesson from his illiterate immigrant mother about the fundamental laws of life. By the time Puzo left his basement "work room," it was late and Erika and the children were all asleep. "I went to bed and slept like a rock," he recalled.

The fact that Puzo had gone straight home to speak with his wife, make phone calls, and eventually go to bed speaks volumes about the major differences between Mario and a great many other writers who at one time or another hit it big. From Jack London to James Jones, from F. Scott Fitzgerald to John Cheever, and from the likes of Lillian Hellman or James Baldwin to Norman Mailer and untold others, the unanimous reaction to any sudden burst of success was binge-drinking and usually a complete collapse of anything resembling common sense or behavioral restraint.

A combination of long-suppressed urges with explosive cravings for instant gratification (knowing full well that large funds were soon to be available) often ensured that in the aftermath of any great-good news about a contract for a book's publication or a play's production, all hell might break loose. And it usually did. A stunning book deal like the one Puzo had just secured would have impelled other authors to embark on a bacchanal. Fast and furious drinking at the very least, followed by carousing and spending sprees or making the scene at Elaine's or the White Horse Tavern or other hotspots for writers desperately seeking a dose of celebrity status. Buying rounds of drinks? Sure. Boasting out loud? Inevitably.

But not with Mario Puzo. On the night of his record-breaking paperback sale, which guaranteed the publicity for the hardcover edition of *The Godfather* would be even more intense, he went home to his wife and kids, called siblings, and went to sleep.

He acted like a man, not a maniac.

And then? Mario later reminisced: "the next morning, my wife and kids circled the bed." The family's moment of reckoning was at hand.

After more than twenty years of dicey economic precariousness, more than two decades of barely making ends meet (most of the time), nearly a quarter century of worry about finances, being dunned, fielding notes and warnings and threats from loan officers, collection agents, and others, there was one question and only one question that Erika Puzo asked Mario in front of their five children on this new morning:

"What was that you said last night?"

Rested now and fully receptive, as Mario later recalled the moment, Erika "had just grasped the whole thing."

A lifetime of dreams now began to come true, even though at first, Mario reflected, "nobody seemed to believe me." But it was fairly easy to demonstrate the truth.

From the house, Puzo made a call to William Targ, his editor at G. P. Putnam's and Sons. After speaking briefly, the arrangements were made with Putnam's business office: "[I] drew an advance check for $100,000," Mario happily recalled, "I paid my debts, paid my agents' commissions, paid my brother his well-deserved 10 percent."

One other reckoning was at hand. And on this occasion, a comeuppance was in order. For more years than he cared to remember, the basic fiscal reality of Puzo's life made unpleasant encounters at banks a sad fact of life. There were no direct deposit payroll protocols for regular customers in those days. Employees from any type of office (or for that matter all types of job) received their paychecks in an envelope that they had to bring to their banks manually for deposit. And that meant person-to-person encounters with bank tellers, who all of sudden knew *every*thing, from what you were paid to what was in (or not in) your checking account or your savings account. A bank customer had to stand there and be seen, no matter what. Drive-thru banking was in its most primitive phase. Online banking did not exist.

Worst of all, the tedious clerical procedures of that era meant that a bank teller also saw on anyone's record just how often there had been overdrafts, bounced checks, late payments, and every other demerit. It was like having to undress for a stranger.

However, the tide had turned. And for once Mario walked into his bank standing tall. He not only held his head high, he left a particular bank teller flabbergasted.

"I brought the check for *The Godfather* paperback sale right to the guy who used to sneer at my overdrafts and reluctantly cash my paychecks and remind me about my late payments. It was so satisfying to watch him grovel," Puzo recalled with true delight.

Unfortunately, there were two specific business matters that Mario signed off on before the extraordinary paperback sale for *The Godfather*. And while that historic paperback sale shone a much bigger spotlight on the imminent publication of the hardcover edition, now scheduled for March 1969, those two other matters were unchanged. One of the issues involved finally reprinting *The Fortunate Pilgrim*.

"Just before *The Godfather* was finished," Mario later lamented, "I sold the paperback rights of *The Fortunate Pilgrim* for a $1,500 cash advance against the usual royalties. I sold them to Lancer Books, and one of the partners, Irwin Stein, was so agreeable he sent me the $1,500 in one whole payment rather than reserving half for publication date."

This meant that no matter how explosively Puzo's reputation grew in the wake of a massive publicity push for *The Godfather*, he could not leverage his second novel for a more lucrative reissue. That was no longer an option.

Meantime, as Puzo once explained, "a bigger mistake was made long before publication when I had the first one hundred pages of *The Godfather* done."

By that time (late in 1966 or early in 1967), Mario "had already switched to Candida Donadio as [my] agent, but [the] William Morris [Agency] had signed the initial book contract and so represented me in the movie deal. They advised me against taking it. They advised me to wait. That was like advising a guy underwater to take a deep breath." A modest offer for the film rights had come when Mario was still on staff at Magazine Management Company, but was also supplementing his income writing "book bonus" adventure stories, varied reviews, and a few articles. After evaluating the first hundred pages of *The Godfather*, the offer from Paramount Pictures was small but firm: "I needed the cash and the $12,500 [from Paramount] looked like Fort Knox." In his own quiet way, Puzo conceded: "the fault was mine."

If the sale of the film rights to *The Godfather* for a mere $12,500, long before the book's publication, proved to be a premature, unlucky turn of events for Puzo—and it was, at bottom, a deal Mario signed off on due simply to economic necessity—then a far luckier twist of fate occurred precisely four months prior to his new novel's appearance in bookstores.

In November 1968, G. P. Putnam's Sons (the same major New York publishing house that was then preparing the first edition of *The Godfather*) released a nonfiction work authored by journalist Peter Maas. It was titled *The Valachi Papers* and in every way it helped whet the public's appetite for *The Godfather*. The timing was not just lucky, it was phenomenal. Synchronicity was at work.

Peter Maas and *The Valachi Papers* shot to the top of the *New York Times Best-Seller List* late in 1968 and early in the winter of 1969. Earlier, between 1966 and 1968, a highly publicized controversy had surrounded *The Valachi Papers*, which originally began as a handwritten manuscript in excess of 300,000 words written in jail by a career criminal named Joseph Valachi. Written while he served a lifetime sentence in a federal prison, Valachi's manuscript then became a typescript of 1,180 pages.

Putnam's publicity machine summed up like this:

The first true story of life inside the Cosa Nostra!

Valachi, the first man to violate the Cosa Nostra (loosely translated, "this thing of ours") oath of silence, was one of the Mafia's most loyal "soldiers," a man who had once given a blood pledge to "live by the gun and knife and die by the gun and knife." He came close . . . While serving time at the Atlanta Federal Penitentiary on a narcotics charge, word went out that Vito Genovese, Mafia overlord, had

conferred upon him the dread "kiss of death." Marked for murder,
Valachi did something unheard of: He turned informer.

It all sounded like a Hollywood movie, except that the constant emphasis was on the true-life nature of Joseph Valachi's confessions, revelations, and innumerable inside scoops. Back in June 1964, Robert F. Kennedy (who was then still the Attorney General) stated that the testimony Valachi had given to a Senate committee, plus the interviews he'd given to the FBI and the officers in the Bureau of Narcotics, provided nothing less than the "biggest single intelligence breakthrough yet in combating organized crime and racketeering in the United States."

In the end, after aggressive interference from the U.S. Department of Justice ("in reference to harsh charges of corruption that Valachi had leveled in his manuscript against some members of the Bureau of Prisons and dubious conduct against others in the Bureau of Narcotics"), an all-out effort was made by then-Attorney General of the United States Ramsey Clark, acting on the direct orders of President Lyndon Johnson's principal aides, including Jack Valenti, to suppress Valachi's book.

That, too, became part of the nonfiction chronicle's blazing publicity:

"For the first time Maas tells the whole story behind the explosive VALACHI PAPERS; how he had to fight a Department of Justice injunction—the sole instance where an Attorney General of the United States, acting on orders of the White House, has ever tried to suppress a book!"

After a great deal of legal wrangling, the actual manuscript written by Valachi had to be superseded by a third-person account of his decades-long Mob life, as written by Peter Maas after many extensive interviews with Valachi.

It all caught on with the public. Readers were fascinated by Peter Maas' portrait of Joseph Valachi, the man "who was the very epitome of the cold, seasoned criminal. His illustrious career encompassed burglary, slot machines, shylocking, numbers, narcotics, the protection racket, ration stamps (which in wartime netted him $150,000 in a good year), and, inevitably, murder."

Publishers Weekly helped to launch *The Valachi Papers* at the end of 1968 with this highly quotable endorsement: "The unadorned revelation of violence, brutality, and the gamut of crime from the numbers game to murder is the landscape of a strange and terrible world."

That same world—the shadowy netherworld of the Sicilian-centered organized crime subculture contrasting the family narrative at the heart of *The Godfather*—had been heavily researched by Puzo as he labored for three years on his new novel.

"I'm ashamed to admit that I wrote *The Godfather* entirely from research," is an oft-quoted statement that Mario Puzo made in one of his autobiographical essays. As was often the case, he exhibited extreme modesty when he made that remark.

It's important to remember that *The Godfather* was written toward the end of the 1960s, and Mario had spent that decade exercising his research skills for the prolific and demanding work quotas at Magazine Management Company. "I used to love to do research," he explained to an interviewer many years later, "like when I wrote an adventure story about the Arctic, I would read all the Arctic books. I became an expert on the Arctic." And this across-the-board research talent lent itself to all the topics that Puzo wrote about, ranging from the Second World War to shark attacks.

"Sometimes I would read 10 or 20 books to do one article," Mario said. "I had to turn out three stories a month, and by doing all that research it wasn't that hard. I'd go to the library and get 'em." Puzo was a man who "loved to read" and he also had a knack for reading fast. "I could read two books a day, so I used to just eat 'em up" he explained: "We were always looking for stuff we could take off on, so part of our job was reading a lot." At home or the office, in the middle of the night, Mario read.

In what has to stand as one of the more compelling coincidences in Americana, it turns out that long before either *The Godfather* or Peter Benchley's *Jaws* became blockbuster novels, Puzo clairvoyantly tapped into the possibilities of terrifying audiences with graphic shark attack material. Using the pen name "Mario Cleri," one of the adventure stories that Mario knocked out in the late 1960s appeared (with grim photos included) under the title: "Killer Sharks That Terrorize Our Shores."

The story's lead paragraph illustrates how Puzo's latter-day action-driven storytelling verve had hit its stride:

> *As carefree summer vacationers frolic on beaches all over America, horrible death waits a few yards off-shore in the maws of giant sharks who've developed an insatiable taste for human flesh.*

But despite a rocketing toll of maimed, crippled, scarred and dead casualties, resort towns everywhere have dropped a blackout curtain on this hideous new menace—preferring to expose millions to death rather than let the frightening truth scare off tourist dollars . . .

In the 1980s, reflecting on his Magazine Management days, Mario said: "I did [that] article on sharks, which was fascinating. It never occurred to me that sharks would make a novel or a movie." Needless to say, others figured out how to achieve that vision.

Although Puzo did conduct a great deal of research in order to write *The Godfather* (especially in relation to the evolution of the Sicilian Mafia in the 19th century and its transformations and adjustments when transplanting itself to America in the 20th century), he also brought to the forefront his innate, organic, rich storytelling skills.

Perhaps most important of all, Mario created a narrative propelled by action and periodic interludes of sex, violence, and bloodshed—but never lost sight of the Corleone family's unconditional love for each other and also for the very notion of the Family as a world unto itself. And yet, it was a tale chock-full of familiar motifs, in tangential ways. An aging patriarch and his trio of sons inevitably suggested the legend of the Kennedys, but it also hinted at a gender-reversed variation on one of Shakespeare's most familiar plays: only instead of King Lear and his three disparate daughters, *The Godfather* presents Vito Corleone with Sonny, Michael, and Fredo.

In March 1969, when the novel was published, its instantaneous success not only startled Puzo and his publisher—it exceeded all expectations. From its cover art, with Neil Fujita's brilliantly stark black-and-white imagery of a closed fist wrapped around a marionette's control bar with seven puppet strings descending in straight lines and merging with the title's unique calligraphy (which has since come to be known as "the Godfather font") to the final line of the novel—" . . . she said the necessary prayers for the soul of Michael Corleone"—the public embraced the book.

So did the first major critic to review *The Godfather*. In *The Saturday Review* on March 15, 1969, Hal Burton, who was the well-known book editor for *Newsday*, offered his praise and admiration in equal proportion.

Mario Puzo's new novel is a big, blunt battering ram of a book, one intended to shock and to stun. It is most certainly the Little Caesar of this generation, though by comparison W. R. Burnett's classic of the bootleg era seems an understatement. The Godfather *is a supercharged account of a family that uses guns, axes, garrotes, and the psychology of fear to achieve dominance over the whole Mafia network in the United States.*

The test of a story of action is whether it convinces the reader while carrying him along. Puzo has wrought his prose so skillfully that the most outrageous episodes seem totally natural. All the blood, all the slaughter, all the raw sex are in consonance with the people about whom he is writing. Yet at the same time he makes his frightening cast of characters seem human and possible.

The power of the reading experience that led to Hal Burton's review was so pulverizing that he inadvertently misrepresented the novel even as he lauded it.

True, there are instances of violence and occasionally an extreme act of grim brutality at staggered intervals in *The Godfather*. But the bulk of the narrative does not depend on dramatizing "a family that uses guns, axes, [and] garrotes." Most of the novel has much more to do with how Don Corleone (and later on, his son Michael) deploy "the psychology of fear," which is often masked as "reason."

In one short paragraph, Puzo had summed up how "reason" is a red flag.

"I'll reason with him," Vito Corleone said. It was to become a famous phrase in the years to come. It was to become the warning rattle before a deadly strike. When he became a Don and asked opponents to sit down and reason with him, they understood it was the last chance to resolve an affair without bloodshed and murder.

And in an equally short paragraph, reviewer Hal Burton succinctly introduced to a great many readers the essence of the iconic character Mario Puzo had created:

The "Godfather" is Don Vito Corleone, a Sicilian-American patriarch, already one of the top men in the Mafia. He dominates gambling but eschews the drug racket as beneath his dignity. His tentacles reach out to policemen, judges, state legislators, U. S. Senators, and labor leaders. Whatever he wants he gets.

Even now, the conclusion of this pivotal, first major review of *The Godfather* echoes with excitement, admiration, a bit of awe, and the kind of appreciation every writer lusts after: "The book pulses with movement, giving the reader scarcely a pause for reflection. Within its genre, which is action rather than philosophy, it is a staggering triumph. Mario Puzo has achieved the definitive novel about a sinister fraternity of crime."

It wasn't just Hal Burton in the *Saturday Review* who was telling the world that Mario's new novel was a triumph. The critic who reviewed *The Godfather* for the *New York Times* topped off his assessment by saying: "You can't stop reading it, and you'll find it hard to stop dreaming about it!" Extraordinary praise by any measure.

Sales were equally extraordinary. Right off the bat. Of course, Putnam gave the book a big push and its marketing and sales personnel all did their best. But the mass public was rarely affected by any publisher's singular campaign. There were thousands of books published annually. Hundreds were lucky enough to snag high-wattage reviews. Dozens were picked for monumental PR blitzes. Yet most of the time, even the books pushed by the muscle of coordinated corporate support did not become best sellers. There was, and still is, a mystery about what ultimately sells.

Once it was published in March 1969, that's all *The Godfather* did. Sell and sell and sell. Reprints were constantly ordered. Stores sold out their supply. Mario's name, the book's title, and graphic artist Neil Fujita's iconic cover image all became as familiar to the public as the logos on *TIME* and *LIFE* magazine.

It was a blockbuster.

Unlike other best-selling books, however, there was no fizzling in the marketplace after a strong season. Not even after two seasons. *The Godfather* stayed near the top of the best-seller's list for well over a year straight: for 67 weeks in a row, it stayed on *The New York Times Best-Seller List*, and for over 20 of those weeks (more than five months) it was America's number-one selling work of fiction.

But it wasn't just an American success. *The Godfather* also landed in the top-spot as a number-one best-seller in France, England, Germany, and elsewhere. When Putnam wasn't cranking up the machines to reprint the book again and again, they teamed with foreign publishers and as swiftly as possible published translations in more than a dozen languages. "It's been translated into seventeen or twenty languages," Mario remarked, "I stopped keeping track."

One year after the hardcover edition appeared, Mario also learned that "it's the fastest and best-selling fiction paperback of all times." Fawcett printed the first paperback edition of *The Godfather* with a

LIFE magazine quotation on a banner printed across the bottom of the book's front cover: "The fastest selling book in history." Multiple dozens of rave reviews; word of mouth; it was a perfect storm.

"Ralph Daigh at Fawcett proved [to be] a straight guy and promoted the book like hell," Puzo recalled. The novel's dizzying success continued all through 1970. Gay Talese, the celebrated Italian-American author and New Journalism innovator, apprehended all this in ethnic terms: "Mario didn't know much about organized crime," Talese noted (at that time Talese was deeply immersed in the writing of *Honor Thy Father*, his own major contribution to nonfiction Mafia history), "but he certainly knew how to depict an Italian family. Take away the gambling and the murder, and it's pretty much a straightforward story about how Italian-American families were assimilated into American culture."

Another Italian-American chronicler, George De Stefano, observed this: "We saw our families in that book, and, for the first time, a great many Americans saw us. It wasn't a pretty image, or a tranquil one, but it was never dull, and it was new to most people." A female voice joined this chorus when Maria Laurino highlighted that "those elaborate passages in 'The Godfather' which describe the family patriarch presiding over weddings and baptisms and then ordering murders gave a new dimension to the image of the Italian father. Movies had always shown the murders but never told us that these men had daughters and godchildren."

On January 23, 1970, Mario took the lead and sent a handwritten letter to Academy Award-winning actor Marlon Brando, touting the idea of Brando as Vito Corleone in the film version of the novel that now seemed inevitable. Writing on his personal stationery (and scrawling with his anything-but-cursive penmanship), Puzo began with a modest "Dear Mr. Brando." Then he continued:

I wrote a book called THE GODFATHER which has had some success and I think you're the only actor who can play the Godfather with that quiet force and irony that the part requires. I hope you'll read the book and like it well enough to use whatever power you can to get the role.

I'm writing Paramount to the same effect for whatever good that will do. I know this seems presumptuous of me, but the least I can do for the book is try. Needless to say, I've been an admirer of your art.

Before signing off, Puzo added: "A mutual friend, Jeff Brown, gave me your address."

That outreach effort to Brando was instinctive, intuitive, clairvoyant, and prescient. It was also an effort rooted in Puzo's anxiety about the possibility of miscasting to an absurd degree.

Mario's jitters derived from the "one day [when] I picked up the paper and it said that Danny Thomas wanted to play the role of *The Godfather*. That threw me into a panic." Such a cute remark sounds like it might have been another throwaway line coughed up by Puzo as he learned to accommodate the vagaries of Hollywood.

But there was real concern on his part. Entertainer Danny Thomas had been a big force in the rise of television throughout the 1950s and early 1960s. He'd made a fortune, many times over, due to syndication rights on programs he produced. Now the word was out that Danny Thomas was thinking of buying a controlling interest in Paramount Pictures, to ensure that he played the lead in the film adaptation of *The Godfather*. (Crazy as it sounds, the truth was that the great big-name studios of the past were all in trouble as the Sixties progressed and as the Seventies dawned; the vast dream factories of prior decades were all hollow shells by 1969; the "star system" was extinct; properties were off-loaded at pathetic fire sales; stock values plummeted; and the movie business was hanging on by its fingernails in yet another example of how a powerful postwar American phenomenon had lost its way amid cultural minefields in the 1960s.)

And so, Puzo initiated a dialogue with Marlon Brando that began with a letter and ended with a phone call: "He was nice enough to call me," Mario said. "We had a talk on the phone. He had not read the book but he told me that the studio would never hire him unless a strong director insisted on it. He was nice over the phone but didn't sound too interested. And that was that."

Such reticence on Brando's part made sense in the context of 1970. By that time, his star had faded. The all-powerful and highly respected Marlon Brando of the 1950s (when his trailblazing performances in films like *A Streetcar Named Desire*, *The Wild One*, *On the Waterfront*, and *Julius Caesar* were cinematic milestones) had been consigned to near-oblivion by 1970. He was considered "box-office poison" after a long series of commercial failures, stretching from the fiscal debacle of his 1962 remake of *Mutiny on the Bounty* (cost overruns and skyrocketing budgets became synonymous with Brando's name after that endeavor) to the mediocrity (or worse) of films like *A Countess from Hong Kong* (in 1966) and the three bombs he starred in during 1968-1969: *Candy, The Night of the Following Day*, and *Burn!*

Yet, it wasn't just Brando who "didn't sound too interested." Mario came to learn after a while that "Paramount had decided not to make the movie." The studio's $12,500 option on Puzo's narrative was chump change. And the pittance that Paramount Pictures paid for the film rights to *The Godfather* seemed like a lucky break in the aftermath of a particularly embarrassing Paramount flop called *The Brotherhood*. Released with great marketing brio in 1968, *The Brotherhood* had starred Kirk Douglas in a big-budget Mafia movie that fell flat with the public. It fell so flat that the studio decided no market for gangster films existed anymore.

That conclusion reinforced the same sense of confusion and despair that plagued all the leftover major studios in early 1970. None of the reliable old forms seemed to draw in the public anymore. Large-scale musicals were a bust, as *Hello, Dolly!* and *Paint Your Wagon* fizzled on the big screen. Aside from John Wayne's turn in *True Grit*, even his Westerns were not doing much business.

Less than a decade earlier, Jerry Lewis had been such a box-office bonanza with his auteur's work as a writer, director, producer, and star in comedies produced by Paramount that one executive was quoted as saying that if Lewis wanted to burn down the studio lot, he would give him the matches. Only a few short years later, Paramount cancelled its contract with Lewis, and his subsequent work at Columbia dovetailed with his own falling star at that time. In the summer of 1970, Jerry Lewis' newest comedy film (a World War Two-related spoof called *Which Way to the Front?*) played only one week at a Los Angeles theater before it was replaced by a smash-hit three-hour documentary called *Woodstock*. That's how drastically the movies (and the culture) had changed.

Mario made sure to go see *The Brotherhood* before it disappeared from movie screens. "The movie was a critical and financial disaster," Puzo remembered. And it annoyed Puzo in particular, because he knew all too well that years earlier, when he blundered by desperately pushing for the sale of the movie rights to *The Godfather* (a purchase that was based on the first hundred pages of his evolving manuscript) he not only sold it cheaply but he helped create the possibility of the material being recycled, so to speak. After all, he was an obscure writer who had been duly paid.

But that was then. As 1969 segued into 1970, the non-stop

blockbuster sales of *The Godfather* made Puzo the most famous writer in the world. Nonetheless, when he bought a ticket to see *The Brotherhood*, he soon bristled. And, later, he fulminated:

> *When I saw* The Brotherhood, *I felt that they had given the first one hundred pages of my book to a real cookie-cutter screenwriter and told him to write a switch. Then they got Kirk Douglas to play the lead, and to show that he was a lovable gangster they always had him kissing little children. Then they had his own brother kill him on orders of the higher ups.*

> *When I saw the picture, I wasn't angry because I thought Paramount hustled me. That was OK. Working for my magazines, I'd written some cookie-cutting switches in my time. But I hated the sheer stupidity of that movie, the writing, the whole concept, the whole misunderstanding of the Mafia world. What I didn't know at the time was that the financial disaster of the film made the studio brass feel that there was no money in Mafia movies. It was only when* The Godfather *became a super best seller (the sixty-seven weeks on the* Times *best-seller list gave it this classification for the money boys) that they had to make the film.*

Paramount's initial plan, however, was to make the movie inexpensively. And the surest way to minimize the budget was to update the story to the present time. As dumb, shallow, and ridiculous as that seems to anyone who appreciates the novel's spellbinding reimagining of Americana circa 1945-1955, the studio's chieftains were committed to re-setting the

Mario Puzo in Hollywood circa 1970-71; photographer unknown

story of *The Godfather* in the early 1970s. (A similarly awful decision had done much to ruin the 1969 film adaptation of Philip Roth's *Goodbye, Columbus*, which was based on a novella steeped in the sensibilities of the 1950s, but ended up reconfigured as a storyline set in the putative Age of Aquarius).

"So I was not interested at all in what Hollywood did to the book as a movie," Mario later admitted, "just so long as I didn't help them do it."

8

Coming Over the Top

I wanted him to get every reward there was. I knew he had seen himself as a fat funny little guy . . . who thought he was an ugly man . . . and I wanted him to know he was loved because he was bigger than his weaknesses and much stronger than his sorrows . . . by his sheer fucking guts he had become the latest Italian-American cut along authentic heroic lines. To the names LaGuardia, Sinatra, DiMaggio, Rocky Marciano . . . you could add Mario, and everyone knew it.

~~~ Seymour Krim

Beginning with *The Godfather*, Puzo's triumph has been to combine a literary sensibility and a steamrolling narrative in almost mathematically equal measures—the dream of every writer.

~~~ Bruce Jay Friedman, "The Don of a New Era"

"This joker is making a fortune off a bastardized version of my life story," [Sinatra] complained, "and I think we should sue him for every fuckin' penny he's got." When told that he would never prevail in a lawsuit against Puzo, Sinatra seethed. "Look, if I ever see this guy . . ."

~~~ J. Randy Taraborrelli, *Sinatra: Behind the Legend*

Agent Candida Donadio learned from the film's producer, Al Ruddy, that he and Paramount wanted Mario to write the script. But Puzo said no after he learned that the low-budget constraints also meant a small screenwriter's fee. "They found more money and a percentage [of the profits]," Mario later recounted, and so he agreed to a first meeting. Puzo found producer Al Ruddy to be "a tall, lanky guy with a lot of easy New York charm" (Ruddy had attended Brooklyn Technical High School and was raised in the city). But the decisive factor may very well have been the meeting's varied quirks.

One quirk that impressed Puzo was how sincerely Al Ruddy apologized for repeatedly being called away from their table. Urgent calls from Hollywood found Ruddy being paged. Although these quick trips to the phone bank at the Edwardian Plaza Room interrupted their luncheon meeting, Ruddy's up-front admission won over the skeptical author. "Christ," Ruddy exclaimed, "this is like the bullshit in the movies, but I really gotta take these calls." That was all right with Puzo, who was then gleefully entertained, thanks to a distraction provided by Al Ruddy's wife.

Mario remembered it like this:

> I chatted with his wife and was charmed when she produced from her handbag a miniature live poodle who let out a yip and had the handbag zipped over his head again before the enraged maitre-d' spotted where the sound came from. It seemed Al and his wife took the poodle everywhere, with nobody the wiser. The poodle never let out a sound while in the handbag. At the end of the lunch I was enchanted by them and the poodle and I agreed to write the script.

Not only was Puzo "enchanted" by the producer and his wife and their contraband poodle, but because Ruddy "was so nice" Mario was quite sure that "it might be fun to go to California." For the first time in his life, he had the freedom to travel.

As 1970 progressed, the astronomical sales of *The Godfather* endured: paperback *and* hardcover. Even when it wasn't in the top spot, it was omnipresent on the *New York Times* Best-Sellers List. The book was reprinted constantly. Then: A promise that Puzo had once made to his wife now found him traveling more than ever before.

"When I was poor and working at home on my books, I made my wife a solemn promise that if I ever hit it big I'd get a studio, [and] get out from under her feet," Mario explained. "She hated having me home during the day."

Elaborating on this domestic tension from days gone by, Puzo later said:

> *I was in the way. I rumpled up the bed. I messed up the living room. I roamed around the house cursing. I came charging and yelling out of my workroom when the kids had a fight. In short, I was nerve-wracking. To make matters worse, she could never catch me working. She claims she never saw me type. She claims that for three years all I did was fall asleep on the sofa and then just magically produced the manuscript for* The Godfather. *Anyway, a man is bound by solemn oaths. Now that I was a big success, I had to get out of my own house during working hours.*

Money was no impediment anymore. Thanks to the six-figure paperback sale and the worldwide blockbuster success of the book (sales in English were extraordinary, and each deal to translate the novel into a foreign language represented a new and separate contract for Puzo's agent to broker), the world was at Mario's feet. At first it was all a bit surreal: "I felt very unnatural being out of debt," he admitted. "I didn't owe anybody one penny." That made it much easier for Erika to enforce the promise that had been made to her. Which led to a revelation in Mario's life:

> *I tried. I rented quiet elegant studios. I went to London. I tried the French Riviera, Puerto Rico and Las Vegas. I hired secretaries and bought dictating machines. Nothing happened. I needed the kids screaming and fighting. I needed my wife interrupting my work to show me her latest curtains. I needed those trips to the supermarket. I got some of my best ideas while helping my wife load up the shopping cart. But I had made a solemn promise to get out of the house.*

By late spring in 1970, Mario finally decided: "OK. I'd go to Hollywood."

Such a trans-continental move was not easy for Mario Puzo. He was almost fifty years old. He had no friends or connections in Los Angeles. And his personality had always been that of a low-key, under-the-radar kind of guy.

But in the wake of the success if his third novel—and the word "success" barely begins to describe the unusual degree to which *The Godfather* buzzed the culture even before the release of its first film adaptation—Puzo's life was changed.

"It's true—success really throws a writer," Mario acknowledged. But in his case it was not the youthful brand of success that had affected other novelists who early on in their careers published a smash-hit novel. (Norman Mailer was twenty-five when *The Naked and the Dead* made him a famous novelist. And James Jones was headed toward his thirtieth birthday when *From Here to Eternity* was published in 1951.)

Mario's mid-life success was an exception to almost all the rules for writers (in many cases, American authors' powers declined as they neared fifty). And it was enough to upend most of his routines and many of his settled, well-worn patterns.

"…for twenty years I had lived the life of a hermit," Puzo explained. "I had seen a few close personal friends on occasion for dinner. I had spent evenings with my wife's friends. I had gone to movies. I had taught my children how to gamble with percentages. But mostly I had been living in my own head, with all my dreams, all my fantasies. The world had passed me by."

This twenty-year period spanned an arc of time that in historical terms was quite vast, as far as Americana was concerned.

It was the period from 1949 to 1969. Which is to say, it added up to two culturally revolutionary decades: From the dawn of the postwar Baby Boom to the summer of Woodstock, the moon landing, and the Manson murders. From the waning era of Hollywood's peak power to the rise of television as America's premier source of entertainment. From President Truman and his crisis with General MacArthur regarding wartime strategies in the unpopular, faraway Korean War (1950-1953), all the way through the varied and escalating crises faced by Presidents Eisenhower, Kennedy, Johnson, and Nixon in the ever-increasingly unpopular Vietnam War that by 1969-1970 was quite literally tearing the nation apart as the antiwar movement was reignited and hundreds of campuses exploded after National Guardsmen in Ohio killed four students at Kent State University on May 4, 1970. That was the same season in which the Black Power movement was calling for violent revolution, the Women's Movement was on the march, and the newly born Gay Rights Movement began making waves in the aftermath of the 1969 Stonewall uprising in New York City.

In his biography of Marlon Brando, author Stefan Kanfer articulated some astute insights regarding the serendipitous timing of *The Godfather.* Kanfer wrote:

> *Unwittingly, Puzo tapped the public's desperate appetite for rationality and control—even at the hands of criminals. Readers, battered by too much news, too much information about strife at home and abroad, made* The Godfather *a phenomenal bestseller. It was as if they needed to believe that a Vito Corleone existed, that violence made sense if you looked at it a certain way, that, for example, a Mafia don could exact revenge against wrongdoers, seeking his own kind of justice, controlling vast swatches of modern life from his living room.*

"I didn't know how much men had changed," Puzo realized. And "women had changed, girls had changed, young men had changed." Now that he was emerging from the hermitage of his writer's workroom at home, Mario saw "how society and the very government had changed."

Nevertheless, Mario Puzo finally discovered that he "had the courage to leave for Hollywood." Doubtless some of that courage arose from the tremendous boosts to his confidence induced by the runaway success of his novel throughout 1969 and straight into 1970. It caused a complete shift in the way that Mario was treated.

"I had always been content to be an observer at the few parties I went to over the years," he said. "I rarely initiated a conversation or a friendship." That was never due to aloofness or arrogance. Puzo's innate shyness was coupled in the past with his lack of all-American "success." It hardly mattered that his first two novels had received royal critical praise . . . even amongst the elite literati, that was not enough to generate true respect. One had to enjoy big sales as well as critical benedictions.

But now spontaneous conversations and new friendships were a breeze. And all Puzo had to do was be present. All of a sudden, as *The Godfather* continued to sit atop the Best-Sellers List, everyone else did all the work. "People seemed genuinely delighted to talk to me, to listen to me; they were charming to me and I loved it. I became perhaps the most easily charmed guy in the Western Hemisphere. It was easy to stop being a hermit, in fact it was a pleasure."

For the most part, every aspect of the making of the first *Godfather* film was fraught with conflict, compromise, and relentless tensions and disagreements. The fact that Puzo worked on the project from start to finish is some kind of testament to Mario's ability to stay calm, keep his cool, and usually appear to make no waves. At any given time, all around him, others were steeped in anxiety, creative chaos, and most of all a desperate sense that nothing much was gelling and all could fade in a hurry.

Up to a certain point, Paramount Pictures had little enthusiasm for the film. Not only was the studio convinced that the failure of *The Brotherhood* was tantamount to a death knell for all gangster pictures, but the ideas put forward from the get-go by director Francis Ford Coppola sent the executives' blood pressure numbers into the stratosphere. Coppola was an Oscar-winning screenwriter (he co-wrote the script for *Patton*, which became a huge hit in 1970), but his track record as a director was not promising. He'd made three prior films between 1965 and 1969 (*You're a Big Boy Now*, *Finian's Rainbow*, and *The Rain People*), none of which were box-office hits.

Nonetheless, because he was an Italian-American (the consensus at Paramount was that a primary reason for the failure of *The Brotherhood* was that no Italians had a role in making the movie) and because he'd work for a low salary, he was courted.

Perceived as a bold renegade (Coppola and his independent production company, American Zoetrope, had set up shop in San Francisco deliberately, to ensure great distance from the Los Angeles scene; and with his long hair and full beard, Coppola seemed to fit right in with the countercultural Zeitgeist of San Francisco at the tail end of the 1960s and the dawn of the 1970s), the thirty-one-year-old director had a kind of confidence that was mesmerizing. Especially for someone who had not yet directed a film that turned a profit. But his passion and his integrity were supreme.

When necessary, Coppola would fight and argue and debate and stand his ground about casting decisions that the Paramount executives disagreed with; and also about how the film ought to be paced, how scenes ought to be lit, shot, edited, cut, and every other imaginable issue.

Almost always, Puzo and Coppola were a harmonious team. However, it wasn't until later in November 1970 that Paramount hired Francis Ford Coppola. For an eight-month period spanning April to November, the sole screenwriter on the project was Puzo. And that whole period turned out to be an eye-opener.

One of the first lessons apprehended by Mario was that money that might seem mightily impressive in a normal milieu disappeared fast in Hollywood. "The deal for the script was agreeable," Puzo recalled: "$500 a week expense money, nice money, up front (sure money), plus two-and-a-half percent of net profit. A fair deal in the marketplace of that time, especially since Al Ruddy had gotten his job by saying that he could produce the picture for only a million."

In 1969 or 1970, most movies cost far in excess of one or two million dollars to produce, and the notion of rushing into production on a shoestring budget of one million dollars was a distressing reminder of how Paramount considered *The Godfather* merely a best seller to exploit. Final budgets and production itself were down the road, though. As for his screenwriter's situation, Puzo learned fast that "the deal was not as good as it sounded." Mario later summed up how his new environment translated into dollars:

> *For one thing, a suite at the Beverly Hills Hotel was $500 a week, so that wiped out the expense money right there. Plus the fact that my two-and-a-half percent was worth zero unless the picture became a big blockbuster like Love Story. The way it works is that the studio usually legally snatches all profits from anybody working on a percentage of net profit. They do this with bookkeeping . . . They have accountants who make profits disappear . . .*

As usual, in his book-centered way, Puzo reflected on others' accounts of writers' lives in the movie business: "I had read the literature about Hollywood," he noted, "how they did in Fitzgerald, Nathanael West, and novelists in general." The grim tales of best-selling authors foundering in the constellation of MGM, Universal, Columbia, Paramount, Twentieth Century Fox, and Warner Brothers were legion. "So I went to Hollywood absolutely sure it held no surprises for me," Puzo said. "I was armored. *The Godfather* was *their* picture, *not mine*. I would be cool. I would never let my feelings get hurt. I would never get proprietary or paranoid. I was an employee."

Like any new employee suddenly set down in an exotic locale, Puzo did his best to immerse himself in all that was new: "California had a lot of sunshine and a lot of fresh air and a lot of tennis courts. (I'd just discovered tennis and was crazy about it.) I'd get skinny and healthy." Although his weight problems now were worse than ever (he was carrying an enormous belly on his five-foot-six-inch frame), Mario did quickly become a tennis aficionado. His agility on the court was remarkable.

Common sense dictated, of course, that one didn't have to stay at a hotel that automatically annihilated a weekly expense account exceeding most Americans' monthly mortgage payments. But in the wake of his success, Mario rationalized:

> The Beverly Hills Hotel is for me the best hotel in the world. It is a rambling three-story affair surrounded by gardens, its own bungalows, swimming pool and the famous Polo Lounge. Also a tennis court whose pro, Alex Omeda, called me Champ. Of course, he called everybody Champ. Still . . . The service is superb and friendly without being familiar. It is the only hotel I've ever been in that made me feel altogether comfortable. But it did wipe out my $500-a-week expense money and more besides.

With the Beverly Hills Hotel as his sanctuary, Mario then learned his way around the Paramount studio lot. "My office was fun," he said: "I loved the Paramount lot with its fake Western town, its little alleyways, its barrack-like buildings, its general atmosphere that made me feel like I was in the twilight zone."

The glory days of Hollywood may have been long gone, but remnants of the old-time magic were there to be seen. It was in a small third-floor office on the lot that Puzo began to transpose his 446-page novel into a screenplay for what was intended to be a two-hour movie.

Producer Al Ruddy had a larger, more elaborate office on the first floor of the same building that Mario was in, and all they had to do to see each other was to walk upstairs or downstairs.

Not only was Mario's little office "out of traffic, just as I liked it," but it also contained "a refrigerator and an unlimited supply of soda pop free." To a man who grew up in New York's Depression-era Neapolitan ghetto, such amenities were still appreciated. Like a dream come true. Free soda!

"And I had an adjoining office for my secretary and a telephone with a buzzer and four lines," Puzo exulted. "This was living." Soon enough, Mario met the executives.

At that time, Paramount's head of production was the young, handsome, and creatively daring Robert Evans. His life story—from garment manufacturer in the early 1950s to being an actor in the late 1950s (he was shot out of a cannon by co-starring roles in 1957's *The Sun Also Rises* and 1958's *The Man with a Thousand Faces,* in which he played the late, great legendary film producer Irving Thalberg) to becoming a studio executive in the 1960s—it was an admixture of Horatio Alger and Walter Mitty. Only forty years old in 1970, Robert Evans had come to personify what the media was calling the New Hollywood. But he had his detractors, too.

Puzo recounted: "I had read once a *LIFE* magazine article on Evans, a savage putdown. So I was surprised to find that he was easy and natural." And then:

> *I liked Evans right off for one reason. There were five of us having a conference in his office. He had to take a private phone call. So he stepped into a little closet to take it. Now Louis B. Mayer would have told the four of us to squeeze into the closet and shut the door so that we wouldn't hear him take the call at his desk.*

> *Evans was unpretentious and usually said or seemed to say exactly what he thought. He said it the way children tell truths, with a curious innocence that made the harshest criticism or disagreement inoffensive. He was unfailingly courteous, to me at any rate. If this seems too flattering a portrait of a film studio chief, let me add that he was so cheap about handing out his Cuban cigars that I had to sneak into his office when he wasn't around to steal some.*

At this early stage of *The Godfather's* pre-production, Mario was included in a series of five-man conferences. In addition to Puzo himself and producer Al Ruddy, there were President of Production Robert Evans, the Vice-President of Production Peter Bart, and also Jack Ballard—about whom Puzo paid this tribute: "Ballard [was] a Yul Brynner-headed guy [i.e., completely bald] who [kept] track of production costs on a movie. Self-effacing, but producers and directors shook in their boots when he totaled tabs on their costs."

Equally impressive was Peter Bart. Mario expressed his admiration for Bart's "cold intelligence" and for the fact that "he liked to think things out before voicing an opinion, and he hadn't yet picked up the trick of being charming while he was thinking." Peter Bart made a highly favorable impression on Mario because "everybody in the movie business is charming, in fact everybody in California is charming, except: Peter Bart . . . the only uncharming guy in the movie business whom I met." In other words, Bart was not a bullshit artist. A rarity!

Their conferences were held "at the Paramount studio's plush headquarters on Canon Drive." After which Puzo and Ruddy would return to the studio's lot, where in Mario's mind they "were just like soldiers returning to the front lines and finally rid of the brass."

At their very first conference, they discussed ideas for casting. Mario chimed in: "I suggested Marlon Brando for the role of the Godfather. They were kind to me but I got the impression my stock had dropped 50 points." Wisely, Puzo did not push. Instead, he listened. He absorbed. He learned by observation. And he held his tongue, except when off-key notes were sounded. "Al Ruddy suggested Robert Redford for the role of Michael," Puzo once recalled, "and I didn't care how nice a guy he was, his stock dropped 50 points. I spoke out and was pleasantly surprised when Evans and Bart agreed with me. It was going to be a fair fight, I thought."

The missing element was that of a director. Million-dollar offers were made to top-tier, established directors like Franklin Schaffner, Costa-Gavras, and others. They all turned down the project. Reasons varied. But gradually two themes emerged: *The Godfather* was misperceived as a trashy film-to-be based on a best-selling book that was too often branded with the misnomer "potboiler"; and it was assumed that *The Godfather* invariably romanticized the Mafia. No director was forthcoming.

And until a strong, compelling script was in hand, no director could be wooed. "I had to write the script before they got a director," Puzo realized. "Directors like to read scripts before they sign. Well, that was what I was in California for." But it wasn't long before Puzo grew homesick. He returned to New York "for a couple of weeks. I missed my wife and kids. And . . . spring is a good time to be in New York."

Producer Al Ruddy expressed his vote of confidence in Puzo by not raising hell about Mario's return to Long Island. "He even kept paying me the $500-a-week expense money while I was living at home," Mario said. Weeks later, after making progress on the script from his home office on Long Island, Mario "flew back to California with a stop at Las Vegas, where I lost what I had saved of my expense money." He shrugged off such losses. His novel was still a best seller.

Month after month in 1970, Paramount Pictures continued to seek an established, well-known, "name" director for *The Godfather*. Without any luck. Astronomical sums were still offered, and still the project was declined by John Frankenheimer, Sidney Lumet, Elia Kazan, and others. A peculiar situation now prevailed. The movie adaptation was tainted by the assumption that the film would be unworthy in the end, primarily because of its unsavory subject matter. And yet, the novel was briskly selling in such vast quantities that Paramount opted not to sell the rights to anyone else, enjoy a huge profit, and let others inherit the trouble. Actor and independent producer Burt Lancaster offered Paramount one million dollars for the films rights to *The Godfather* (which had cost Paramount $12,500) but the studio declined. The common practice of "turnaround" was not an option on this.

The search for a director continued. And Mario Puzo was having one hell of a good time. He later summarized his newfound idyll:

> *So from April to August I led an ideal existence: California, tennis and sunshine—until I got homesick, then home again. Then when home life got on my nerves—back to California. Nobody knew where I was or when. Meanwhile I was being charmed out of my shoes by all the people I met in California. Socially, I had round heels, there was no other word for it. I wasn't getting much work done, but nobody seemed to be worrying about it.*

He may not have been pounding out pages as fast as an experienced screenwriter could, but in truth Puzo was getting plenty of work done—it just happened to be the kind of writer's work that appears to others to be idleness. He was taking in, sorting out, processing, mentally editing and filing away in his memory an enormous inventory of behavior patterns, quirks and foibles, patterns and protocols, varied types (stereotypes and archetypes), and general Hollywood atmospherics. Such material was not germane to *The Godfather*, but in his future novels (Hollywood subplots would be a major narrative element in *Fools Die*, *The Fourth K*, and *The Last Don*) this inventory of material drawn from Puzo's up-close and personal observations in America's film headquarters in 1970 proved to be invaluable.

Mario discovered that he felt tremendous sympathy for the Hollywood rank and file, whose lives were consumed by their career quests. "One of the greatest surprises for me was to find actresses and actors so sympathetic," Puzo noted. "Writers and directors and producers always put performers down. Star actors are considered dunderheads. Actresses are always to be manipulated by power, in their personal and professional life. They are supposed not to have intelligence or sensitivity."

But, in his own way, Mario had "quite simply found the reverse to be often true. I found many of them intelligent, quiet, sensitive, and shy. I observed that at the beginnings of their careers and afterward they are badly exploited by their producers, studios and agents and assorted hustlers."

His innate empathy for the strivers in Hollywood—the hopeful underdogs who had only the slimmest chances of any kind of breakthrough (let alone any careers) in the film industry— dovetailed with the preoccupation Mario had always had in his novels regarding characters embroiled in negotiations of power. Negotiations of differences. Such negotiations of power were Puzo's ultimate variations on a theme, informing significant episodes in *The Dark Arena* and *The Fortunate Pilgrim*, and serving as a primary leitmotif in *The Godfather*. Such negotiations (in all of their subtle forms, as well as in blatant manifestations) were everywhere in Hollywood.

"I used to enjoy watching the pretty girls making the rounds of producers' offices to read for parts," Mario recalled. But it wasn't just actresses constantly auditioning.

A battalion of hopefuls was forever immersed in the realm of "development hell."

Writing later on about his debut year in Hollywood, Puzo summed up this realm.

> *Every studio has a gang of producers who rent offices on the lot while getting a picture ready for production. Nine hundred and ninety-nine out of a thousand of these pictures never get made, but meanwhile the producers have people coming in to read and rehearse parts, study scripts, and have long and earnest discussions on how to play the parts. Outside the studios there are another 10,000 hopefuls who have written scripts and carry three containers of film to shoot their own independent movie. They, too, are interviewing and rehearsing the 1,000,000 pretties, young women and men in America who have flocked to LA to get in films. All this combined with the great weather and sunshine, gave Hollywood an ambience that was to me at least interesting.*

Of course there was a degree of respect accorded to Mario Puzo that few writers in Hollywood could even imagine. Although he was a New Yorker (ergo "an outsider" through and through, which in clubby, clique-centric Hollywood is usually the kiss of death) and because writers are always near the bottom of the Hollywood hierarchy, unless they're also accomplished directors and producers à la Spike Lee or Julie Taymor, most writers in the film industry are reminded in myriad ways that they remain "schmucks with Underwoods!" as Harry Cohn once said while ruling his fiefdom at Columbia Pictures; it's easily updated to "schmucks with laptops!"

However, during Puzo's first hiatus in Hollywood in 1970, his novel continued to sell in extraordinary numbers and a major photo-essay about Mario and his new blast of middle-aged success appeared in *LIFE* magazine in July of that year. The text of that essay was written by Mario's old friend George Mandel (it's safe to assume that Puzo made a specific request to *LIFE* to commission Mandel for the assignment).

And Mario later assessed the period that Mandel's essay captured:

"From April to August of 1970 I commuted back and forth from New York to Los Angeles, working on the script, playing tennis, getting a taste of the social life in Hollywood. All very pleasant. The time before a writer delivers the script is sort of a honeymoon time. Love is everywhere."

Certainly it was a bit of an exaggeration to claim that "Love is everywhere," especially when so many dice were being rolled on *The Godfather*. However, contradictory assessments *were* everywhere in the culture at large that summer.

On July 10, 1970, the latest issue of *LIFE* magazine featured a cover that was gloriously schizophrenic in its contrasting elements. The full-cover photo was that of a bikini-clad young California woman, emerging from the surf with free-swinging arms and a Pepsodent smile; her gorgeous legs, taut stomach (clearly unburdened by childbirth or any other signs of stress), and the two ample breast-cups of her blue bikini top held in placed at the center of her cleavage by a gold ring. A sea goddess.

Yet, the headline directly beneath the famous LIFE logo read: "Report on Cambodia: The tottering wreck we leave behind." More lousy news about Southeast Asia and the forever-embroiled ill fates of Vietnam, Cambodia, and Laos.

While scoring points for placing such a serious headline beneath its logo, *LIFE* also cued readers as to what the sexy, buoyant, mermaid-caliber photo led to: down below, to the photo's lower left, another headline promised a pictorial spread: "California Girls Spangle the Beach." A brazen reminder that many young Americans were consumed by typical coming-of-age enjoyments; not by radical movements, racial furies, or combat.

In the middle of that *LIFE* magazine from July 10, 1970, there appeared a photo-essay titled "Wealthy Father of 'The Godfather.'" And along with a selection of pithy, insightful, humorous quotations from the days that George Mandel spent with Mario out in California, there also appeared eight illustrative photos by Bob Peterson.

There was no article in the traditional sense. The photographs are the focus of the feature. But LIFE ensured that readers apprehended how far Puzo had traveled to now find himself ensconced on the Paramount Pictures lot, transposing his novel for the big silver screen. Beneath a close-up picture of Puzo in profile, sitting like a hefty sultan before a Royal typewriter in his Hollywood office (and brandishing a ten-inch cigar like a scepter), a one-paragraph mini-bio was provided by LIFE:

"A minor classic" is what the New York Times *called Mario Puzo's 1965 novel,* The Fortunate Pilgrim, *a sensitive, bitter-sweet story of an Italian immigrant family in New York in the first three decades of this century. But the book's main payoff was in praise; Puzo had to borrow money to live. For a while he wrote perceptive literary reviews—and had to borrow money to pay the mortgage. Then he sat down to write a best-seller . . . and out came* The Godfather *. . . a novel about the Mafia. It became the fastest-selling book in history, No. 1 best-seller 22 consecutive weeks, in the top 10 for 67, five million sold in paperback while the hardcover was selling a million, a movie in the works and a TV series being discussed. To find out how he's getting on with his new-found affluence, LIFE asked Novelist George Mandel, an old friend of Puzo, to visit him in Los Angeles. This is the Puzo picture he saw.*

It is a picture of long-overdue success commingled with newfound pleasures and just the right indulgence of latter-day confidence. One photo shows Mario on a tennis court, corpulence be damned, swinging a racket with gusto in the company of his new secretary: "I told Paramount I wanted a tennis-playing secretary," Puzo is quoted as saying. And George Mandel also recorded Mario's punch line: "'Where can we find a pretty stenographer who's a good typist and can play tennis?' they asked. Who said anything about pretty or stenography or typing?"

Another picture shows Mario sampling a dish of Rigatoni Siciliana pasta at an upscale Italian restaurant in Los Angeles, where he quipped: "The best way to launch an Italian restaurant is to have it raided because the Mafia eats there. Everybody knows they eat well."

As always, Mario was eating very well. It showed not just in the close-up photograph where he's seated in profile, his colossal belly forming a basketball's shape beneath his stylish button-down sports shirt, but also in a medium shot taken in producer Al Ruddy's handsome, well-furnished office. Mario is seen reclining on a couch, a hardcover copy of *The Godfather* on his lap, as Al Ruddy stands nearby in the middle of their dialogue. Once again, Puzo's imposing physique is on display, but the picture's most telling detail is that Mario's bare feet are propped up on a table that's set in front of Ruddy's couch.

The attribute explains: "Puzo sheds shoes (he never wears socks)," and that would remain true for as long as he lived. Fellow authors (and pals) Joseph Heller, John Bowers, and Bruce Jay Friedman all quipped that Puzo's love of Bally slippers was utilitarian, because his belly precluded leaning down to tie shoelaces. The last picture in the photo-essay shows Puzo visiting with Joseph Heller at Heller's home in New York, where the two thriving novelists are seen in conversation as Mario (cigar in hand) drops nickels into a vintage slot machine that Heller had acquired.

It's the second-to-last picture, however, that speaks volumes. To accommodate LIFE's wishes and to make the photo-essay not just a writer's success story, but also a human-interest feature on a family man, all five Puzo children joined Mario and Erika for a snapshot out in the yard behind their home on Long Island. In an era of relentless negativity in the media over the subject of the Generation Gap, the photo of the Puzo clan was a tonic to LIFE's millions of subscribers. All five children look comfortable and youthful with their contemporary hairstyles and trendy clothing.

But they also look just as comfortable surrounding their older, square-looking mother and father. There was no effort expended by Erika or Mario to "get with it" and sport anything like the "hip" or "mod" looks that had slowly infiltrated Main Street USA. Superficialities aside, one salient detail gives the photo its sweetness.

With four of their five children arrayed around them, daughter Dorothy stands in between her parents and wraps her arms around each of them. So, in order to be photographed still touching each other, Erika and Mario extended their arms in front of Dorothy's midriff, and they're seen clasping hands. They had triumphed.

One man who had sustained a lifetime of triumphs (with a few low points as well) took a special interest in disliking *The Godfather*. That man was Frank Sinatra.

In Puzo's novel, far more than in the films that resulted from his book, the character of Johnny Fontane is a significant presence. And everyone in the era of 1969-1970 who had any sort of working knowledge of cultural Americana in the prior two decades (or anyone who kept up with the news through the years, wherein gossip and stories and PR defenses and general information about Sinatra were abundant) had no trouble seeing the many similarities between the life and times of the self-anointed Chairman of the Board (Sinatra's hubristic self-assessment) and Johnny Fontane, who in Mario's novel sometimes receives chapter-length explication.

While Puzo worked on the earliest drafts of the screenplay in Hollywood during his 1970 West Coast hiatus, the word was out that Frank Sinatra detested the book and turned livid whenever he was asked about the correlations between his own career and his private life and the dramatized exploits of Johnny Fontane. The connections seemed more than random. And many readers who had come of age in the 1950s or early 1960s could spot the linkages. Older readers found even more to chew over.

Just a few pages into *The Godfather*, readers see Johnny Fontane in a drunken state of disarray. It's explained that his career is in crisis, much like Sinatra's career was in crisis in the very early 1950s, when his Columbia Records recording contract was not renewed, his TV show was cancelled by CBS, his talent agency dropped him, and movie offers were scant. That downward spiral had commenced when MGM invoked its "morals clause" as the married Sinatra cavorted in a scandalous affair with Ava Gardner, making a spectacle of his philandering to a world that had been plied with years of PR about his love for his wife, Nancy, and their three children. In short order, MGM tossed him off the lot and "Frankie" went from earning $150,000 per film to being stranded without any significant movie offers at all.

Until late 1952, that is, when Sinatra and Ava Gardner (by then they were married, briefly) lobbied heavily to persuade the chief of Columbia Pictures, Harry Cohn, to give the greenlight to a screen test for Sinatra. The blockbuster James Jones novel *From Here to*

Eternity was ramping up for production and Sinatra coveted the role of Maggio, the loudmouth enlisted soldier (an Italian-American from Brooklyn) in the pre-war epoch, stationed in Hawaii at an Army base adjacent to Pearl Harbor.

In the end, it wasn't a horse's head found in the bed of any studio executive that ensured Sinatra was given the role. Harry Cohn's approval of Sinatra in a straight dramatic part was granted after director Fred Zinnemann was awed by an improvisation that Sinatra had spontaneously performed during his screen test (when he used olives in lieu of dice to shoot craps in the middle of a barroom scene). Matters were helped along when Ava Gardner (who was then as big a screen star as Julia Roberts at her peak) quietly assured Cohn that she'd owe Columbia a picture if they'd contract Sinatra for *From Here to Eternity*; and helped furthermore when Sinatra agreed to play the part for a total of $8,000 (co-stars Burt Lancaster and Montgomery Clift were each being paid $150,000).

The film version of *From Here to Eternity* was shot in March and April of 1953, quickly and brilliantly edited, and released to stunning success in August of 1953. It was as big a movie in its day as *Titanic* was in the late 1990s or as *The Godfather* turned out to be as a cinematic sensation in the early-to-mid 1970s.

Nominated for eleven Academy Awards in the spring of 1954, the movie *From Here to Eternity* won eight Oscars (including Best Motion Picture) and ignited a bona-fide renaissance in the career of Frank Sinatra. Winning the Oscar for Best Supporting Actor revived Sinatra's fortunes (having clearly proved that he had talent as a dramatic actor, post-Oscar film offers for dramas, musicals, and boozy romantic comedies were forthcoming), and seemingly overnight (after having been branded as a washed-up has-been a few years earlier) he had a new recording contract and television specials in the pipeline. It was well known as a great comeback story.

And the general outline of that story was akin to Johnny Fontane's tale of early success as a "crooner" with a famous band à la "Frankie" and the Tommy Dorsey Orchestra circa 1940-42; a slew of failures in later years; and then his rise back to the top. With a great deal of help from Don Vito Corleone, pulling all the strings.

The fact that millions of copies of *The Godfather* continued to sell as the 1970s got underway enraged Sinatra. Invariably, the ways in which the affairs and struggles and Mob-related business of Johnny Fontane resembled the legend and the mystique of Sinatra's own career trajectory made for inglorious gossip.

How could it not? In 1970, Sinatra was one of the most famous men on the planet. And his brief marriage to Ava Gardner (back in 1952-53) was still talked about as a myth of star-crossed lovers. Gardner's notoriously impassioned behavior and her famously hyperactive libido (just like Sinatra's) made the similarities between Johnny Fontane and his cheating second wife, and the Sinatra/ Gardner legend, inevitable.

But in Puzo's novel there were also affirmative aspects to the character of Johnny Fontane, who is a doting father to his children and a reliable supporter to his former wife (whom he still obviously loves, though platonically). Such traits were often reported in the press when Sinatra's life was summed up in articles, which appeared with great frequency. The life of Frank Sinatra was an open book.

In Mario's novel, Johnny Fontane is a highly sympathetic figure. A complex man.

That was Puzo's intention all along. "Now the thing was," Mario recalled, "in my book, that I had written the Fontane character with complete sympathy for the man and his life-style and his hang-ups. I thought I had caught the innocence of great show biz people, their despair at the corruption that their kind of life forces on them and the people around them."

Early in the book, when Fontane appears as a wedding guest on the day Connie Corleone is married, his vulnerability is on full display as he consults with the Don.

When total despair is expressed by Johnny Fontane—"It's too late . . . All the contracts have been signed and they start shooting in a week. It's absolutely impossible."—he is reassured by Don Vito Corleone with the chilling (yet comforting) first utterance of the novel's most famous line: "He's a business man . . . I'll make him an offer he can't refuse."

Just those few exchanges seemed to signify (or at least echo) common knowledge about Sinatra's works and days. The ethos of the Rat Pack is outlined (gambling, boozing, loose "broads" for the taking). And *From Here to Eternity* is alluded to in relation to "the biggest novel of the year" (Jones's debut novel was the best-selling novel of the year when it was published, and also won the National Book Award). Most telling is the Sinatra/Maggio linkage: "I wouldn't even have to act, just be myself," which most filmgoers assumed was the reason that the role was apt for Frank Sinatra to such a startling degree.

Somehow, word of the Fontane character had leaked even

before the novel was published. "Before the book came out," Mario remarked, "my publisher got a letter from Sinatra's lawyers demanding to see the manuscript. In polite language we refused." Distinct resemblances between Sinatra and Johnny Fontane to the side, it's worth noting that the Fontane character also reminds one of Dean Martin, whose own career was in many ways cut from the same cloth. Ironically, it's because the legend of Sinatra's Oscar-winning comeback performance in *From Here to Eternity* was so engrained in pop culture history that Dean Martin's equally fine dramatic debut in another World War Two-related film (*The Young Lions*) never received the attention it deserved. It still doesn't. Nonetheless, Puzo knew he was walking a fine line: "I thought I had caught the inner innocence of [Fontane]. But I could also see that if Sinatra thought the character was himself, he might not like it—the book—or me."

That observation was put to the test one night in New York City. Inevitably. As Puzo once remarked about the possibility of being introduced to Sinatra: "Of course some people wanted to bring us together." The first effort to do so occurred at Elaine's.

By 1970, Elaine's was already one of Manhattan's premier high-profile celebrity hangouts, and it became even more famous throughout the 1970s and 1980s as magazine articles and paparazzi photos forever reinforced the gossip and the scoops about who was seen at "Woody Allen's table" (always reserved for the diminutive wunderkind of American cinema) or who was spotted dining with whoever the hottest celebs were at any given time. The seating arrangements at Elaine's were a reliable barometer of who was hot and who was not amid America's media-crazed, hierarchical culture of fame and fortune. A table up front was akin to royalty.

"At Elaine's in New York one night Sinatra was at the bar and I was at a table," Mario recalled. Not surprising at all. The bar at Elaine's was where high-wattage hotshots often held court. Norman Mailer was no stranger to that bar, and his pontifications blended right in with the smoke-filled ambience and the competition for attention. Long-established American icons like Walter Cronkite or Bob Hope could easily move about and be assured of deferential treatment. And then there was Frank.

That's all: "Frank." Calling him by his last name was common enough, but those who really wanted to reassure themselves that they had "arrived" at some elevated level in America's status-addicted glitterati could not be satisfied by saying that they had crossed paths with Sinatra . . . they had to cross the threshold allowing them to aver that yes, indeed (and saints be praised!), at long last they had been blessed by "Frank."

This was a transitional time in Sinatra's career. Record sales were down and his most recent TV specials suffered poor ratings. Things were so bad that a couple of years earlier, in 1968, prodded by the network and doubtless a crew of obsequious advisors, Sinatra at age fifty-three appeared on a television special (*Francis Albert Sinatra Does His Thing*) wearing an Indian-style Nehru jacket and sporting "hippie beads" fit for Jerry Garcia. That absurd get-up was intended to make the self-aggrandizing Chairman of the Board (stuck with his omnipresent toupee) somehow appealing to younger viewers. Equally idiotic efforts were made by desperate others elsewhere. On one album cover around that time, legendary jazz drummer Buddy Rich (also older than fifty) posed not only in a jet-black Nehru jacket with a psychedelic background of *Sgt. Pepper*-era colors, but also wore "love beads" in his own quest to be thought of as "groovy" and "with it" by "the kids." Fat chance.

But who could blame them? The oppressively moronic media focus was on the youth market. By the early 1970s, Duke Ellington and Tony Bennett were without recording contracts. Concert performances kept them going. Ditto Sinatra. It was clear that with wretched films like *Dirty Dingus Magee* (which managed to be even worse than *Marriage on the Rocks* or the subpar movies in which Sinatra starred as a detective named Tony Rome), there was no place in the New Hollywood for "Frank."

But he always had Las Vegas, concert halls, and a spot like Elaine's to draw forth the worship he thrived on. Sycophants abounded. "Frank" exerted Pope-like authority.

Except with Mario Puzo. And it's to Puzo's credit that he really didn't give a shit.

That particular night at Elaine's, the famously gregarious and charismatic owner herself stopped at Mario's table and made the pitch: "Elaine asked if I would object to meeting Sinatra. I said it was OK with me if it was OK with him. It was not OK with Sinatra. And that was perfectly OK with me. I didn't give it another thought."

Until more than a year later, that is. "I was working on the script in Hollywood," Mario recalled. And though his routine was to stay in his room on almost all nights and read as much as possible, he made the occasional exception and stepped out.

One night Mario attended a party at Chasen's, which regularly hosted Hollywood royalty the way that Elaine's served as the Pantheon in Manhattan. It was a party for producer Al Ruddy's friend, who was celebrating his birthday. "A party for twelve given by a famous millionaire," Puzo later dubbed it: "Just an agreeable dinner. Everybody had been so charming to me in the past six months I had gotten over some of my backwardness. So I went."

Puzo sensed quickly that things might go awry. For starters, the millionaire who was hosting his own birthday party turned out to be "one of those elderly men always trying to be youthful." But that was part of the Zeitgeist. In one of the weirdest episodes of American cultural and social history (and the magazine ads for clothes, cars, and cigarettes and booze illustrate this with only a cursory review), the trend by 1970 was for adults—even "senior" adults—to adopt fashion choices which derived from the Haight-Ashbury hippie efflorescence that flourished briefly a few years earlier in San Francisco. Clear overtones of Swinging London's "Mod" scene from the mid-Sixties finally transferred to Main Street, USA. Business suits all of a sudden featured "flair bottom" pants for men; and boots were "in" for guys who were "with it." Wingtips? No. Colorful shirts and psychedelic ties? Yes. Women's fashions in 1970 were also a sign of the triumph of the omnipresent youth culture influence: funky belts, wild patterns, sashes and headbands and suede and denim, with accoutrements like wire-rimmed glasses and shoulder bags with fringe.

As for the glad-handing, backslapping geezer hosting the party that night at Chasen's, Mario recalled: "he wore red slacks and a miniature Stetson and had that five-martini affability I dread more than anything else in the world." Gradually, inexorably, things happened. The die was cast.

"As we were having a drink at the bar," Puzo explained, "he said that Sinatra was having dinner at another table and would I like to meet him. I said no. The millionaire had a Right-Hand Man who tried to insist. I said no again. We finally went to dinner." The dinner party featured one thrill amid a disappointing meal. Puzo, however, was emotionally moved by a magic moment. He later elaborated:

> *During the dinner there was a tableau of John Wayne and Frank Sinatra meeting in the space equidistant between their two tables to salute each other. They both looked absolutely great, better than on the screen, twenty years younger than they really were. And both beautifully dressed, Sinatra especially. It was really great to see. They were beribboned kings meeting on the Field of the Cloth of Gold; Chasen's is regally formal.*

But then there was the food. "It was lousy," Mario recalled. "I'd eaten better in one-arm Italian joints all over New York. This was the famous Chasen's? I was glad when we finished and I started to leave."

Quickly now, the trouble began. As Puzo recalled the incident, it was when "the millionaire took me by the hand and started leading me toward a table." That was when Mario realized that the birthday boy's "Right-Hand Man" had grasped Puzo's other hand. Suddenly, the host insisted: "You've gotta meet Frank . . . he's a good friend of mine."

Momentum was swift. "We were almost to the table," Mario remembered years later, "[and] I still could have wrenched loose and walked away, but it would have been an obvious snub. It was easier, physically and psychologically, to be led the few remaining steps."

Nothing good came from it. Although he claimed to dislike the press, Sinatra kept a close eye on newspapers and magazines. When he wanted or needed to, he played the media like a master pianist plays Chopin. By this time, the July 1970 issue of *LIFE* magazine with its photo-essay on Puzo was in circulation. There could be no doubt about who was suddenly being pulled toward the table where sat the most famous singer in the world. "Sinatra never looked up from his plate," Puzo recalled.

The millionaire completely missed that cue, and spoke gregariously: "I'd like you to meet my good friend, Mario Puzo." Sinatra sat there like a Sphinx. And finally said: "I don't think so." Instantly, Mario turned and stepped away. Then he heard it again.

The millionaire offered another introduction. It was clear that in all of his "five-martini affability," the host "didn't get the message. He started over again."

This time Sinatra was adamant: "I don't want to meet him." Space was tight and Puzo could not make a quick, inconspicuous exit. "I was trying to get past the Right-Hand Man and get the hell out of there," he said. Amid the discomfort all around, the scene became farce. Realizing that he had transgressed and possibly offended the

Chairman of the Board, the millionaire host "began stuttering his apologies . . . to Sinatra. [He] was actually in tears. 'Frank, I'm sorry, God, Frank, I didn't know, Frank, I'm sorry—'"

The mood shifted. Mario had begun his retreat. Now Sinatra was conciliatory toward his crestfallen acquaintance. And Puzo's antenna picked it all up. He may have been stepping away, but Mario noted that "Sinatra cut him short and his voice was . . . soft and velvety. He was consoling the shattered millionaire. 'It's *not* your *fault*,' Sinatra said."

It appeared that Sinatra assumed that Puzo had choreographed the encounter.

All of a sudden, Mario turned on a dime and returned to the table long enough to say: "Listen, it wasn't my idea." Total confusion reigned. Mario later explained: "[Sinatra] completely misunderstood. He thought I was apologizing for the character of Johnny Fontane in my book." Adopting a kind mien on the assumption that Mario wished to atone, Sinatra asked Puzo: "Who told you to put that in the book, your publisher?"

Puzo clarified what he had meant when he said: "Listen, it wasn't my idea." He clarified it by doing the unthinkable. He spoke straight talk to a man who wasn't used to such a thing. "I mean about being introduced to you," he said to Sinatra.

That set off Sinatra's apoplectic fit. The very idea that the minion in his midst had not been keen to meet the king was even more offensive than Johnny Fontane. But what Puzo recalled with real surprise was that "contrary to his reputation [Sinatra] did not use foul language at all. The worst thing he called me was a pimp."

Their encounter ended as "Sinatra started to shout abuse . . . [he said] that if it wasn't that I was so much older than he, he would beat the hell out of me." Such idiocy is unintentionally funny. First: Sinatra was five years older than Puzo, but as Mario once noted: "OK, he looked twenty years younger." Still, the absurdity was off the charts. Puzo framed matters in relation to their shared ethnic heritage: "What hurt was that here he was, a Northern Italian, threatening me, a Southern Italian, with physical violence. This was roughly the equivalent of Einstein pulling a knife on Al Capone. It just wasn't done. Northern Italians never mess with Southern Italians except to get them put in jail or deported to some desert island."

That was a polite way assessing matters. In truth, Sinatra (despite his vaunted reputation as a tough guy) couldn't fight his way out of a tuxedo, unless he was hitting a woman (for which he was rather well known). Several times he had paid off low-life goons to come from the shadows and beat the daylights out of his male enemies. He was not only a pampered man whose idea of roughing it was running out of ice cubes, but he was too busy with valets, massages, saunas, manicures, and other forms of prissy self-indulgence to learn how to throw a real punch. Sinatra wouldn't have lasted two weeks with the Fourth Armored Division in World War Two (a perforated eardrum, which oddly never affected his musical expertise, kept "Frankie" out of the military in the 1940s), yet Puzo lasted more than two years.

Their dismal chance encounter ended awkwardly, Mario remembered:

> *Sinatra kept up his abuse and I kept staring at him. He kept staring down at his plate. Yelling. He never looked up. Finally I walked away and out of the restaurant. My humiliation must have showed on my face because he yelled after me, "Choke. Go ahead and choke." The voice frenzied, high-pitched.*

At least one of the two men had the decency (and balls) to look at the other.

Varied and contradictory accounts of that imbroglio were reported in the media. Mario noted: "Different versions of this incident appeared in papers and on TV," with the winner-or-loser verdict "depending on who was doing the planting."

Another lesson was quickly absorbed by Puzo, who admitted: "It was at this time I realized how important a public relations apparatus is. Sinatra [had] a guy named Jim Mahoney and he must [have been] good because every story version made Sinatra a hero. Which made me think: Was everything I had admired about Sinatra a creation of Mahoney?"

There was no doubt that Mario truly did hold Frank Sinatra in esteem. He had no qualms about expressing such admiration in print, either. Even after the untoward incident at Chasen's, when Mario wrote an autobiographical essay for *New York* Magazine in 1972, he plainly stated: "I just believed he was a great artist (singing, not acting) and that he had lived a life of great courage. I admired his sense of family responsibility, especially since he was a Northern Italian, which to a Southern Italian is as alien as being an Englishman."

The irony is that as far back as August 1967, more than a year and a half before *The Godfather* was published, Puzo's respect for Sinatra made its way into print at the beginning and the end of a lengthy article that he wrote for the *New York Times Magazine*. But for every affirmation, there was a tweak. A contrasting critique.

Titled "The Italians, American Style," the essay presented what Puzo called an "impressionistic portrait" of American Italians and their storied history. The news hook was the national fundraising drive underway by "the newly formed American Italian Anti-Defamation League, headed by Mr. Frank Sinatra."

As for the purpose of such an American Italian Anti-Defamation League (clearly modeled on other ethnically defined civil rights organizations for Jewish Americans or African Americans), it was described in Puzo's article as a mission "to persuade book publishers, movie studios, TV producers and magazine editors not to call criminals by names ending in *i* or *o*."

In the context of that article, Mario had assessed for an international general readership the unique stature of Frank Sinatra not only in the imagination of the American-Italian demographic, but American life at large:

> And the national chairman of the American Italian Anti-Defamation League, Mr. Sinatra himself, is not only the most sought-after entertainer in show business today but the secret idol of every guilt-ridden American male. No other famous man has managed to divorce his wife yet retain control of her life and the lives of their children, guiding them all to happiness and success while jealously guarding his own personal freedom.

> The league knows very well what it is about. Sinatra is, in this country, the most powerful American of Italian descent. He is also, it would seem, a man of extraordinary force, having burst the shell of a callow crooner to become the shrewdest and richest executive in the movie world. Interestingly enough, he has very obviously modeled his personal behavior on that of the great Mafia chiefs who reigned in Sicily—let me add hastily, on their best behavior.

It's important to stress that in this era the stature of the *New York Times* was unsurpassed. And *The New York Times Magazine* was no mere appendage. The *Times* was not only "the paper of record," but its international reputation derived from the assumption that its pages presented ultimate authoritative content. Thus "The Italians, American Style" was perused by a worldwide readership (not just the showbiz crowd) and Puzo later confirmed: "I was deluged with letters. Some good. Some bad. Some Italians were infuriated."

Chances are, one who was angered was Sinatra. True, Puzo made a flattering comparison between the Old World "Mafia chiefs who reigned in Sicily" and the legend of Sinatra's own making: "These Mafia chiefs were men who inspired a fierce loyalty, and an enormous amount of fear. They did so by giving unstinting aid to followers who were completely faithful to them . . . Sinatra, too, has helped talented people up the ladder of success and has befriended the famous who have fallen on hard times. He would also seem to have that special quality all great Mafia chiefs possessed: the ability to inspire respect and affection in men of equal power and rank." And yet, toward the end of "The Italians, American Style" there was also Mario's observation about "the evidence that he is a rash man. (In this he differs from the Mafia chiefs he emulates.) Recently [in 1966], he married a girl [Mia Farrow] almost thirty years younger than himself. In the Nevada affair that lost him his interest in a profitable gambling casino, he refused to publicly disown his friendship with [Chicago-based Mob boss] Sam Giancana."

Fury resulted from such reminders of two of the most embarrassing episodes in Sinatra's life in the 1960s. His two-year marriage to Mia Farrow (whom he referred to as his "child bride") between 1966 and 1968 was a major demonstration of his desperate urge to defy age, transcend time, and most of all to somehow dovetail with the newly dominant youth culture—needless to say Sinatra did not travel to India in 1967 to cavort with Mia in the company of the Maharishi and the Beatles.

That excursion occurred during the same month—August 1967— that "The Italians, American Style" appeared in the *New York Times Magazine*. And while Mia, the Beatles, Donovan, and others (including Mia Farrow's sister, who inspired the *White Album* song "Sexy Sadie" after trysts with the Maharishi were suspected) had their short-lived hippie hiatus, Sinatra (still married to Farrow) was not pleased by this kind of a backhanded compliment in Mario's long-form article: "[Frank] is loyal to his friends, generous to any cause he champions, and, above all, he performed the astonishing hat trick of remaining a good husband and father after getting divorced. That alone endeared him to thousands of American Italians."

That was almost as bad as the widely quoted remark by Ava

Gardner, the still glamorous, buxom, and brash second wife of Sinatra, who commented on the third Mrs. Sinatra by noting Mia's crew-cut hairstyle and petite physique: "Ha! I always knew Frank would end up in bed with a boy!"

The notoriety of the 1970 confrontation between Mario Puzo and Frank Sinatra certainly provided grist for the gossip mill. It also validated Puzo's instincts about a couple of issues. Issue number one was his basic desire for solitude and quiet (as opposed to indulging in the party scene), and issue number two was his lack of desire when it came to seeking the approval of others. Any craving to be part of the "in" crowd failed to galvanize him. Still, he pondered the confrontation, musing about it.

> It must be pointed out that this incident was not Sinatra's fault. He was eating dinner, minding his own business. The fault is partly mine. I could have pulled away and I wonder to this day why I did not. I was really beginning to think I was important. [But] now I [had] an accepted excuse for not going to parties. Before that it was always hard to explain why. Now all I [had] to do was tell the Sinatra story and [I was] excused.

If nothing else, such a flashpoint inspired Mario to retreat (as always) to his typewriter, and his voracious nighttime reading. He later said: "Incidents like this send a writer scurrying back to his workroom for safety. Make no mistake, writers become writers to avoid the pains and humiliations of the real world and real people. I started rewriting the script, playing tennis, and reading quietly at night in my suite. If I was going to be a hermit, the Beverly Hills Hotel was a great hut."

After reading an advance copy of a new memoir by one of his former colleagues at Magazine Management Company, a generous blurb was provided by Puzo. The memoir was *The Colony*, and its author was John Bowers. He told the story of his early life and his quest to be a writer; a quest that included a lengthy spell at the writers' colony founded (and funded) by novelist James Jones and his mercurial, incendiary, controversial mentor Lowney Handy in downstate Illinois back in the 1950s. Puzo's endorsement—"The wittiest and most touching and most honest book about writers I've ever read"—helped to launch Bowers' memoir in 1971.

Still and all, in a private, personal way, Puzo was wounded by Sinatra's rage. "I felt depressed too," he once said, "because I thought

Sinatra hated the book and believed I had attacked him personally in the character of Johnny Fontane."

Soon enough, there was no time left for hurt feelings. At long last, Paramount's executives had finally succeeded at recruiting Francis Ford Coppola to direct *The Godfather*, and suddenly even Frank Sinatra was yearning to participate. Mario recalled: "a few weeks later [after Francis Coppola] was named as director of the film, he too had an incident with Sinatra. They ran into each other in an LA club one night, and Sinatra put his arms around Coppola's shoulders and said, 'Francis, I'd play the Godfather for you. I wouldn't do it for those guys at Paramount, but I'd do it for you.' "

Once Coppola was on board, everything about the making of the first *Godfather* film became an admixture of kismet and serendipity, endless debates, high anxiety, constant conflict, and relentless second-guessing. Decades later, in 1996, Puzo (on *The Charlie Rose Show*) described Coppola as "a genius moviemaker."

Dozens of other biographies (about everyone from Coppola or Marlon Brando to Al Pacino) as well as chronicles about filmmaking at large have recounted and recycled the contrasting versions of the innumerable anecdotes about the gradual emergence of what's commonly considered one of the greatest achievements in cinematic history. Suffice to say—for the purpose of assessing Puzo's life— that Mario and Francis worked together with mutual respect and harmony as the co-screenwriters for all three of the major films yielded by the novel *The Godfather*.

One spring night, on April 8, 1975, Mario Puzo stood on the stage at the Dorothy Chandler Pavilion in Los Angeles, California. Beaming, he held his Oscar for Best Adapted Screenplay (which he shared with director Francis Ford Coppola, who co-wrote the script for which they were being honored). Mario wore a tuxedo and he looked splendid. He'd grown his dark hair quite long in the back, but still brushed it up and over his ears. Old school. And his large black-framed tortoise-shell glasses were also a throwback to an older style. It was "Hollywood's biggest night," as the Academy Awards ceremony is often called. Puzo glowed. And he beheld his Oscar.

It was the second Oscar he'd won, much to his own amazement. Two years earlier, he won for the screen adaptation of *The Godfather*, which had become throughout 1972 and 1973 the most popular, profitable, and exceedingly successful film since *Gone With the Wind* decades earlier.

And Puzo and Coppola thus won the Academy Award for co-writing the screenplay for *The Godfather*. The success of that film was so phenomenal that Paramount Pictures granted director Francis Ford Coppola his every wish, and a sequel was written, filmed, edited, and released just in time for Christmas 1974.

The Godfather: Part II didn't catch on with the mass public as immediately as its predecessor had, yet over time *The Godfather: Part II* earned not just universal critical respect as a towering artistic achievement, but also great popular renown.

Unlike most sequels that are geared to a certain formula, there are vast swaths of *The Godfather: Part II* harking back to the middle chapters of Mario Puzo's novel *The Godfather*. The scenes in *Part II*, in which a then-new young actor named Robert De Niro played the part of Don Vito Corleone as a youthful Italian immigrant evolving from a poor workingman into a "man of respect" on the Lower East Side of New York City in the World War One era. Those scenes derive almost entirely from Book III: Chapter 14, which is so vividly detailed in Puzo's novel.

Taken together, the two *Godfather* films released in 1972 and 1974 became a dual cinematic touchstone globally. Both movies received the Academy Award for Best Picture. Each of the films received Oscars in other categories. Books galore, several documentaries, innumerable magazine articles, and hundreds of interviews through the years with actors and actresses, and with Coppola and his army of filmmaking allies, have chronicled and recorded, assessed and recounted, analyzed and duly recapitulated the panoramic and quasi-mythic tales of the who, what, when, where, how, and why those two films evolved and emerged as they did. Those valuable books have rightly celebrated Francis Coppola's visionary leadership (his audacity as a young director who had not yet helmed a hit was mind-boggling), as well as the casting-call legends, infighting during the meticulous editing process, the musical score (which was also globally embraced), the PR, and other cinematic issues.

For more than forty years now, the first two films spawned from Mario Puzo's third novel have shimmered in the public imagination and are enshrined in the highest critical echelons. There is a mystique about the unique power and glory of the first two *Godfather* films. There's also a canard too often reiterating that it was solely Coppola's talent unilaterally creating the artistic cinematic triumphs, and that Puzo's novel was—at best—upgraded "schlock." Francis Ford Coppola himself has debunked that stupid, oft-repeated notion, going on the record to say: "Everything that's wonderful about the *Godfather* movies comes from the book."

And it was at Coppola's insistence that Paramount Pictures, in later years, reconfigured the credits of the movies so that Puzo's name always appears above the title. As in: "Mario Puzo's *The Godfather*." There was justice in that gesture.

However, long before either film was released, long before the first film was ever cast, even before the hiring of Francis Ford Coppola had occurred late in 1970, the international success of Puzo's novel was a phenomenon unto itself. More than one million copies of *The Godfather* sold in hardcover (a rare achievement for any fiction). Paperback sales eventually exceeded twenty million copies and reprints continue to this day. On one day, when his blockbuster novel was ranked as the world's #1 best-selling work of fiction, Mario Puzo received a call from a former colleague at Magazine Management Company—Jules Siegel was checking in. He asked Puzo how it felt to be the author of the most famous book in the world.

Mario's mordant reply was swift: "I am still fat," he said.

Mario Puzo won Academy Awards for Best Screenplay (Adaptation) for THE GODFATHER and THE GODFATHER: PART II. Puzo and Francis Ford Coppola shared the writing credits for both scripts; each film also won for Best Picture; photographer unknown

9

Wrap

Mario Puzo lit a Rey del Mundo that looked as long as Merlin's wand, puffed contentedly, and said: "When I wrote 'The Godfather' I took dead aim at the public. I was determined to write a book that would sell . . . But I wrote 'Fools Die' for myself. I wanted to say certain things about gambling, Las Vegas, and the country. I used to be a fairly constant gambler in Vegas. I knew that I would use it in a book someday. I even had a rationalization for losing all that money—I told myself I was really researching. But I'm aging out now as a gambler—it isn't what it used to be for me."
~~~ Herbert Mitgang, BEHIND THE BEST SELLERS,
The *New York Times* (1979)

Coppola remembers visiting Las Vegas with Puzo when "some thug-like guy came over and said to me, 'Just remember, he made you, you didn't make him!' I said, 'Fine.'"
~~~ Michael Sragow, "Godfatherhood,"
The *New Yorker* (1997)

"I fancy myself an Italian peasant who's living comfortably on his little farm," Mr. Puzo remarks. Four of his five children live within 45 minutes of his house, which is run like a self-sufficient "patriarchy" (Ms. [Carol] Gino's word) into which no stranger need step. Even the newspaper is delivered by a family member ... " 'Stay at home,' my mother always said," Mario Puzo declares, "'Only bad things happen to you outside.'"
~~~ Camille Paglia, "It All Comes Back to Family,"
The *New York Times* (1997)

Long ago and far away, the ultimate symbol of recognition, importance, and influence in American life was to be on the cover of *TIME* magazine. In prior decades, other writers at the peak of their careers had been featured on TIME's cover, with a lengthy essay inside the magazine to complement their appearance beneath the magazine's iconic logo. John Dos Passos appeared on the cover back in 1936. J. D. Salinger was there in 1961. James Baldwin in 1963. Hemingway, of course—twice (first in 1937 and then again in 1954). Now it was Mario Puzo's turn.

The perennial popularity and the lingering impact of favorite words, phrases, and expressions from *The Godfather* ("*Leave the gun, take the cannoli*" and many others) had infiltrated American culture to such a degree that there could be no question about the meaning of the cover-story's title: "Paperback Godfather." Nor was any confusion likely when readers saw the tag line at the top of the article: "Meet Mario Puzo, the author you can't refuse." The passage of time had only increased the popularity of Puzo's third novel, and the first two *Godfather* films were increasingly exalted the world over. Ratings skyrocketed when they were broadcast on TV.

The long-form essay about Puzo that ran in *TIME*'s issue dated August 28, 1978, revolved around the high-priced bidding war that led to Mario's new novel, *Fools Die*, setting yet another record in the publishing industry in the summer of '78. A dramatic, tense, exciting recapitulation gave the article a compelling You Are There feel. And readers learned not just about the record-shattering price paid for the paperback rights to *Fools Die* ($2.55 million) but that the deal also included another $350,000 "to reprint his all-time bestselling saga, *The Godfather.*" In the end, it was "the most expensive paperback auction in publishing history." No surprise there. It would be Mario Puzo's first new novel since *The Godfather* appeared back in 1969.

A triangular theme emerged in the *TIME* cover story, with its focus shifting between the phenomenal level of commercial success that Puzo sustained throughout the 1970s (he'd acquired multiple screenwriting deals in addition to his work on the two *Godfather* films); plus an assessment of how blockbuster deals were altering the publishing industry ("paperback publishers were bidding that day on futures, as if [*Fools Die*] were listed on the commodity exchange . . . With good reason. The booming paperback business can become as risky, and profitable, an arena as the stock market and the gambling casino"), topped off by a biographical summation of Mario's rags-to-riches life story. An American triumph, in spades.

It read like an admixture of Horatio Alger, the legend of Walter Mitty, and *Rocky* with a manual typewriter: "The paperback millionaire estimates that in the past ten years he has made at least $6 million from his books and movies. Before *Godfather*, his combined income from two previous novels was $6,500."

Mario's generosity in the wake of his bountiful mid-life success was legendary among his closest allies. Bruce Jay Friedman was once entangled in a fiscal bind and he asked Puzo for a $10,000 loan. Mario sent a check with a note that read: "Your credit is still good." Friedman was stunned by such confident generosity, and he asked their mutual friend John Bowers if that was a quip or if Mario meant it. John Bowers (speaking from experience) assured Friedman that it was no joke, adding that Friedman had low-balled himself: "The going rate for a Puzo loan," Bowers said, "is twenty-five thousand."

It was during these years—throughout the 1970s and the 1980s— that Mario indulged regularly in trips to Las Vegas for brief forays into the realm of gambling. He refused to allow himself to become what he called a "degenerate gambler" (which he defined to the *TIME* reporter as "a guy who would rather gamble than do anything else"), and usually limited his junkets in Vegas to a few days. Tops. When he did journey there, *TIME* noted, "[Puzo] can usually be found prowling the Tropicana, one of the older casinos off the glittering Strip, where he has invested in the hotel's new tennis facilities."

In Las Vegas, a celebrity aura glowed around Mario. He was known as "Mr. P." to all the dealers. When he was not preoccupied at the baccarat or blackjack tables, the roulette wheel beckoned. Ditto the dice at the craps tables.

A senior vice president of a New York advertising agency that employed Erica Heller (Joe's daughter) witnessed Puzo's multitasking in Las Vegas. He reported his avid observations to Erica back in Manhattan: "Mario was actually playing dice and roulette simultaneously, prancing nimbly while moving back and forth between the tables." Although the *TIME* cover story claimed that gambling for Puzo was budgeted as "a $20,000-a-year relaxation and a chance to visit with Las Vegas friends," it seemed to Erica that far more was often at stake.

"Dad [Joseph Heller] called Mario a philanthropist," Erica Heller later said, "because he provided such constant, excessive support to 'needy casinos.' Tony Puzo told me that he and his two brothers had estimated . . . that over the years Mario had probably lost at least $200,000 to $500,000 gambling." Pro-rated over the twenty-five year period spanning 1970 to 1995, that more or less aligns with *TIME*'s data.

"But money wasn't real to Mario," Erica later said. "Once during the [1980s] . . . we chatted for a few minutes, and he told me he had lost about $30,000 of some advance money he'd recently gotten, at a casino in Puerto Rico. I quickly calculated how much time it would take me to earn such money at my advertising copywriter job and groaned. 'Aren't you sick over it?' . . . [Puzo] looked at me squarely and imparted to me in a few quiet sentences what his son Tony says was pretty much Mario's *Guide to Gambling, Living, and Losing* . . . 'Look, kid . . . I didn't have that advance money before. Now I don't have it again. Nothing's different.'"

And yet, despite his extraordinary latter-day success, *TIME*'s reporter noted Puzo's disregard for domestic extravagance. The article highlighted that "Mario and his German-born wife Erika, whom he met while serving with the Army in World War II, live with two of their five children in a white colonial tract house on Long Island. The house was a contractor's model, and the author bought it furnished." Also noted was "what Puzo calls his 'peasant's study.' It is a no-frills working area with an oak desk . . . A small table holds a worn portable Olympia [manual typewriter]. 'If anything ever happened to it I would have to stop writing,' he claims. Old personal objects have a talisman's significance." And rightly so. When anyone chided Puzo about his hefty periodic gambling losses (which did add up to significant sums), Mario often retorted: "I may be losing thousands in the casino, but I'm making millions at my typewriter."

On the home front, the singular sign of Puzo's wealth (aside from building additions onto the house for guest rooms, plus some extra wings) was the tournament–caliber tennis court that he had constructed in the backyard of his Long Island haven. In comparison to the indulgences of others, that accoutrement may have endeared Mario to millions of *TIME* subscribers. Elsewhere in the article, however, there were numbers—staggering numbers—that doubtless caused envy, spite, jealousy, rage, and contempt to arise in the minds of critics, fellow writers, and others who felt that Puzo's success in the wake of the phenomenon of *The Godfather* (a cultural phenom that showed no signs of abating) was now ridiculously outsized.

Most published authors never earn much in royalties. The sad fact is that the vast majority of books issued within the traditional business model of publishing never "earn out"—that is, they don't sell enough copies to reimburse the publisher for the advance that the writer was paid—let alone turn a profit. And most critics accept book review assignments for the stipend paid, however small, just as most writers who go into teaching do so for the guaranteed income (again, however small). The truth is that English departments (at every level) and magazine and newspaper staffs have always been populated by underpaid, resentful, striving authors who scrounge to earn a living. They're primed to resent others' successes.

And they were loaded for bear when it came to a writer like Puzo, who did not merely succeed at long last, but had become a one-man corporation. The content of Mario's fourth novel, *Fools Die*, was outshone by *TIME*'s emphasis on his income in the mid-to-late 1970s. Book deals and paperback records aside, Hollywood gushed.

And even though Mario openly criticized the film world's chicanery ("It's the most crooked business that I've ever had any experience with. You can get a better shake in Vegas than you can in Hollywood . . ."), the reportage in *TIME* pushed hot buttons.

"The money machine has been exceptionally kind to Puzo. He made about $1 million for his work on *Godfather I*. For *Godfather II* he received a $100,000 script fee plus a promise of 10% of the net— which he has yet to see. There is another $1 million, minus legal expenses [Mario sued Universal Pictures re: unpaid dividends] for *Earthquake*, and $350,000 plus 5% of the gross on *Superman I* and *II*, the forthcoming spectaculars about The Man of Steel. On top of this, Puzo will earn $250,000 in increments and a gross percentage for his treatment for *Godfather III*."

Even now, such sums are hefty. Forty years ago, they were astronomical. The most fiscally robust of fellow authors seemed like pygmies by comparison. Money, of course, was always (and remains to this day) a squeamish, discomfiting, toxic, ego-bruising sore subject for writers. Revealing such details in *TIME* was unwise. But the enviable facts were already out there in showbiz gospels like *Variety* or the *Hollywood Reporter*. Nonetheless, such lucrative spoils did much to whet the appetite of highbrow critics and competitive authors. What they hungered for was the chance to defecate on *Fools Die*. And to ridicule and belittle Puzo in the process.

Mega-success like the international sales enjoyed by *The Godfather* (between 1973 and 1978, for five years in a row, only the Holy Bible sold more copies than *The Godfather* on an annual basis), well, that was simply beyond category. Puzo now had to be punished. And he was. Payback time, with vengeance. With interest.

The history of American literature is littered with prior examples of the beatings that soon were inflicted on Mario and his new novel. Oftentimes, it's after a smash-hit debut novel that an author must cultivate a thicker skin and a Buddha-caliber level of detachment, because in most instances a highly successful first novel is inevitably followed by what can often feel like the Second Book Blues. For any number of reasons (lack of innovation, flagging imagination, repetitious themes, recycling the first work's essential elements, or some other flaws), there is a tendency for one's second novel (this problem seems particularly knotty for fiction writers) to not live up to the achievement or the expectations of the well-received first one. All of a sudden, in many cases, the authors who somehow managed to write and publish a highly admired novel end up being taken to task when their follow-up work is branded as a disappointment or a letdown or in some way as unworthy.

What's never made sense is why a major success for many novelists has to be followed by punishment in the critical arena. Of course it's true that there can be a sense of weakness or ineffectiveness about any given book. Fair enough. But the ugly truth is that a monumentally successful novel—and we can define that as a work embraced by the public and many critics alike—that's published by a first-time author (or by a breakout writer à la Puzo, whose prior novels faded away) almost always leads to critical slaughtering when the writer's next book appears.

In the epoch of Puzo's own career, this entrenched pattern had manifested time after time. A few examples had become the stuff of legend to Mario's generation. Back in 1947, *The Gallery* by John Horne Burns caught on with the public and was instantly acclaimed by critics all over America. Two years later, Burns' second novel (*Lucifer with a Book*) was treated like sewage by the critical establishment, who utterly failed to see how in many ways it was a more daring, ambitious novel than *The Gallery*. Similarly, in 1948 Norman Mailer's *The Naked and the Dead* made him a star. It was beloved by many critics and a bestseller with the public. Yet, three years later Mailer was treated like a fluke of a one-hit wonder, when his second novel (*Barbary Shore*) was crushed by bad reviews, none of which hurt more than the beat-down in *TIME* magazine, branding the book "tasteless, paceless, and graceless." Burns never recovered from such a roller-coaster ride, wherein one year he was America's most promising new novelist and then, suddenly, persona non grata. Mailer's ego would not have it; he fought back, and eventually triumphed.

Two other authors for whom Mario had the greatest admiration had endured this highly public ritual humiliation. There could not have been a more wildly disparate reaction to two novels than the critical responses to James Jones's *From Here to Eternity* in 1951 and then the publication in 1958 of Jones's second novel: *Some Came Running*. Jones was not just reviewed harshly throughout 1958; he was personally attacked by critics claiming that he was a primitive, ill-educated, semi-literate (or even illiterate) writer, who in no way deserved the phenomenal success engendered by his first book. Wisely, it was then that Jones moved to Paris.

Closer to home, and much closer to Mario's own personal life, was Joseph Heller. As the decade of the 1960s had evolved, Heller's *Catch-22* had proved to be the rarest kind of success. Published in 1961, it did not hit big right away. But kismet and the Zeitgeist soon conspired. By the mid-to-late 1960s, *Catch-22* was a cultural touchstone.

Thirteen years passed before Heller's second novel (*Something Happened*) was published in 1974. By that time, he and Mario had become the best of friends. They played cards with a passion and routinely met for long, slow meals (with other selected friends at the table).

As a friend and colleague, Puzo had every reason to carefully note the way in which vast expectations for Heller's follow-up to *Catch-22* had set the bar for a successful reception increasingly higher. Critical opinions were mixed over *Something Happened*, but on the strength of *Catch-22's* perennial popularity (and with the thirteen-year wait finally over), there had been a mighty dose of media hype regarding Heller's long-awaited second novel. Thus sales were instantly strong.

And yet, compared to the elevated (even iconic) status of *Catch-22*, which over time had assumed the stature of a classic play or a favorite symphony, there was invariably a sense of disappointment. The expectations were unreasonable.

Something Happened, by any normal measure, had done very well.

Yet it was soon perceived as being a so-so success, compared to its predecessor.

A similar fate awaited *Fools Die*. Then Erika died.

The death of Erika Puzo at the end of November 1978 concluded that year on a low note. Breast cancer was the cause. At that time, the mortality rate for breast cancer was frighteningly high; multiple protocols and therapies administered today with curative intent were unavailable then. Erika was only in her mid-fifties when she died. Mario was just one month past his fifty-eighth birthday. Their marriage had endured for more than thirty years. And their five children were all healthy and in different ways thriving. Still, Erika's death brought 1978 to a somber, forlorn, disconsolate end.

No allusion to Erika's illness was in the *TIME* magazine cover story that was published four months earlier in August. As always, when it came to his wife and his children, Mario was circumspect. That aspect of his personality was nicely assessed in one of the biographical passages of the *TIME* article: "Pretentiousness and a flashy style disturb him . . . 'More pasta and less panache is a good saying to remember' [Puzo advises] . . . It is a godfather's view of the world. Indeed, the old don embodies Puzo's heroic ideal. 'A hero,' he insists, is a guy who is very, very careful. He takes risks while he takes precautions. "Like in my own family, I am very careful with my kids and my wife. My idea of a hero is a guy who never discloses any of his responsibilities or duties but glories in fulfilling them.'"

Having fulfilled his professional obligation to deliver a new novel to Putnam's (*Fools Die* was published in October 1978) and having further reinforced his personal policy of duty and responsibility regarding his family members (according to *TIME*'s essay "Puzo glories in monetary gifts to relatives, and in large trust funds for his children . . . The generosity amounts to workmen's compensation for years of deprivation"), Mario sat back and let the critics have their say.

Unwise as *TIME*'s multiple references were to the record-setting 15-hour book auction that climaxed with Puzo's 2.55 million-dollar paperback deal for *Fools Die*, it would have been pointless to try to ignore such a monumental element. Back on June 17, 1978, scant days after the auction concluded, its staggering terms were disclosed in a Herbert Mitgang column that the *New York Times* published.

When *TIME* used the breathtaking details of the latest Mario milestone as a framing device for its cover story in their August 28th issue, the news was already trumpeted. And it became such a talking point that when novelist, dramatist, and short-story master Irwin Shaw reviewed *Fools Die* on the front page of the *New York Times Book Review*, the first point he stressed was the need to erase the deal from memory.

> *The first thing to be done is to ignore the event. The event in the case of Mario Puzo's first novel since "The Godfather" is the highly publicized sale of "Fools Die" at a record figure to a paperback house before its publication. Apropos of events such as this one, it must be noted that for some literary critics writing a book that is popular and commercially successful rates very high on the list of white-collar crimes. Needless to say, I do not agree. The public, in its blind groping for entertainment, may fix on the good as well as the bad. To be readable is not always a badge of disgrace. Dickens and Dostoevski come to mind.*

Irwin Shaw was no stranger to the critical barbs and brickbats that often struck authors who had achieved enormous popular success. Although Shaw's early career was met with huzzahs and high praise from literary critics who wrote glowingly of his famous one-act play *Bury the Dead* and also his best short stories (a great many of which first appeared in *The New Yorker*), the transition that Shaw made in the 1950s and 1960s (becoming a high-priced screenwriter and authoring increasingly commercial novels) was met with derision. He understood Puzo's problem.

Shaw also understood just how capacious and vertically in-depth *Fools Die* was as a picaresque novel in the tradition of Henry Fielding's *Tom Jones* or Miguel Cervantes' *Don Quixote*. In a sweeping flourish, Irwin Shaw summed up the following . . .

> *The surprises include two suicides, one murder, described, in a Japanese country inn, others, in Las Vegas, hinted at, bribery in the U.S. Army Reserve, a grand jury hearing, skullduggery and pimping and cheating in the Nevada casinos, plus a full and fascinating account of how Las Vegas is run (not for children), the betrayal of the artist in Hollywood (nothing new here), several involved love affairs and carnal arrangements, secret Swiss bank accounts and*

how they are nourished from America, the smuggling of millions of dollars through Hong Kong from Tokyo, influence peddling and subornation of witnesses, placid family life, the care and feeding of children, reflections upon the relations between the races (impossibly complex), the uses of fame and wealth, a scarifying portrayal of the New York literary establishment, adorned with a malicious but affectionate and witty picture of a writer who might just as well have been called by his own name, one scene following another pell-mell, all written with unflagging vitality, the points of view constantly changing, the language flowing, bawdy, comic, highly colored, exaggerated, hypnotic. It would be a very cool reader indeed who did not devour the whole rich mix greedily.

Turns out there were plenty of "very cool reader[s]" in the upper decks of the literary community, but their disdain had no effect whatsoever on sales, popular opinion, or the immediate need for reprints. Although it never seized the public's imagination the way that *The Godfather* had, *Fools Die* was a best seller for months.

The hostile content of several high-profile reviews was often encapsulated in the brutality of the reviews' headlines. Case in point: "Nothing in the Hole" was the headline for a bruising, derogatory review by Joe McGinnis (author of *The Selling of the President, Fatal Vision*, and other books). Published in *The Nation* magazine's issue of November 11, 1978, the critique offered by McGinnis was scathing: "a hodgepodge . . . a lump . . . an unfinished, undisciplined, disorganized . . . clarion call for the return of the editor, any editor."

In the opinion of Joe McGinnis, *Fools Die* was a novel consisting of "one very . . . short story buried among 500 pages of debris." In truth, *Fools Die* is a sprawling, loosely written picaresque novel, a deliberate throwback to an out-of-fashion form and style. "Picaresque" is defined as "relating to an episodic style of fiction dealing with the adventures of a rough and dishonest but appealing hero." And the adventures explored and related in *Fools Die* revolve around the three primary milieus of Puzo's own life as a man: the world of writing and publishing in New York; the demesne of big-time Las Vegas gambling; and the netherworld of Hollywood screenwriting. All three environments come in for scabrous and abrasive commentary, as the storytelling oscillates between Puzo's usual omniscient narration and also a series of first-person narrators (male and female).

Fools Die is Puzo's most transparently autobiographical tale, and in its unwieldy structure and digressive patterns it is also his most fabulously unbuttoned novel.

Unfortunately, with months of advance publicity feverishly stressing that this new novel by the author of *The Godfather* had already generated mega-deals and big-time buzz, there awaited a battalion of reviewers whose mission was to not only derogate Puzo, but to scoff at the notion that he was a serious writer.

An English professor named Roger Sale, writing for *The New York Review of Books*, immediately categorized *Fools Die* as worthless: "a publishing event rather than a novel," he called it. He followed up with these rhetorical questions: "As I stumbled my way through *Fools Die* I kept asking myself who could possibly enjoy reading such gloomy trash. Of course it will be a hit because of *The Godfather* . . . does Puzo himself think *Fools Die* is a good novel?"

Twenty years later, near the end of his life, Mario called it "my personal favorite."

Many newspaper reviewers *did* think it was a good novel, or at least worthy of some praise as well as thoughtful criticism. A chasm existed between the highbrow critics writing for magazines and journals noted for their intellectual patina and the writers whose verdicts of *Fools Die* appeared in other periodicals and newspapers:

"An epic novel about fame and fortune in contemporary America . . . Puzo is a gifted writer . . . a lusty chronicler of our times whose writing style bulldozes its way through pretense and hypocrisy."
~~ *St. Louis Post-Dispatch*

"Master storytelling . . . sensational reading!" ~~ *Los Angeles Times*

"Fascinating . . . brilliant . . . this is Puzo at his best . . . the feverish world of gambling, of big-time hustlers, men and women, comes across as excitingly as anything in *The Godfather* and as gruesomely."
~~ *Publishers Weekly*

"Convincing and fascinating . . . Puzo is a skilled craftsman . . . . There is a Balzacian fascination in seeing the inside workings of the casinos." ~~ *The Wall Street Journal*

"Riveting, rousing . . . Puzo's gift as a storyteller shines!"
~~ *Hartford Courant*

Such affirmative remarks notwithstanding, the knives were out in other quarters.

If Joe McGinnis sneered in his review for *The Nation*, then Barbara Grizzuti Harrison was downright contemptuous when she wrote about *Fools Die* for *The New Republic*: "a big bad book . . . boring . . . in large part illiterate . . . as if it were the product of an empty brain, an empty heart, and an empty soul." That species of ad hominem attack inspired literary scholar Richard Greifner to sum up in a judicious way the curious (and bilious) scorn heaped upon *Fools Die* by apoplectic critics in the periodicals favored by the Ivy League literati. Greifner explained:

> *While an exorbitant publishing deal fed a media frenzy eager for a second coming of* The Godfather, *it was those same excessively lofty expectations that lay the foundation for a merciless reception.*

This constant media attention certainly contributed to the novel's steady sales rate. Continuous press coverage kept *Fools Die* in the forefront of America's consciousness, and enabled the novel to retain its top-five hardcover fiction best-seller status for months. However, not all of this coverage was supportive of Puzo's latest effort. The eager anticipation for the novel that characterized early accounts of the publishing deal quickly turned into critical disdain and pointed personal attacks upon Puzo following the novel's release.

One of the reasons that a re-evaluation of *Fools Die* is a compelling idea, four decades later, is that no one, back in 1978, put the spotlight on how pugnaciously humorous Puzo's writing is in that novel. Gallons of ink were spilled praising the novel for varied reasons or heaping scorn on it for other reasons—but the zest of its humor and Mario's oft-times acidic observations about human foibles in regard to money and gambling, marriage and sex, ambition and careers, and the male ego in particular make *Fools Die* a laugh-out-loud reading experience at times.

TIME's cover story pointed to one aspect of the novel where furtive humor was deployed—yet *TIME*'s writer pulled punches and simply offered this preview: "The ambiguous hero of the book is a writer named Osano, a ruthless genius who pursues his dreams of potency, fame and fortune by living out his darkest instincts. Osano is constructed of some cast-off parts of Norman Mailer and some full-blown fantasies of Mario Puzo. The character is a grand fool, but also a brutally honest observer."

That barely scratches the surface. In chapter-length storytelling bursts, Puzo wrote with saturated detail about Osano's ego-driven pontifications and his multiple marriages; the forever-elusive "great novel" that will cap his career and win him the Nobel Prize; his televised rants, vivid party-circuit brawls, and anti-feminist tantrums —it's all a Jonathan Swift-level of ridicule and characterization, and it's all Norman Mailer in triplicate. To Mario's credit, there are no wife-stabbing allusions or exploits. (Mailer twice-stabbed and almost killed his second wife in a berserk drunken fit in 1960.)

Puzo sidestepped any potential libel suits by naming his character in a way that cannot be an anagram for Mailer—yet by using only a one-word-last name tactic, given the perennial notoriety of Mailer in the 1960s and 1970s (his infamous 1981–1982 advocacy for convicted killer Jack Henry Abbott topped off Mailer's many years of dubious behavior), it was easy to ascertain that Osano = Mailer.

Here's how Puzo introduced one of his most energetically drawn, vigorous characters. "He was, of course, the most famous writer in America. Praised for his string of successful novels, notorious for his scrapes with the law and his revolutionary attitude toward society. Infamous for his scandalous sexual misbehavior. He fought against everybody and everything."

Later in *Fools Die*, after all sorts of misadventures together (in the text, Puzo's doppelganger, John Merlyn, takes a staff job writing for a weekly New York periodical obviously modeled on the Sunday *New York Times Book Review*, where Osano is ensconced as the top editor—a fictional ploy that further prevented a possible libel suit, because Mailer never helmed a review), there's a passage that again makes Mailer grist for Puzo's mill:

> *It was easy to see that he was coming apart in some way. I thought maybe he was going crazy. But I didn't know from what. His face looked unhealthy, puffy; his green eyes had a glitter that was not really normal. I worried about him. Because despite my disapproval of his writings, his striving for the Nobel with all his cutthroat maneuvers, his trying to screw every dame he came into contact with, I had an affection for him. He would talk to me about the novel I was working on, encourage me, give me advice, try to lend me money though I knew he was in hock up to his ears and spent money at an enormous rate supporting his five ex-wives and eight or nine children. I was awestricken by the amount of work he published, flawed though it was . . .*

When *Fools Die* is centered on John Merlyn's early struggles as an author and Osano's larger-than-life escapades, the pages brim over with raw, juicy humor.

TIME's cover story was spot-on with this summary: "Puzo's descriptions of Las Vegas, its Strip, showgirls, characters, and the variety of ways one can lose money swiftly and painlessly, are carried off with brio. The green baize world of casino management has never seemed more professional, entertaining and lethal."

The word "lethal" probably best describes how Norman Mailer reacted to the ways in which Osano is presented as his alter ego in *Fools Die*. Writing a piece in 1980 for *New York* magazine, Mailer let fly with this digression: "Mario Puzo once portrayed me as a fat man who smoked cigars and strangled a poodle with his bare hands on an airplane. That sounds more like a description of Puzo than myself. I also resent what Puzo's fiction had me doing. I owned a standard poodle once, and he was a great dog and lived to be eighteen years old. I do not go around killing poodles." Five years later, in a 1987 interview with Barry H. Leeds, Mailer's anger was still evident. Leeds had said " . . . in *Fools Die* you probably know that Mario Puzo's got a character called Osano who bears some resemblance to you," to which Mailer replied: "Well, very little in a funny way because he smokes cigars which I hate . . . I can think of three things I don't like. Cigars are probably the first, and the other is he has me killing a poodle. I had a poodle for eighteen years, so I resented that directly. You know, if I were ever to kill a dog, a poodle would be the last one."

As an unintentionally funny encore, Mailer then added: "I never read *Fools Die*."

Throughout every subsequent year during the next two decades, there were two constants in Mario's life. No matter what else he wrote, no matter what else he did, and regardless of where he lived, visited or traveled, he was always—first and foremost—the father of *The Godfather*. It couldn't be helped. The legend prevailed.

The second constant, between 1979 and 1999, was Carol Gino's companionship.

Born in 1941, Carol Gino was twenty-one years younger than Mario. She had made his acquaintance while working as a private nurse for Erika in the twilight of Erika's fatal illness. By the end of 1979, one year after the death of Erika Puzo, the warmth and rapport between Mario and Carol was there for all to see, whether they were dining at Elaine's in Manhattan or traveling together to the Cannes Film Festival. Carol was a short, dark-haired, highly intelligent woman whose coming of age between the 1950s and the mid–1970s contrasted Mario's old-school upbringing back in the 1930s. Friends who observed the new couple noted her positive influences on him.

In Carol Gino's life, a career in nursing led not only to meeting Mario Puzo as a private-duty nurse for the ailing Erika, but also to a latter-day career as a writer.

Beginning in the later 1970s, Gino had started to compose prose vignettes that evolved into short stories (sometimes writing in the wee small hours by the bedside of terminally ill patients). Before she ever met Mario, she sold her first pieces to *New York* magazine and also to the *Chicago Tribune*. The overwhelming stress, chronic anxiety, and burdensome fatigue induced by the regular demands she felt in her nursing milieu impelled Gino to write with vehement intensity.

"There was a tornado of death and disease sweeping around me constantly," she once said, when asked about her duties at varied Long Island hospitals. "I found myself living with fear all the time. I face my own mortality every day. If something was not measured by life or death, I would refuse to consider it important."

By the time she was romantically linked to Puzo, her unique perspective was made clear to Mario. He noted: "She is really terrific but you have to be seriously ill to get her attention." His incisive sense of humor was at play, but there was surely a tinge of hard-earned truth about his assessment: "If you want a little tender, loving care or feel a little sick, forget it. You have to be terminal to get her sympathy."

In high school back in the late 1950s, Carol Gino had envisioned a career as either a teacher or a lawyer. Neither materialized. Instead, in the spirit of the times, she married not long after her high school graduation and had two children (a daughter and a son) before divorcing in 1966. A brief second marriage that began in 1975 also ended in divorce shortly thereafter, and by then Gino was not just focused on nursing and writing, but on hiring out as a private nurse. Thus she met the Puzos.

In the early 1980s she was sedulously at work on an autobiographical novel titled *The Nurse's Story*, and Mario wasn't the only one who believed in her. Introduced by Puzo to his agent, Candida Donadio, it wasn't long before Carol had earned for herself a contract with Simon & Schuster. "The more she worked on the book, the less she listened to me," Mario said, "but I'm very proud of her."

With good reason. *The Nurse's Story* was chosen as a selection by not just the Book-of-the-Month Club, but also the Macmillan Book Club. *People Magazine* featured Gino in a photo-essay published on November 29, 1982, and there was even talk of a film.

"I think her book would be a hell of a movie if they did it right," Puzo told *People* magazine. "It's like those old Clark Gable and Spencer Tracy movies that are all about male bonding. I'd like to write the screenplay."

No film was ever made (like most of the properties that are optioned for the movies, a production did not result). But the prospect of co-screenwriting with Puzo added to Carol Gino's stress levels because she feared that any success she might have could create jealousy between them. Even a chasm. "Mario got a big kick out of that," she later realized. "He's at the age now when he's thrilled to death over a woman who is solvent and independent. I think he's really a feminist hiding in an old Italian ginzo uniform." She wasn't far off the mark.

Puzo adamantly supported abortion rights: "I thought the male sex had a lot of balls to pass laws restricting a woman's right to abortion" he wrote in his long-form essay "Confessions of a Male Chauvinist," in which he assessed his generation's need for a major transformation regarding gender roles. The essay began with research intended for his novel *Fools Die.* Then Mario's humor and autobiography emerged.

> *The first thing I learned from my research was that I would have to change a whole lifetime's style of thinking. I'm glad that today my daughters can claim a modern form of sexual freedom and are no longer victims of those old shames. But I also know that I'll never really be comfortable without a sense of sexual possessiveness. Which is my tough luck. Most of my generation's marriages are falling apart, seemingly for no obvious reasons. Even the good marriages. For men of my generation our only hope may be to adopt the following slogan to live by: Sex ain't serious. Gentleman, the jig is up. The line can no longer be held. Here I have to be a little personal.*

I am not altogether innocent. I have exploited one woman.

I exploited my wife in that I subordinated her wishes to my desire to write books. I made her totally supportive to my ambition. She took it well but promised to pay me back in spades when we reached sixty. (She was too busy with the five kids to plan an earlier revenge. I was too busy supporting them all to worry about even living that long.) My pleas for mercy included the fact that I never chased women, never got drunk, always gave her house money on time, and bought her gifts on Christmas, Easter, our wedding anniversary, her birthday and whenever she had a baby. Also: I worked twenty years on jobs I hated.

But now I know that she is right and I am wrong. Her life was a limited life . . . in good Southern Italian style, I had her locked in pretty good and she never achieved her true potential. And this of course is a major complaint Women's Liberation has against the male sex. Anyway . . . my wife, the kids almost grown, had a little time on her hands and hinted that she was moving up her game plan to age fifty. Obviously so were millions of other women in America.

Although he never remarried, there was a consistency to Carol's presence in his life that signified their love for each other. Her sympathetic interpretations of feminism and the Women's Movement galvanizing America in the 1970s updated Mario's ideas about the roles of women in the home and in society at large. Puzo confessed more than once that until he met Carol Gino, he was content to be an old-fashioned male chauvinist—with a twist: "I decided I had to become a 'liberal' male chauvinist," he wrote.

And in other ways, he credited his more progressive ideas about women's rights not just to his association with Carol Gino, but also to what he heard and what he learned from conversation with his adult daughters: Dorothy and Virginia. By the very early 1980s, both of Mario's daughters were past their thirtieth birthdays, and their perspectives were steeped in the tumultuous social upheavals of recent years. Over dinner one night with some fellow male writers, Mario once recalled a turning point in his evolution as a father: "I picked up the phone by accident one day," he explained, "and overheard my teenage daughter discussing boys with her friends. It took me years to recover from what I heard." Bruce Jay Friedman later said: "When it came to sex, [Puzo] was generationally trapped. To an extent, all of us were."

After Erika had died, Mario was unique among his peers in that he decided never to marry again. Over the years, his rapport with Carol Gino developed a rhythm and a pattern of its own. They never lived together as a full-time couple, but overnights were always an option; and travelling the world together was a routine. One of their extended journeys was a particularly vivid (and informative) research trip to Sicily. During that 1982 tour of the island, Mario soaked up a great deal of atmosphere and local color that helped him complete his next novel.

Published in November 1984, *The Sicilian* marked an ambitious return to the kind of densely textured narrative that Puzo had achieved with *The Dark Arena* and *The Fortunate Pilgrim* decades earlier. It told the true-life tale of Salvatore Giuliani, the legendary postwar Sicilian renegade who was akin to Robin Hood in relation to the poor and oppressed people of Sicily. In the end Salvatore Giuliani was killed by his enemies in the Sicilian Mafia, and in Puzo's fifth novel there manifested a profound connection between the real-life Giuliani and the fictional Corleones. Recognizing that untold millions of readers (and filmgoers) were acutely aware of how Michael Corleone had been exiled to Sicily in *The Godfather* (after killing the corrupt Captain McCluskey and the heroin-trafficking Virgil Sollozzo, not long after Sollozzo's failed attempt to kill Don Vito Corleone), the narrative of *The Sicilian* was framed by Puzo in a way that offers new material about Michael Corleone's exile and the goings-on of Don Vito, Tom Hagen, Clemenza, and a number of others from *The Godfather*.

Publishers Weekly expressed admiration for the deft way that Mario structured, configured, and bookended his new novel:

"*The Sicilian* is not so much a sequel to as a mirror of *The Godfather*, with all the winning elements of the American epic reflected in the homeland: treachery, passion, Puzo's calculated drama put into full effect again . . . . So continues a monumental and riveting saga."

In an equally decorous tribute, the book critic for the *New York Daily News* said:

Once again, Puzo has created a story that will keep a significant portion of the world up at night. But it is not only the intricate plot that compels; above all, the novelist is a master of character and the noble and treacherous souls who people The Sicilian *are even more alluring than the men who made* The Godfather *a modern-day myth. Myth, of course, the novel is—again, and magically so.*

While ambling about and quietly researching in dusty, Old World towns in Sicily, absorbing the grief-stricken, dolorous, and fatalistic ethos of the island's innermost denizens, Puzo walked through history. As the author of *The Godfather*, he was treated like visiting royalty. And in the company of Carol Gino, he evinced improved health. His overweight condition had yet to improve, but the fact that Carol had him walking at varied times around parts of Sicily was in itself a triumph. As a historical novel, *The Sicilian* was resoundingly triumphant.

It enjoyed more than one year of best-seller status and for several weeks sat at the #1 spot on the most prestigious lists. Reviews were powerfully affirmative. One particular write-up that drew attention came from the pen of esteemed author Gay Talese, whose contributions to the New Journalism were seminal and whose book-length works (*The Kingdom and the Power, Honor Thy Father*) were landmarks. In his front-page review for the *New York Times Book Review*, Gay Talese not only evinced appreciation for *The Sicilian*, but also for Mario himself. Talese wrote:

"Dramatic. . . . perhaps only an American writer with deep Sicilian roots and passions could have succeeded as Mr. Puzo has in symbolizing a desperate society through the deeds of a desperado, and in revealing how thin is the line that often separates a freedom-fighter from a terrorist. . . . A fine, fast-paced novel."

Mario agreed to do some book signings (a rare event for him) in public venues.

One particularly striking photo shows Puzo at a table in the midst of signing copies of *The Sicilian*, and his beautifully tailored clothes are not just colorful and handsome, they are vivifying. "She's trying to doll me up," Mario explained to his surprised and delighted old friends. And he looked resplendent, with his gorgeously tailored sports coat and a finely crafted dress shirt. Looking over his shoulder in the photo is Carol Gino, wearing a multicolored ensemble to set off her strong Mediterranean profile. It's clear from the body language in the picture that she's committed to watching over Mario. Her protective, comforting affection is palpable.

Equally protective and just as comforting throughout the 1980s were the deep male friendships Mario sustained with his pals Joseph Heller, Bruce Jay Friedman, and a small circle of allies who continued to enjoy each other's company in what they finally dubbed The Gourmet Club. Their mutual love for bountiful long meals would carry on until, one by one, ill health thinned out their numbers. Age was threatening.

For Mario, the decade of the 1980s was bookended by two separate (yet oddly related) Hollywood commitments that reminded one and all of the sheer lunacy you might encounter if, in a case such as Puzo's, you had authored a novel with its own mystique. When the onset of the home-based videocassette revolution turned the first *Godfather* film into 1980's top-selling VHS tape, the world at large was reminded that Mario had created a genuine American myth. Compared to the Corleones, no other American narrative had such durable heft.

And it was at the dawn of the 1980s that Robert Evans (now an independent producer, having vacated his executive role at Paramount years earlier) made Mario an offer that he could not refuse. It was too lucrative. Evans was now smitten with a coffee-table tome, a photo-history of the Harlem Renaissance amply illustrating the legendary Cotton Club in Harlem of the 1920s and '30s. The vivid, sepia-toned photos inspired Evans' imagination. Then: Evans contracted Puzo for a flat one million dollars to create an original story and to write a script that brought such images to life.

In the end, after endless rewrites and varied drafts by others, not one word of Mario's screenplay was heard in the film *The Cotton Club*, which appeared as a Christmas release in 1984. But Puzo still banked his one million dollar paycheck. The vagaries of Hollywood and the surreal craziness of the protocols that often found a select minority of writers receiving astronomical sums for work never produced, or for writing that disappeared as other scribes in the collaborative process superseded them, never ceased to leave Puzo baffled and oftentimes amused, unless he had to sue for the monies owed to him.

In a funny way, this pattern summed up (with the exception of his work on the three *Godfather* films) Mario's lucrative screenwriting endeavors throughout the 1970s and the 1980s. In almost every situation, it was Puzo's blockbuster name (and his Oscar-winning credibility) that usually caused high-rolling producers to recruit him to write first drafts of *Earthquake*, *Superman* (eventually released as two films), *Christopher Columbus: The Discovery*, and other major motion pictures.

Invariably, after Mario's initial drafts were found wanting for one reason or another, the Hollywood rigmarole commenced. New scribes would write revised drafts and, eventually, Puzo's script would be abandoned. The 1978 blockbuster *Superman* is a perfect example. Puzo retained his Story credit and is listed as one of four screenwriters on the finished film, but Tom Mankiewicz (son of Oscar-winning director, producer, and screenwriter Joseph L. Mankiewicz), serving as a "Creative Consultant" on *Superman*, said: "Not a word from the Puzo script was used."

And yet, during a twenty-year run spanning 1972 to 1992, Mario earned a fortune writing first drafts for producers who knew that if his name was an "element" that was "attached" to the project—any project—it would be easier to secure financing for the film. Although Evans's dream of another *Godfather*-caliber blockbuster didn't quite pan out (even though Francis Ford Coppola was hired on to direct), *The Cotton Club* has its admirers.

At the end of the 1980s, when Puzo and Coppola reunited to the fullest extent to co-write and ramp up production on Paramount Pictures' dream come true—a.k.a. *The Godfather: Part III*—they brought the story of Michael Corleone and his ill-fated family forward in time to 1979. To this day, *The Godfather: Part III* incites debate.

For many, it's a failed film that can't be compared to its two predecessors. But for others, who note the myriad ways in which *Part III* breaks new ground while at the same time offering significant connective elements to the films from 1972 and 1974, *The Godfather: Part III* deserves better than the tepid critical reception and the lack of popularity it suffered after its Christmas Day release in 1990.

Because they had mined just about all that they could from Mario's 1969 novel, it was essential for Puzo and co-screenwriter Francis Ford Coppola (also directing and co-producing) to create an entirely original screenplay for *The Godfather: Part III*. What they wrote was a vastly ambitious storyline involving the denouement of the Corleone Family circa 1979, as the now-aging patriarch Michael Corleone confronts everything from his own mortality (health issues are affecting him profoundly) to a number of psychological crises resulting from his prodigious guilt over his past.

Having ordered the execution of his own brother in *The Godfather: Part II* (a harrowing plot point that Puzo opposed, but about which Coppola was adamant; thus their brilliant compromise—at Mario's insistence—that Fredo not be killed until after Mama Corleone had died), the Michael Corleone we witness in the third installment is a man buckling under both psychic and physical oppression. There is a funereal tone in much of *The Godfather: Part III*. Lamentations abound. And the intertwined themes of sin and redemption, past and present, aren't meant for fun. Audiences expecting any presentation of "gangster life" that might be considered whimsical, cool, or at least semi-macho . . . well, they were resentfully crestfallen.

Regardless of any critical opinions, the completion of the most beloved trilogy in American cinema was by any measure an extraordinary achievement for Mario Puzo and Francis Coppola. It was also an opportunity for Mario's oldest daughter, Dorothy, to induce an impromptu tribute to her father. One day, during the film's principal shooting period, Dorothy (who was steeped at that time in learning all she could about filmmaking) was visiting the set. Before an outdoor scene was shot, Al Pacino asked that something be done about a distracting group of onlookers in the near distance. Francis Coppola excused himself to go ask the gawkers to please exit.

It was then that Dorothy decided to introduce herself to Pacino, who was alone and standing still and merely looking around. Coming out from around the sound table 15 yards away from Pacino, it took Dorothy only a few moments to quietly approach him. She introduced herself by using her full name, said hello, smiled, and then told Pacino that her father sent greetings. While walking back toward the sound table, she heard Al Pacino—to everyone's delight—call out to her: "I love that man!"

Another achievement for Mario was the 1991 publication of *The Fourth K*. For Puzo, it was a matter of coming full circle because Random House published the novel, his sixth, and now well over three decades after Random House had issued *The Dark Arena*, way back in 1955 when Mario was a hopeful "first novelist."

The Fourth K is rooted in the legacy of the Kennedy Family, and yet Mario steered clear of familiar anecdotes regarding JFK or RFK. Instead, he created a high-wire political thriller built around a new fictional Kennedy Administration with a nephew of JFK and RFK now sitting in the Oval Office. There were overlapping plots about international terrorism that some critics called implausible. That is, until after 9/11.

More than a decade after it was first published, when Ballantine Books issued a new Mass Market Edition of *The Fourth K* in paperback in 2004, their marketing riff shone a light on how events

in the recent past had been imagined in fiction by Puzo long ago:
"A Presidential Dynasty. An Arab Terrorist Attack. Democracy Under
Siege. Mario Puzo envisioned it all in his eerily prescient 1991 novel,
The Fourth K." Surprisingly, no film version of *The Fourth K* has ever
been made.

"Who knows what sells to the movies?" Mario commented to a
friend in 1996. "I was totally convinced that *The Fourth K* would
produce an automatic film sale—and I was wrong." Perhaps it was
for the best. Back in the late 1980s, without Mario's participation
in the screenwriting, two other Puzo novels were reconfigured by
writers for television and film. Neither was received particularly
well. A four-hour TV mini-series adaptation of *The Fortunate Pilgrim*
was broadcast in 1988, and though Sophia Loren was superlative
as Lucia Santa (and other fine actors were also involved), more
than one critic noted that the warmth and the authentic narrative
integrity of Puzo's novel were lost in translation. Similarly, when
director Michael Cimino helmed a movie version of *The Sicilian* that
fared poorly at the box office in 1987, the absence of a script that
reflected the tension, the texture, and the sweeping narrative verve
of Mario's novel had much to do with the film's weakness.

Other than selling the film rights, Puzo had nothing to do with
Cimino's movie.

Ill health plagued Mario during the early 1990s (a massive heart
attack in 1991 almost ended his life, and his Type I Diabetes and
obesity issues also demanded a reformation), but with a great deal of
nurturing (and nursing) from Carol Gino and with the omnipresent
support of his loving children and eight grandchildren, he slowly,
incrementally recovered from quadruple coronary bypass surgery.

Two decades earlier, Puzo more or less shrugged off a first heart
attack. At that time, his publisher (and Putnam's Editor-in-Chief)
William Targ had written in his diary on July 24, 1974: "A visit from
Mario Puzo this morning; he's taken off over forty pounds since his
heart attack five months ago; looks great in his new beige 'bush suit'
. . . says Mario: 'There's only one way to lose a lot of weight—have
a heart attack!'" Unfortunately, by the end of that year Puzo had
reverted to his well-known patterns of overindulgence, as Targ also
recalled: "On Tuesday, December 10, 1974, Mario [hosted] a Chinese

banquet . . . with his family and Francis Ford Coppola . . . We spent two hours gourmandizing." Puzo gained all his weight back.

In the early 1990s, he also survived a wicked bout with depression, which hit hard after his bypass surgery. When discussing a variety of issues with talk-show host Larry King in 1996, it was important to Mario to end the interview by paying tribute to Carol Gino—"she saved my life," he explained. First, by noting the signs of a cardiac arrest that afflicted Puzo when they were out gambling together at a Las Vegas casino on New Year's Eve in 1991: "[Carol] noticed my fingers were blue and other signs, and she dragged me to [Los Angeles] and I immediately had heart surgery. But also . . . I was very depressed after my heart operation. I couldn't write. And she got me [on] Prozac . . . it was Carol that really brought me through."

In 1995, when it had become clear that his difficulty walking was only to worsen over time, Mario had an elevator installed at home, thus allowing him to glide down from the second floor of his Long Island house right into the kitchen. Puzo's new editor at Random House, Jonathan Karp, often visited Mario at home and fondly recalls seeing how the elevator trips brought forth a godfather-like mien from Puzo: "As he aged, his round face had begun to resemble that of Vito Corleone at the end of 'The Godfather,' and Mario himself observed that in his hand gestures and facial expressions, he was behaving more and more like a don. When it became too difficult for [him] to use the stairs, he installed an elevator to take him from his bedroom to the kitchen. He would wave to me grandly from the elevator as he made his descent."

In fact, not only did Mario recover, he experienced a renaissance of creative energy and public popularity. *The Last Don*, published by Random House in August 1996, enjoyed monumental international success. It shot up to the number-one spot on most best-sellers lists, and CBS Television acquired the film rights for $2.1 million dollars.

By that time, with the 25th anniversary of the premiere of the first *Godfather* film right around the corner, the very title of Mario's newest novel (and its evocative story about how the Mafia is part and parcel of what goes on behind the scenes in Las Vegas and in Hollywood) caused terrific excitement. As did the rave reviews in the media, along with superlative interviews with Puzo on television.

While visiting with Bruce Jay Friedman for a day-long interview in 1996 (Friedman, on assignment for the *Los Angeles Times*, was assured by Mario: "You were the boss, and you're still the boss"), Puzo was still preoccupied with how he had chosen to end *The Last*

Don. Friedman recounted: "I have to laugh. The book was bought by CBS Television for $2.1 million (after a bidding war with Francis Ford Coppola); it's been sold to a long list of foreign countries; it's already received several enthusiastic reviews—and he's worried about the ending." Friedman averred: "It works, Mario."

Much to Mario's surprise and delight, the 1997 CBS mini-series *The Last Don* induced the highest television ratings enjoyed that year by any adaptation.

After decades of shying away from almost all interviews and refusing to have his picture appear on the dust jackets of his books, Mario yielded to his advisors and he made memorable appearances as a guest with talk-show journalists Charlie Rose and Larry King. Puzo's storytelling savoir-faire was on full display.

In the process of answering questions that were posed by King or Rose and also by callers, Mario calmly explained that some of the most celebrated and oft-referred to episodes in the *Godfather* films derived from stories he heard in his Hell's Kitchen youth. In fact, the beloved episode in *The Godfather: Part II* wherein young Don Vito Corleone hides guns for a neighbor he doesn't even know, and is then rewarded by acquiring an expensive stolen rug that he's unaware has been pilfered . . . well, that episode, Puzo explained, was easy to conjure up because it happened within his own family when he was a boy. After helping a neighbor in a similar crisis, Mario's older brother had ended up coming home with a fancy rug that was not purchased in a traditional manner.

Questions still arose about the origin of the "horse's head scene," and Mario explained that it was a Sicilian folk tradition for those in power to sever the head of an adversary's most beloved animal (a dog, oftentimes) and to nail that head to the door of the home of whoever it was that needed persuading. When interviewed by national Public Radio's host Terry Gross, the inevitable question induced Mario's pedagogy and his dry wit: "The horse's head thing," Puzo explained, "was strictly from Sicilian folklore, only they nailed the head of your favorite dog to your door as the first warning if you didn't pay the money. They were great believers in collecting money before doing the job."

Callers were delighted and appreciative of Puzo's commentaries, and Mario himself—by all accounts—was startled and deeply moved by the fulsome affection that greeted him on his one and only book tour in 1996. At every locale where he appeared for book-signings, there were massive crowds in attendance and many of those fans had stood in line for several hours. One day in Los Angeles such an overflow audience was present that Mario ordered pizza for the throngs and happily picked up the tab.

His generosity (not just generosity of spirit but also cash) continued to be a saving grace in his inner circle. Friend and fellow novelist Joseph Heller freely spoke of how unstinting Mario Puzo was with large cash infusions early in the 1980s. For well over a year, beginning early in 1982, Heller suffered the stupefying immobility caused by his bout with Guillain-Barre syndrome, a devastating illness that at its worst can leave a victim completely paralyzed. Due to a clerical error and a missed deadline, Heller's health insurance had lapsed.

While Heller was hospitalized for almost six months (and still in a wheelchair, partially paralyzed, and in need of caregivers when he returned home), Puzo came through with more than one five-figure loan. Mario also made sure to slip cash gifts to one of Heller's closest friends, Speed Vogel, who had evolved into a de facto full-time housemate and caregiver. Those cash gifts made it possible for Vogel to travel with Heller for salutary episodes on the French Riviera. Heller gradually recovered, and was able to resume an active life—and his writing. Although known for his acerbic wit, cutting remarks, satirical fiction, and sharp elbows, Joseph Heller evinced nothing but mature, respectful admiration for Puzo as a man and a friend: "He never asked a favor," Heller said, "and he always granted a request." Nor did Heller ever forget the power of Mario's literary integrity earlier in his career. *The Fortunate Pilgrim* had inspired Heller to say: "No one I know can create a city scene with more vivid accuracy, and there is not a character in [that] novel of New York City Italians who does not give me the feeling that I had met him in life."

In the mid–1990s, Mario seemed healthier than he had in years, having slimmed down considerably. Still, Bruce Jay Friedman noticed, as the decade drew to a close, that infirmity was Mario's new normal. When observing Puzo as 1997 approached, Friedman said: "[He] looked frail. He could hardly walk. No longer could he smoke his beloved Dunhill cigars; he was reduced to chewing them or so he claimed. I was convinced he took a surreptitious puff now and then."

And it wasn't just Mario who was aging in a hurry. One night, after their ritual extended meal, Friedman recalled: "The streets were icy. Puzo and [Joseph] Heller both asked for help getting to their cars. I walked to the parking lot with an icon on each arm." It was twilight time for Puzo's generation.

Most poignant of all was that one year later, in 1997, Random House published anew a beautifully designed hardcover edition of *The Fortunate Pilgrim*, with a preface by Puzo. In his brief introductory remarks, Mario made a confession. For more than twenty-five years, he'd been asked time after time about whom it was who truly inspired the iconic persona of his mythic Don Vito Corleone.

Perennially, it was assumed that the Don's essential character derived from true-life Mob legends like Frank Costello, Sam Giancana, Santo Trafficante, and Carlos Marcello. Each of those once infamous men had been a sworn witness during the televised hearings that drew massive audiences back in the 1950s and 1960s, and they'd often been the subject of newspaper and magazine stories. But Mario's confession trumped all:

> *Whenever the Godfather opened his mouth, in my own mind I heard the voice of my mother. I heard her wisdom, her ruthlessness, and her unconquerable love for her family, and for life itself, qualities not valued in women at the time. The Don's courage and loyalty came from her; his humanity came from her. Through my characters, I heard the voices of my sisters and brothers, with their tolerance of human frailty. And so, I know now, without Lucia Santa [the heroine of* The Fortunate Pilgrim, *modeled on Puzo's mother], I could not have written* The Godfather.

The year 1997 was also highlighted by cultural critic Camille Paglia's superb portrait of Mario, written for the *New York Times*. Her assessment of Puzo's works and days was a tonic after all the critical slights and insults coughed up by others in the past. In the course of her interview with Puzo (and Carol Gino), the inquisitive Paglia hit it off so well with everyone that multiple insights emerged. For example, Paglia noted that "he had his First Communion and Confirmation, [but] he inherited his mother's (then radical) skepticism about the Catholic Church, which was, in his words, 'very domineering and always against progress.'" And yet, a spiritual serenity was in the air and thanks to Carol Gino's observation, one assessment was proffered: "When Mario gambles, it's like Zen. Writing and gambling—that's his religious experience!"

Such a pithy summation may have sounded cavalier, but, back in 1977, when Puzo wrote the text for a richly illustrated coffee-table book titled *Inside Las Vegas*, he had, in fact, repeatedly stressed the notion Carol Gino alluded to. Time after time, in his *Inside Las Vegas* narrative, Mario had noted how for innumerable individuals, the focus, absorption, succor, mystery, periodic epiphanies, and occasional spasms of doubt experienced at the gaming tables or slot machines were a secular version of what so many others experienced in churches, temples, and mosques.

"I think of myself as a working-class novelist," Mario told Camille Paglia. "It's a craft." What Paglia marveled at was the capacious nature of Puzo's daily and nightly reading patterns. "[He] reads 16 out of 24 hours a day and calls himself 'addicted' to books, 20 of which must be available at all times: 'I'm just as bad as a guy who takes cocaine,'" he said to Paglia. Such concentration, solitude, and mental liberty were all ensured by the infrastructure of Puzo's own Don-like *la famiglia* in the 1990s.

By that time, with the exception of his lawyer (Bert Fields) in Los Angeles and of course his Manhattan agent and Random House allies, all of the domestic engineering one might require was handled for Mario by his immediate family members. Daughter Virginia presided over the running of the house in terms of shopping, cooking, and secretarial duty. Eldest son Anthony (a.k.a.: Tony) watched over the particulars of budgets, finances, and the monitoring of various family properties. Additional assistance came from son Eugene in relation to everything from landscaping and tending the garden to the maintenance of all interiors. Meantime, youngest son Joseph had become a lawyer and handled the details of Mario's expansive estate, along with a nephew in the family who was also an attorney. And eldest daughter Dorothy continued her studies in acting, writing, and also filmmaking, living for lengthy periods in Los Angeles, but often visiting Long Island. It's no wonder that the title of the *New York Times* profile of Puzo was "It All Comes Back to Family."

"He calls himself 'a Romantic writer,'" Camille Paglia wrote in her 1997 piece on Mario. Surely Puzo was not alluding to Wordsworth, Shelley, or Keats. For more than 200 years now the continental

European arts movement called Romanticism has been endlessly debated and even today its defining terms and individual personae (in poetry, prose, painting, music, and drama) are fodder for academic cannons (and canons). The literary prototype of that Romanticism that Mario most resembles is personified by the universally embraced 19th–century French novelists Alexandre Dumas (whose historical adventures *The Three Musketeers* and *The Count of Monte Cristo* were templates for the durability that *The Godfather* has shown) and Victor Hugo, the towering author whose beloved works (*The Hunchback of Notre Dame* and *Les Miserables*) continue to enthrall readers and avid theatergoers.

Puzo, however, cited another romanticism in his autobiographical novel *Fools Die*.

As a child I used books as magic . . . I could spirit myself away and escape by reading and then weave my own fantasies. The books I loved best at that early age of ten, eleven or twelve were the romantic legends of Roland, Charlemagne, the American West, but especially of King Arthur and his Round Table and his brave knights Lancelot and Galahad. But most of all, I loved Merlin because I thought myself like him. And so I came to love King Arthur's magician, Merlin, who had lived through the past, could foresee the future, who was immortal and all-wise.

It was then that I developed a trick of actually transferring myself from the present into the future. I used it all my life . . . I would make myself into a young man with clever bookish friends. I could make myself live in a luxurious apartment and on the sofa of that apartment make love to a passionate, beautiful woman.

During the war on tedious guard or patrol duty I would project myself into the future when I would be on leave in Paris, eating great food and bedding down with luscious whores. Under shellfire I could magically disappear and find myself resting in the woods by a gentle brook, reading a favorite book.

It worked, it really worked. I magically disappeared. And I would remember in actual later time, when I was really doing those great things. I remembered these terrible times and it would seem as if I had escaped them altogether, that I had never suffered. That they were only dreams.

Perhaps Mario Puzo did have something in common with John Keats, whose work to this day dominates the English Romantic Poets canon. Keats wrote about "the truth of the imagination" and, against all odds, Puzo lived by that credo. And with a flourish unique in America's literary history, Mario used "the silent work of the imagination" to keep readers enthralled. As one of the first readers, and as editor and publisher at Putnam's, William Targ concluded: "*The Godfather* is a perfect example . . . *Power and crime.* We all identify with Don Corleone who exemplified both elements. Crime fiction and true-crime narratives, when done with skill and strong narrative power, will titillate the reader like catnip; most readers have fantasies about committing the perfect crime, solving the unsolvable crimes, or exercising power of a supernatural order. In *The Godfather* we also find the element of *magic* . . . the Don can grant any wish; he can pull a rabbit out of a hat or he can secure a major film role for a has-been. All he requires in payment is some 'service' at some undetermined date. Payment deferred."

In what is probably Mario's most succinct, definitive statement about his most successful book, he once said: "I was looking to present a myth . . . a legend . . . To me *The Godfather* isn't an exposé; it's a romantic novel."

Fathers Day 1999 was nothing less than a full-on family reunion for the Puzo clan. All five of Mario's children gathered at the Bay Shore compound, along with his nine grandchildren and a wide array of tribal relations. Although it was the middle of June, a blanket covered Mario throughout the day—which he spent in a wheelchair. Even that new level of frailty, however, did not spoil his generosity of spirit or love for life. He conscientiously made sure to greet each of the assembled guests, and took the time (and expended the energy) to autograph some of his books. Within a week, a speedy decline set in and Puzo quietly admitted to one of his sons that he was, at bottom, unable to go on much longer. Age, illness, fatigue, and all the ancillary issues of his dim prognosis now induced a sense of resigned acceptance.

Morphine and a respirator were essential new elements by July 2. Family members kept constant vigil, and Carol Gino was omnipresent. When editor Jonathan Karp called that day, hoping to discuss some basic editorial issues regarding *Omerta* (a posthumously published novel that Puzo had revised through eleven drafts in the prior three years; it's the capstone to his Mafia trilogy), the phone was handed to Gino. She, in turn, explained to Karp: "You'd better get out here fast if you want to say goodbye." Karp rushed to Bay Shore. There was just enough time left to hold one of Puzo's hands, and offer assurances. "I told him how much I loved *Omerta*," he later reminisced, adding: "I told him I would do everything in my power to make sure it was published well, and that his legacy would live on."

Later that day, on July 2, 1999, Mario Puzo died of heart failure at the age of 78. A private funeral service followed.

In her eulogy for Mario, his integrity and dignity were summed up by Carol Gino. She said:

> *He believed that hurting another was the greatest 'sin' and thought losing his temper unforgivable. He believed in no special God, no dogma, and had no faith except in the basic goodness of humanity. And though he distrusted religion, he lived as good and moral a life as anyone I've ever known. He had . . . an elegant empathy. Mario was on all counts both eccentric and authentic—and he always tried to be a 'reasonable' man. But, in truth, he was so much more. He was a man who dared to dream and make his dreams come true. And he was an ordinary man, but he lived in an extraordinary way.*

In the public arena, in addition to worldwide obituaries that highlighted *The Godfather* and its never-ending status as an American milestone, an elegiac commentary by Jonathan Karp (who was then a rising star in Manhattan as a Random House editor) was published in *The Washington Post*. Karp's thoughtful remarks convey an elevated, deeply appreciative assessment of Puzo's legacy:

> *He was acutely aware of his own strengths and weaknesses as a writer . . . it is equally true that Mario came to realize that his true gift was for creating mythic morality plays in which only the most ferocious and cunning would survive. He thought a lot about mortality, and his later books are filled with wonderful scenes of old men confronting death. What Mario Puzo will leave behind are his stories—glorious, romantic myths of thieves and heroes, and the perplexing ambiguities that exist between them.*

Today, every novel he wrote remains in print. Mario Puzo lives.

Mario Puzo and Carol Gino circa 1996;
photo courtesy of Carol Gino

Epilogue

When we attended the New York premiere of the [first] *Godfather* film, Mario stole the show. Among the guests were Henry Kissinger and Raquel Welch and most of the *Godfather* cast, but Mario was the only man in the room with charisma. (And he wore a rented tuxedo, he refused to buy one. He also refused to wear socks.) When asked to make a speech, he first removed his tie.
　　~~ William Targ
　　　　(*Indecent Pleasures: The Life and Colorful Times of William Targ*)

The heavy dose of fatalism that pervaded peasant life in southern Italy had placed little or no emphasis on education. In the peasant worldview, what was the point of books? Books didn't provide food, and all the education in the world didn't matter: *il destino* ("fate") controlled all.
　　~~ Tom Santopietro
　　　　(*The Godfather Effect: Changing Hollywood, America, and Me*)

. . . and most of all I love my mother and hold her in true reverence. She lived a life of tragedy and still embraced life. She is, I can see from this vantage point, in every one of the books I have written. And I know now that I am not the hero of my life, she is. All these years later, her tragedies still make me weep.
　　~~ Mario Puzo, 1997

Don't disregard the element of luck in moviemaking. To have that cast, [and] to have Mario Puzo, who was the most wonderful, helpful man, who had written that book—but even beyond [that] . . . in the collaboration and friendship [Puzo] was just the greatest possible person to work with.
　　~~ Francis Ford Coppola
　　　　(interviewed by Paul Thomas Anderson in 2011)

Books by Mario Puzo

NOVELS

The Dark Arena. New York: Random House, 1955.

The Fortunate Pilgrim. New York: Atheneum Books, 1965.

The Godfather. New York: G. P. Putnam's Sons, 1969.

Fools Die. New York: G. P. Putnam's Sons, 1978.

The Sicilian. New York: Simon & Schuster, 1984.

The Fourth K. New York: Random House, 1991.

The Last Don. New York: Random House, 1996.

Omerta. New York: Random House, 2000.

The Family (completed by Carol Gino).
New York: HarperCollins, 2001.

NONFICTION

The Godfather Papers & Other Confessions. New York: G. P. Putnam's Sons, 1972.

Inside Las Vegas. New York: Grosset & Dunlap, 1977.

CHILDREN'S BOOK

The Runaway Summer of Davie Shaw. New York: Platt & Munk, 1966.

Bibliography

Aldridge, John W. *After the Lost Generation: A Critical Study of the Writers of Two Wars* (New York: McGraw-Hill, 1951)

----------. *In the Country of the Young* (New York: Harper's Magazine Press, 1970).

----------. *In Search of Heresy: American Literature in an Age of Conformity* (New York: McGraw-Hill, 1956).

----------. *The Devil in the Fire: Retrospective Essays on American Literature and Culture 1951-1971* (New York: Harper's Magazine Press, 1972)

Bart, Peter. *Infamous Players: A Tale of the Movies, The Mob (and Sex)* (New York: Weinstein Books, 2011).

----------. *BOFFO! How I Learned to Love the Blockbuster and Fear the Bomb* (New York: Miramax Books/Hyperion, 2006)

----------. *Dangerous Company ~ Dark Tales from Tinseltown* (New York: New York: Miramax Books/Hyperion, 2003).

Bosworth, Patricia. *Marlon Brando* (New York: A Lipper/Viking Book, 2001).

----------. *The Men in My Life: A Memoir of Love and Art in 1950s Manhattan* (New York: HarperCollins, 2017).

Clarke, Donald. *All or Nothing at All: A Life of Frank Sinatra* (New York: Fromm International, 1997).

Coppola, Francis Ford; Puzo, Mario. *The Godfather Notebook* (New York: Regan Arts, 2016).

Coppola, Francis Ford; Phillips, Gene D.; Hill, Rodney. *Interviews* (Jackson: University Press of Mississippi, 2004).

Cowie, Peter. *The Godfather Book* (London: Faber & Faber, 1997).

Dallek, Robert. *Camelot's Court: Inside the Kennedy White House* (New York: HarperCollins Publishers, 2013).

Damone, Vic (with Chanoff, David). *Singing Was the Easy Part* (New York: St. Martin's Press, 2009).

Ellis, Douglas; Hulse, Ed; Weinberg, Robert; Wilson, F. Paul (editors). *The Art of the Pulps: An Illustrated History* (San Diego: IDW Publishing, 2017).

Evans, Robert. *The Kid Stays in the Picture* (New York: Hyperion Books, 1994).

----------. *The Fat Lady Sang* (New York: HarperCollins Publishers, 2013).

Ferraro, Thomas J. *Feeling Italian: The Art of Ethnicity in America* (New York: New York University Press, 2005).

Frankel, Nat; Smith, Larry. *Patton's Best: An Informal History of the 4th Armored Division* (New York: Hawthorn Books, 1978).

Friedman, Bruce Jay. *Even the Rhinos Were Nymphos: Best Nonfiction* (Chicago and London: The University of Chicago Press, 2000).

----------. *Lucky Bruce: A Literary Memoir* (Ontario: Biblioasis, 2011).

Fussell, Paul. *The Boys' Crusade: The American Infantry in Northwestern Europe, 1944-1945* (New York: A Modern Library Chronicles Book, 2003).

----------. *Doing Battle: The Making of a Skeptic* (Boston: Little, Brown and Company, 1996).

Geismar, Maxwell. *American Moderns: From Rebellion to Conformity* (New York: Hill and Wang, 1958).

Gino, Carol. *Me and Mario: A Memoir* (Texas: Aaha! Books LLC, 2018).

Goldfarb, Ronald. *Perfect Villains, Imperfect Heroes: Robert F. Kennedy's War Against Organized Crime* (New York: Random House, 1995).

Goodwin, Michael; Wise, Naomi. *On the Edge: The Life & Times of Francis Coppola* (New York: William Morrow and Company, 1989).

Gray, Francine du Plessix. *Simone Weil* (A Lipper/Viking Book, 2001).

Grobel, Lawrence. *Al Pacino: In Conversation with Lawrence Grobel* (New York: Simon Spotlight Entertainment/An Imprint of Simon and Schuster, 2000).

----------. *Al Pacino: The Authorized Biography* (New York: Simon and Schuster, 2006).

Guthman, Edwin. *We Band of Brothers: A Memoir of Robert F. Kennedy* (New York: Harper & Row, 1971).

Haberman, Clyde. *The Times of the Seventies* (New York: Black Dog & Levanthal Publishers, 2013).

Hamill, Pete. *Why Sinatra Matters* (New York: Little, Brown, 1998).

Heller, Erica. *Yossarian Slept Here: When Joseph Heller Was Dad, the Apthorp Was Home, and Life Was a Catch-22* (New York: Simon and Schuster, 2011).

Heller, Joseph. *Now and Then* (New York: Alfred A. Knopf, 1998).

Heller, Joseph; Vogel, Speed. *No Laughing Matter* (New York: G. P. Putnam's Sons, 1986).

Hersh, Burton. *Bobby and J. Edgar: The Historic Face-Off Between the Kennedys and J. Edgar Hoover That Transformed America* (New York: Carroll & Graf, 2007).

Holmes, John Clellon. *Nothing More to Declare* (New York: E. P. Dutton & Co., 1967).

Hotchner, A. E. *Everyone Comes to Elaine's* (New York: HarperEntertainment, 2004).

Hoyt, Edwin P. *The GI's War: The Story of American Soldiers in Europe in World War II* (New York: McGraw-Hill Book Company, 1988).

Johnson, Joyce. *The Voice is All: The Lonely Victory of Jack Kerouac* (New York: Viking, 2012).

Jones, James. *WW II ~ A Chronicle of Soldiering* (New York: Grosset & Dunlap, 1975).

Jones, Jenny M. *The Annotated Godfather* (New York: Black Dog & Leventhal, 2007).

Kaplan, James. *Frank: The Voice* (New York: Doubleday, 2010).

------------. *Sinatra: The Chairman* (New York: Doubleday, 2015).

Kanfer, Stefan. *Marlon Brando* (New York: Vintage Books, 2008).

Kazin, Alfred. *On Native Grounds: An Interpretation of Modern American Prose Literature* (New York: Harcourt, Brace & World, Inc., 1942).

Krim, Seymour. *You & Me* (New York: Holt, Rinehart and Winston, 1974).

Lebo, Harlan. *The Godfather Legacy* (New York: Simon and Schuster, 1997).

Levinson, Peter J. *Tommy Dorsey: A Biography* (Boston: Da Capo Press, 2005).

Levy, Shawn. *King of Comedy: The Life and Art of Jerry Lewis* (New York: St. Martin's Griffin, 1997).

Lewis, Norman. *In Sicily* (New York: Thomas Dunne / St. Martin's Press, 2000).

Lingeman, Richard. *The Noir Forties: The American People from Victory to Cold War* (New York: Nation Books, 2012).

Maas, Peter. *The Valachi Papers* (New York: G. P. Putnam's Sons, 1968).

Mailer, Norman. *Conversations with Norman Mailer [ed. by J. Michael Lennon]* (Jackson, Mississippi: University Press of Mississippi, 1988).

Mailer, Norman. *Pieces and Pontifications* (Boston: Little, Brown & Co., 1982).

Mangione, Jerre; Morreale, Ben. *La Storia: Five Centuries of the Italian American Experience* (New York: HarperCollins Publishers, 1992).

Manso, Peter. *Brando: The Biography* (New York: Hyperion, 1994).

Maran, A. G. D. *Inside the Dark Heart: The Rise and Fall of the Sicilian Mafia* (New York: Thomas Dunne Books/St. Martin's Press, 2008).

Margolick, David. *Beyond Glory: Joe Louis vs. Max Schmeling, and a World on the Brink* (New York: Alfred A. Knopf, 2005).

"Mario Puzo's Brush with the Law." *The Smoking Gun* (July 20, 2000). www.thesmokinggun.com/documents/crime/mario-puzos-brush-law-0)

McDonald, Brian. *Last Call at Elaine's* (New York: St. Martin's Press, 2008).

O'Brien, Glenn (ed.). *The Cool School: Writing from America's Hip Underground* (New York: Penguin Group / The Library of America, 2013.)

Paglia, Camille. "It All Comes Back To Family" (*The New York Times*, May 8, 1997).

Parfrey, Adam. *It's a Man's World: Men's Adventure Magazines, The Postwar Pulps, Expanded Edition* (Port Townsend: Feral House, 2015).

Perlstein, Rick. *Nixonland: The Rise of a President and the Fracturing of America* (New York: Scribner, 2008).

Petkov, Steven; Mustazza, Leonard. *The Frank Sinatra Reader* (New York: Oxford University Press, 1995).

Phibbs, Brendan. *The Other Side of Time: A Combat Surgeon in World War II* (Boston: Little, Brown and Company, 1987).

Phillips, Gene D., and Hill, Rodney (eds.) *Francis Ford Coppola: Interviews* (Jackson: University Press of Mississippi, 2004).

Phillips, Gene D. *Godfather: The Intimate Francis Ford Coppola* (Lexington: The University Press of Kentucky, 2004).

Prose, Francine. *Anne Frank: The Book, the Life, the Afterlife* (New York: HarperCollins Publishers, 2009).

Reavill. Gil. *Mafia Summit* (New York: Thomas Dunne Books/St. Martin's, 2013).

Santopietro, Tom. *The Godfather Effect: Changing Hollywood, America, and Me* (New York: Thomas Dunne Books/St. Martin's Press, 2012).

Schapiro, Steve; Duncan, Paul. *The Godfather Family Album* (Koln: Taschen, 2010).

Schickel, Richard. *Brando* (New York: Thunder's Mouth Press, 1999).

Schumacher, Michael. *Francis Ford Coppola: A Filmmaker's Life* (New York: Crown Publishers, 1999).

Summers, Anthony. *Sinatra: The Life* (New York: Alfred A. Knopf, 2005).

Taraborrelli, J. Randy. *Sinatra: Behind the Legend* (New York: A Birch Lane Press Book, 1997).

Targ, William. *Indecent Pleasures: The Life and Colorful Times of William Targ* (New York: Macmillan Publishing Co., 1975).

Thomson, David. *Marlon Brando* (London: Avalon Publishing Group, 2003).

Torgoff, Martin. *Bop Apocalypse: Jazz, Race, the Beats, and Drugs* (Boston: Da Capo Press, 2016).

Wakefield, Dan. *Between the Lines* (New York: New American Library, 1966).

Waldoff, Leon. *Keats and the Silent Work of Imagination* (Urbana: University of Illinois Press, 1985).

Weintraub, Stanley. *11 Days in December: Christmas at the Bulge, 1944* (New York: Free Press, 2006).

----------. *Pearl Harbor Christmas: A World at War, December 1941* (Boston: Da Capo Press, 2011).

Welsh, James M.; Phillips, Gene D.; Hill, Rodney. *The Francis Ford Coppola Encyclopedia* (Lanham: The Scarecrow Press, 2010).

Mario Puzo's novels; photo courtesy of J. Geoff Malta

CPSIA information can be obtained
at www.ICGtesting.com
Printed in the USA
FFHW020010050319
50863630-56263FF